The
Winning Performance

The Winning Performance

HOW AMERICA'S HIGH-GROWTH MIDSIZE COMPANIES SUCCEED

Donald K. Clifford, Jr.
and
Richard E. Cavanagh

BANTAM BOOKS
TORONTO · NEW YORK · LONDON · SYDNEY · AUCKLAND

THE WINNING PERFORMANCE
A Bantam Book
Bantam hardcover edition / November 1985
3 printings through November 1985
Bantam trade edition / March 1988

Library of Congress Cataloging-in-Publication Data

Clifford, Donald K.
    The winning performance.

    1. Industrial management—United States   I. Cavanagh.
Richard E.   II. Title.
HD70.U5C543   1985   658   85-47651
ISBN 0-553-34463-3

Published simultaneously in the United States and Canada

PRINTED IN THE UNITED STATES OF AMERICA

FG   0   9   8   7   6   5   4   3   2   1

For Marvin Bower, who taught us
the values that underpin
professionalism and entrepreneurship
DKC, Jr., and REC

To my parents, who made it all possible,
and to Mary, who makes it wonderful
DKC, Jr.

To my mother, who taught me that
compassion and courage are as
important as competence and
achievement
REC

And to Dee d'Arbeloff, whose inspiring
courage, wisdom, and friendship will
live on.

CONTENTS

PREFACE

Since its first appearance, *The Winning Performance* has enjoyed a large circulation. The proposition underlying the book—that entrepreneurship is alive and well in America—was a message that many in and out of business were ready to hear.

Now, two years later, the central role of entrepreneurship in America's economic development has gained increased urgency. If we are to solve the dilemma posed by record domestic and trade deficits without sustaining a substantial decline in our standard of living, the United States must supply en environment that nurtures the sort of innovative manufacturing and service companies profiled in this book. These are the companies that are making a disproportionate contribution to the creation of jobs, to the development and deployment of new technologies, and to the growth of exports. They represent our nation's economic future.

The American Business Conference (ABC), a coalition of one hundred midsize, high-growth companies, promotes macroeconomic, regulatory, and trade policies designed to stimulate entrepreneurial opportunities and accelerate economic growth and employment. Much as our members take a long-term perspective in their business plans, so too ABC's horizons extend beyond the immediate, special interest agendas characteristic of other business groups. The central premise of ABC is that our members' self-interest, properly construed, is congruent with general economic progress equitably distributed throughout society.

ABC is proud to have sponsored the initial research by McKinsey & Company that undergirds this volume. We believe that with *The Winning Performance*, Don Clifford and Dick Cavanagh have made a significant and lasting contribution to the literature on entrepreneurialism. It is our hope that readers will find the managerial commitments described in these pages—commitments to quality, to value, to hard work, and to meaningful participation by all within the organization—both illustrative and inspiring.

Arthur Levitt, Jr., *Chairman*
William Lilley III, *President*

The American Business Conference

NEW YORK AND WASHINGTON

ACKNOWLEDGMENTS

Many people contributed their thought, time, and talent to this book.

Three McKinsey colleagues merit special mention. Bob Waterman was the spiritual and intellectual godfather to the effort. He gave unstintingly—ideas, support, and critical review. Jon Katzenbach, master of transforming the ideal into the practical, offered exhaustive substantive and personal sustenance. Marvin Bower was our professional mentor—as leader, consultant, and communicator.

Tom Peters and Allan Kennedy were present at the creation—and their thinking and approaches helped to frame the effort in fundamental ways. Fred Gluck contributed his state-of-the-art expertise in business strategy; Julien Phillips helped us understand how change is managed. Terry Williams was the project's earliest champion and served as a critical reviewer. Later, colleagues such as Doug Axsmith, Jim Balloun, Jim Bennett, Steve Coley, Nathaniel Foote, Dick Foster, Max Geldens, Quincy Hunsicker, George Norsig, Bob O'Block, John Stewart, Mac Stewart, and Don Waite challenged our thoughts and offered their own. Robert Higgins, a venture capitalist and entrepreneur, shared his wisdom and ideas.

The McKinsey study team that worked with us on the initial research assignment for the American Business Conference brought extraordinary skill and spirit. It combined the analytic rigor of Kevin Coyne, the research ingenuity of David Mark and Bruce Roberson, the creative insights of Jon Winder, and the heavy hand but light touch of Cindy Perrin. Professor Harvey Wagner contributed his considerable capabilities to make sophisticated statistical analysis not only possible but insightful. Ann Robertson helped collect facts, and Ralph Romano figured out how to display them graphically.

Ron Daniel provided sympathetic support to this many-year effort and exhibited the patience and hope that makes writing a book possible in a busy professional firm. Warren Cannon and Roland Mann—skilled at ideas and words—contributed both.

There were several day-to-day heroes of this volume, whose energy, enthusiasm, and just plain hard work made it happen. Ted Barnett, who coordinated research, made sure that facts were facts and marshaled evidence with skill and creativity (and Carol B. White checked those facts again). Yolande Lynch and Emilia Diez not only painstakingly produced and assembled the manuscript—they organized the authors' work lives and kept the faith. Yo Lynch and Arlene McCarthy proofread meticulously; throughout the entire process, Mrs. Lynch served as the project manager of the effort with devotion, effectiveness, and good cheer.

Rafe Sagalyn, our literary agent, represented the best of that profession, contributing as much to the book's substance as to its arrangements. And despite the heavy burden of her other responsibilities as editor-in-chief and publisher at Bantam Books, Linda Grey helped two new writers understand how to become authors.

Last but by no means least, we owe a special debt to Robert Keefe, our general editor, who devoted months of effort to this book. In addition to challenging and structuring our thinking and doing his best to straighten out our writing, Bob brought his considerable wit, perspective, and personal organization to the task. We had sought from Bob a high standard of professionalism—and got even more than we expected.

To these men and women, and to countless others who have been associated with this project, such as the McKinsey information services and report production staffs in New York and in Washington, we are indebted. But despite their best efforts, this book, like any other human endeavor, will have its share of shortcomings—which are ours, not theirs.

DKC, Jr.
REC

WASHINGTON AND NEW YORK

SPECIAL ACKNOWLEDGMENT TO THE AMERICAN BUSINESS CONFERENCE

We are especially grateful to the leadership and members of the American Business Conference—a coalition of one hundred leaders of midsize high-growth companies who represent the interests of the entrepreneurial growth sector of the nation.

Although the American Business Conference is a relatively new public-policy organization, in its short history it has achieved great success, acclaimed by *The New York Times* and *Fortune* as one of the top five business groups in Washington.*

The ABC is the product of the vision of Arthur Levitt, Jr., the energy of Jack Albertine, and the wisdom of one hundred successful leaders. Levitt, the chairman of the American Stock Exchange, firmly believes that the nation's economic future lies in the ambitions and dreams of entrepreneurs. Earlier in his career as the founder and leader of a Wall Street firm (now Shearson Lehman Brothers, Inc.), Levitt played a leading role in building that firm as well as arranging the financing for a host of newer enterprises who were its clients. In 1978, in recognition of his interest and expertise in the area, Levitt was named chairman of the White House Conference on Small Business, responsible for advising the president and the Congress on how the nation could help foster small business—and benefit from its energy, resourcefulness, and contribution.

*"Business Chiefs Ask Budget Cuts," *The New York Times* (November 15, 1982), p. D1; "The Impresario of Corporate Rate Cuts," *Fortune* (June 13, 1983), p. 32.

During his Washington service, Levitt found government was becoming an increasingly not-so-silent partner of business and that an important sector of the economy—midsize companies—was not recognized for its contribution, fully considered in public-policy decisions, or represented in the highest councils of government. Giant enterprises, the household names of business that populate the upper reaches of the *Fortune* 500 list, were ably represented. The smallest business (such as those who were members of the National Federation of Independent Businesses) received institutional attention from Congress's small-business-oversight committees. And individual sectors—from the Air Conditioning Contractors of America to the Writing Instrument Manufacturers—fill the Washington telephone directory's fourteen hundred listings of trade associations. But the midsize companies—like middle-class Americans—were without focused and organized representation in the capital.

Hence Levitt began his effort to give the midsize sector—especially its vital high-growth segment—a voice in Washington. He organized meetings of forward-thinking business leaders like Lee Brown, Bob Chilton, Barrie Damson, George Dillon, Mel Klein, Norman Miller, Bob Mosbacher, Ernie Nagy, and Red Scott. Arthur Andersen & Company, the accounting firm, surveyed a sample of midsize companies and found they believed their message needed to be aimed at Washington. McKinsey & Company interviewed Washington decision-makers who confirmed that the midsize sector was not effectively represented.

Eligibility for membership in the ABC is limited to leaders of midsize firms whose businesses have grown at least 15 percent annually for the past five years—in other words, companies that have doubled in size in five years or less.* To ensure a truly representative group, members were sought from all sectors of the economy—manufacturing, services, retailing, natural resources, and the like—as well as from all regions of America. Finally, although its founder led the American Stock Exchange, the ABC deliberately sought to attract firms that were privately held, traded on the over-the-counter markets, and listed on the New York or American stock exchanges.

While the new group searched for a full-time operating officer based in Washington, the ABC's initial efforts were ably coordinated by Dorothy Drummer, then a vice president of the American Stock Exchange. Jack Albertine, at the time executive director of the Congress's Joint Economic Committee, was attracted to the new, unknown group. A former professor with a doctorate in economics from the University of Virginia, Albertine was struck by the need for entrepreneurship to be

*The ABC members as a group far exceed these minimum standards.

better understood in Washington. Once he was named president of the ABC, he attacked the task with single-minded dedication, political savvy, and creativity—leading *Fortune* to report him two years later as "the hottest business lobbyist in town."*

The founders of the ABC decided to concentrate on the few issues critical to entrepreneurship in America—tax policy and capital formation, international trade and regulatory reform. And they decided the group should operate with a small staff and a modest budget.

As the ABC was launched, the Congress had grown weary of bad news about the economy and the competitiveness of its industries. Memories of federal assistance to troubled businesses were still fresh, and congressional patience was being tested by the relentless drumbeat for special preference—such as trade protection and tax provisions—for business. In the midst of this pessimism, the Joint Economic Committee scheduled hearings to explore and learn about the healthy and promising elements of the economy. In preparing for these hearings, entitled "Business Management Practices and the Productivity of the American Economy," it was not surprising that the committee sought the insights of members of the ABC. So on May 11, 1981, five chief executives, each a founding member of the ABC, testified.† Jack Albertine helped coordinate the testimony so it presented a focused picture of how and why the ABC companies performed.

At about the same time, two of our McKinsey colleagues, Tom Peters and Bob Waterman, were completing their research on the practices of high-performance large companies. This research would ultimately appear in their book *In Search of Excellence: Lessons from America's Best-Run Companies.* Albertine and the ABC members had drawn upon Peters and Waterman's excellent-company findings for their testimony, and—looking for ways to keep the momentum going—became excited at the idea of a parallel study about successful midsize companies. So the ABC, under the guidance of its Research Committee, authorized the study and invited McKinsey & Company to conduct it. With the support and help of the ABC Research Committee, led by D. V. d'Arbeloff, we undertook the study.

Our report, *The Winning Performance of the Midsized Growth Companies,* was completed in May 1983. Although it had not been evident to any of us at the outset, this inquiry appears to be the first comprehensive examination of midsize high-growth companies. In June the ABC held a public briefing on its findings. The report was well received, and

---

Fortune, op. cit.

†D. V. d'Arbeloff; Don L. Gevirtz; Melvyn N. Klein; Abraham Krasnoff; and Arthur Levitt, Jr.

with the encouragement of the ABC and McKinsey, we decided to forge ahead to write a book on the lessons from the midsize growth companies. The support, enthusiasm, and insights of ABC members who served as a laboratory for our study were of great value, and to them we express our appreciation.

*   *   *

As this book went to press, we were saddened to learn of the death of D. V. ("Dee") d'Arbeloff following a courageous seven-month battle with cancer. The loss of this great friend, entrepreneur, leader and business statesman is particularly acute and painful for the authors. Dee was unusually well qualified to provide leadership to the original ABC study effort, and later—as vice chairman of the American Business Conference—to serve as one of our chief counselors and constructive critics in the writing of this book. He was chief executive of Millipore from 1971 to 1984, guiding that company through its critical formative years. He was a co-founder and later chairman of the Massachusetts High Technology Council, the group that pioneered tax and education reform in that state. Dee served as chairman of the Health Industry Manufacturers Association and as a Member of the President's Commission on Industrial Competitiveness.

We shall miss him.

The
Winning Performance

Authors' Introduction

Example is a powerful way to learn.

Children learn through example, observing the successes and failures of their parents, brothers and sisters, playmates, teachers, classmates, and neighbors. Craftsmen serve apprenticeships. Lawyers and business students study by the case method. Physicians serve internships and residencies. Almost all of us have profited from mentors—successful practitioners who share the wisdom of their experience and serve as examples for us. Learning by example is simple in concept but difficult in execution. It's the process of discovering what works and doing more of it; discovering what doesn't work and doing less of it. Learning by example is not mindless imitation. To learn by example, one must understand best practices, applying them selectively, always testing and challenging.

To help others learn about the management of midsize high-growth companies, we selected the examples for this book with care. Most, but not all, participated in McKinsey & Company's project for the American Business Conference in 1981–83. Almost all are good examples of enterprises that have grown very rapidly in sales, employment and profits—good examples of how entrepreneurship and innovation work. Most, though not all, have encountered major problems during their march toward success, and most of these have overcome their problems and returned to outpacing the economy and their industries in growth and profitability.

How and why these companies achieved their winning performance—

and the lessons to be drawn from their example—are the subject of this book. Our approach has been quite straightforward, and is similar to that of our McKinsey colleagues Tom Peters and Bob Waterman, who searched memorably for big-company excellence earlier in the 1980s,* as well as to the approach the postwar Japanese industrialists followed in visiting the United States and taking copious notes about how leading American companies worked.

Our initial sample of companies consisted of members of the American Business Conference (ABC)—companies whose sales, when we began our project, ranged between $25 million and $1 billion and whose growth in earnings or sales had exceeded 15 percent annually for the preceding five years. Overall, in fact, their performance was much better even than that: among the publicly held ABC members, on average, sales increased by 18 percent, earnings by 20 percent, and market value by 38 percent in the five years ending in 1983. This sample group of successful businesses was very much representative of the top quarter of all midsize companies in the nation in terms of industry or service sector, geography, and ownership.

It comes as no surprise that in the time since we began that work in 1981, much has changed in the economy and within the ABC member companies, and we expanded and updated our inquiry in writing this book. Several of our sample companies have outgrown the ABC's billion-dollar ceiling—not unexpectedly, because by definition, growth companies grow. A handful have merged or been acquired. A few are even on the ropes financially; success is rarely, if ever, eternal. And we have added new companies along the way. A few of the companies we discuss were or are McKinsey clients, and with their permission we have included the fruits of our observations and analysis that at times have involved many years of service. But in the vast majority of cases, our examination was new. We recognize that some examples are better than others, and we take full responsibility for the choices.

We first read everything we could find about the companies, their leaders, their competitors and their markets. We then launched a massive program of interviews and visits. Of particular importance were interviews with chief executives—more than one hundred in four years. But talking with the boss doesn't always tell the whole story, and we supplemented these discussions with hundreds of other fact-finding conversations—with former CEOs and founders, other members of management, alumni, down-the-line workers, customers, competitors, industry observers such as journalists and financial analysts, and anyone else who

---

*Thomas J. Peters and Robert H. Waterman, Jr., *In Search of Excellence* (New York: Harper & Row, 1982).

might have a firsthand perspective. We also administered an eighty-two-question survey that collected detailed operating, financial and marketing data, and provided an opportunity for each CEO to confirm or challenge our early findings.

Some of the management practices we found are familiar. In some cases they are similar to the findings Peters and Waterman reported in *In Search of Excellence*. For example, our smaller but better-performing corporate cousins of the "excellent companies" are also masters of autonomy, experimentation, action, and value-driven management. They also keep close to their customers and they stick to their knitting. That we should find similarities—and even more obsessive pursuit of these attributes—is unsurprising; our discussions with Tom and Bob confirm that the largest, best-performing companies typically developed their management philosophies, practices, and values during their threshold years—the subject of this book.

But many of the strategic, organizational, and leadership traits we encountered flatly contradicted the conventional wisdom of how to succeed in business that prevailed while our companies were recording their winning performances, and even transcended more recent research. To confirm the validity of these ideas, we cast our fact-finding and analytical net further. Because we had gained our insights about how to succeed from those who have succeeded, it was necessary that we test those findings against other groups with diverse records of performance to make sure that the traits we observed were common among winners but uncommon among also-rans. We traced industry trends and examined large populations of midsize companies, drawing on the Standard & Poor's Compustat data base (six thousand companies) and Dun & Bradstreet (five million enterprises) to compare and contrast our winners with groups that didn't perform so well. In addition to these statistical analyses, McKinsey's collective experience and our own personal experience in having served clients with all sorts of performance records for more than forty years were invaluable to us as we sought to draw contrasts between successful and less successful companies.

We were fortunate to enlist the cooperation of the Profit Impact of Market Strategy (PIMS) program, a respected academic and industry research-and-application program operated by the Strategic Planning Institute in Cambridge, Massachusetts. PIMS granted us access to its data base and software, enabling us to unlock detailed operating and performance information on a group of some 200 participating companies consisting of 2,500 business units. And as the reader will see, we tested the findings of our sample with the larger PIMS group exhaustively—analyzing how the traits we discovered among winning performers correlate with the performance of 525 midsize enterprises over a four-year period.

An extensive literature search into business success directed us to sources ranging from articles in the popular press to doctoral dissertations. We found little, other than Don Clifford's writings in the 1970s,* that focused on midsize enterprises. But we gained much insight about management of large and small businesses that helped us generate ideas. Two seminal bodies of work—Joseph Schumpeter's views on entrepreneurship, first published seven decades ago, and Peter Drucker's contemporary works on management, entrepreneurship, and innovation—figured prominently in our thinking.

Our book is organized by findings, not by examples. The first chapter introduces the winning performers and summarizes how they do it. The next chapter provides some perspective on the obstacles that stand in the way of winning and the transitions and thresholds through which these companies must pass. Three subsequent chapters provide more detailed examples of their business strategies, organization practices, and leadership traits. We then look at instances of companies that have gotten into trouble (as most seem to do): why it happened and how they recaptured success. An examination follows of three companies we believe illustrate the full range of practices that win. Finally, we offer a set of observations about the most important lessons we learned and their implications for smaller and larger enterprises.

It is important to note that we do not attempt to tell fortunes in this book. The companies we use as examples have achieved remarkable records of success and growth by most any measure. But if history is a guide, not all of them will keep it up. Business success is really the practice of innovation and creating new tradition. What we offer here is the current tradition of entrepreneurial management as a departure point for those who will challenge, strengthen, and reform it as they become the winners of the '90s.

---

*"Growth pains of the threshold company," *Harvard Business Review* (September-October 1973), pp. 143–54; "The Case of the Floundering Founder," *Organizational Dynamics* (Autumn 1975), pp. 21–33; "Thriving in a recession," *Harvard Business Review* (July-August 1977), pp. 57–65.

CHAPTER I

Toward a New Tradition of Management

We think of this as a book about mavericks.

The mavericks whose stories it tells constitute perhaps the least known but most successful sector of the American economy: its midsize high-growth companies, its winning performers.

They have made their considerable mark by overturning the conventional wisdom of the 1970s. In its place, they have created a new tradition of management practice for the '80s.

At first glance, the winners have little in common. We find them not only in the Sun Belt or Silicon Valley; they span the continent. They are neither too young nor too old; they range in age from 10 to 150 years. They are high tech *and* they are smokestack. Some make products and others deliver services. They compete in virtually every sector of the economy.

What they do share are superior track records. By all the measures of economic growth that count, they outpace their larger competitors; they outpace their industries; they outpace the entire economy.

These winning companies, all between $25 million and $1 billion in sales at the time we studied them, are on the threshold of bigness—in the stage of corporate metamorphosis when systematic management and shared leadership become necessary to meet the challenges of growth and complexity that result from early success.

But the most important characteristic these winners share—important because it holds lessons for every manager of every business, whether threshold, mom-and-pop, or General Motors—is in the way they have won.

1

They are dyed-in-the-wool entrepreneurs in the classic tradition.

Entrepreneurship is hardly new. Mankind's drive to create new institutions and to renew existing ones is as old as mankind itself. Before World War I, Joseph A. Schumpeter, the eminent economist, defined the role of the modern business entrepreneur: "to carry out new combinations" that will create new products, new methods of production, new markets, new systems of organization.*

We owe Schumpeter a greater debt, though, for his observation about *how* entrepreneurs succeed. They do it, he said, "precisely in breaking up old, and creating new, tradition"—exactly how today's entrepreneurs succeed.

They win because they succeed in developing and executing business strategies, management practices, and personal leadership programs that often contradict the popular axioms of management orthodoxy. They do all sorts of things "wrong," and yet measured by any yardstick you care to name, they nevertheless (or perhaps therefore) run laps around the competition.

THE NEGLECTED SECTOR

Although the number can't be calculated with absolute precision, our best research suggests that there are about 19 million businesses in America, ranging from the giant multinational corporations at the top of the *Fortune* 500 list to millions of one- or two-person shops that operate in somebody's basement. About 15,000 of those 19 million—0.08 percent— are, by our definition, independent midsize companies.

In terms of sheer numbers, then, it's not surprising that researchers, journalists, the financial community, and academics have focused their attention almost exclusively on the two extremes, the established big and the emerging small. Pick up just about any periodical and there's sure to be a story about the problems and power of the nation's giant enterprises or the promise and potential of small new ventures. There are *Fortune* and *Forbes* for the former and *Inc.* and *Venture* for the latter. But there isn't a *Threshold*—yet.

Although America's 15,000 midsize companies represent less than 1 percent of all businesses, this minuscule minority is responsible for about a quarter of all sales and accounts for a fifth of all private-sector

*Joseph A. Schumpeter, *The Theory of Economic Development: An Inquiry into Profits, Capital, Credit, Interest and the Business Cycle* (New York: Oxford University Press, 1934; first published in German in 1911), p. 92.

employment. Furthermore, the midsize segment is very much a microcosm of the U.S. economy in general in terms of industry composition, geography, and overall business and financial performance.

THE BEST OF THE BUNCH

The companies we call winning performers substantially outperform that midsize economy and the best of the rest as well. The top 25 percent among all midsize companies have achieved records of growth that exceed the top quarter of the economy and the top quarter of the *Fortune* 500.

Exhibit I-1
COMPOUND ANNUAL GROWTH RATES, 1978-83
Percent

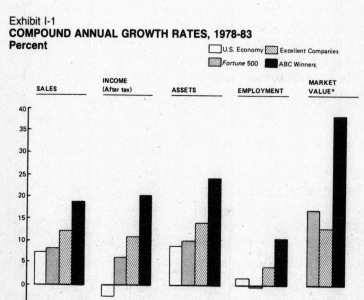

*Does not apply to U.S. economy

GROWTH RATES

1978–83

Performance Measure	U.S. Economy	*Fortune* 500	Excellent Companies	ABC Winners
Sales	7.1	7.9	12.0	18.4
After-tax income	−2.7	5.9	10.4	19.7
Assets	8.3	9.5	13.5	23.6
Employment	1.0	−.5	3.6	10.0
Market value	NA	16.3	12.5	37.8

Our analysis of the 6,117 midsize companies whose data have been compiled by Dun & Bradstreet for five years showed that even during the 1981–82 recession, revenues increased among the top midsize quartile by 43 percent—4 times the growth rate of the comparable quartile of the *Fortune* 250 (11 percent) and 3½ times the growth rates of the two middle quartiles of all midsize companies (12 percent).

The sample that serves as the focus of this book were members of the American Business Conference (ABC)—the by-invitation-only coalition of presidents, chairmen, or chief executive officers of 100 of the nation's highest-growth midsize companies.* In the half-decade 1978 through 1983, the collective performance of the ABC companies in sales, profits, assets, jobs, and market value outpaced the performance of the economy, the *Fortune* 500, and even the "excellent companies" chronicled by Tom Peters and Bob Waterman in *In Search of Excellence,* often by factors of two or more.† (See Exhibit I-1.)

If there had been such a thing as a winners' mutual fund consisting of stock of publicly traded ABC members, a $1,000 investment in it in 1973 would have grown to $22,742 a decade later. By contrast, the best-performing real mutual fund, Fidelity Magellan, grew by less than a third as much over the same period: It would have delivered $6,319 for the same $1,000 investment. And the Standard & Poor's 500 and Dow Jones Industrial Average performed dismally by comparison: Their respective ten-year results would have been just $2,239 and $2,046.

The performance of these corporate superachievers is impressive. More important, though, in the course of achieving those levels of performance, they are establishing the new tradition that is the subject of this book.

WHERE AND HOW TO COMPETE

Anyone who has had a smattering of business strategy training can tell you that the success of any enterprise is explained by the answers to two questions: *Where* to compete, and *how.*

---

*A list of the American Business Conference membership is found in Appendix A.
†Percentage increases as a measure of performance risk at least one distortion. Every additional dollar for a small concern is a bigger percentage increase than the same dollar is for a larger company. For example, a $10-million increase in sales for a $50-million company is 20 percent; for a $1-billion company, the same $10-million increase is just 1 percent.

The questions are right, but too often the conventional answers have been wrong.

WHERE TO COMPETE

Business-school students a decade or so ago had it drilled into them that success in business meant identifying attractive sectors and betting on them. The reasoning still permeates the conventional wisdom of many sharp-penciled business strategists today: To get a lucrative piece of the action, invest in high-growth, exciting, fashionable markets.

By the 1970s, sophisticated planning tools with names like growth/ share matrixes and sectoral analysis frameworks were standard-issue equipment in every strategist's tool kit. Companies, mutual funds, even governments tried to profit by applying them. Companies jockeyed to enter the growth markets (at least 150 companies market personal computers as this book goes to press). Countless state and local governments tried to become high-tech meccas. Mutual funds were created exclusively to assemble portfolios of health-care, energy, and high-tech investments. While some succeed, most don't.

The new tradition the winning entrepreneurs have established, however, recognizes that *broad sectors of the economy don't win. Companies do.* Even the dullest sectors yield companies with exciting growth and profitability.

The winners we studied are not concentrated in the supposedly "exciting" growth sectors; they compete everywhere across the economy. We expected to find winners in computers, health-care delivery, communications, and high technology generally—and we did. But we also found companies with exceptional records of growth and profitability in such unglamorous, mature sectors as textiles, furniture, fasteners, and credit reporting. In fact, there isn't a single SIC sector where you *won't* find a winner.*

Unifi, Inc., a Yadkinville, North Carolina, producer of texturized polyester yarn, is one example of a company that did well in a decidedly unglamorous sector. Although several of the major chemical companies abandoned this seemingly unexciting, unpromising, and unprofitable

*The Standard Industrial Classification (SIC) system, adopted by the federal government's Census Bureau in 1940, has become the principal basis for monitoring microeconomic trends. In short, it is a Dewey Decimal System for economists. At the two-digit level, it divides and measures the nation's economy by sectors ranging from amusement and recreation services to wholesale trade. In our research, we excluded the nonprofit SIC groups (such as government and education), and finance and real estate and focused on the 58 major SIC codes in the economy's profit-seeking sectors.

market, Unifi's founder and chief executive, G. Allen Mebane, decided to invest heavily in it, and he turned the company from a 2-percent-share also-ran into a $200-million business that may be the largest company of its kind in the world.

During the period 1977–82, Unifi more than tripled its sales and saw profits increase eightfold—averaging a return on equity of more than 20 percent. Though its sector of the textile industry was plagued perhaps even more than most by foreign competition, about one third of Unifi's sales were to foreign markets, including mainland China. In 1983, *Forbes* admiringly pointed to Unifi as an example of a company that defied conventional wisdom by taking a low-share, stagnant-market "dog" business and turning it into a roaring success.*

Or take Safety-Kleen Corporation of Elgin, Illinois. It supplies little red tubs filled with solvent to clean greasy machine parts and tools— about as unglamorous an enterprise as we can think of. Yet Safety-Kleen, unconcerned for glamor, has watched its revenue grow from $100,000 in 1968 to $185 million in 1984. Safety-Kleen's success is measured in fourteen consecutive years of more than 20 percent net earnings growth since 1971 and a 28-percent return on equity during the 1979–83 period.

Or consider William Farley, son of a Providence postman, scholarship student at Bowdoin, now listed by *Forbes* as one of the four hundred richest people in America. He built his personal fortune and his $800-million privately held company, Farley Industries, on mature businesses their original owners cast off—a die-casting company, a maker of screws, a manufacturer of paper-folding machines. Farley's two-pronged formula calls for investing in the businesses and revitalizing the spirit of the workers, and it has, on average, increased the sales and profitability of these leveraged buyouts by a factor of two to three.

These achievers know that, in the end, deciding where to compete doesn't mean choosing an industry sector at all, glamorous or otherwise. It does mean finding the right specialized (usually small) segments of the market—the right *niches*. To A. T. Cross, it means high-quality pens, not throwaway ballpoints or plastic felt-tips. For Dunkin' Donuts, it means just what the name suggests, doughnuts and coffee to dunk them in.

More than 90 percent of the highly profitable midsize growth companies we studied, it turned out, are niche players that compete by segmenting the market and figuring out how to meet the special needs of their customers.

---

*"The market share myth," *Forbes* (March 14, 1983), pp. 109–10.

HOW TO COMPETE

The new tradition of the winning entrepreneurs finds at its heart six principles of competition—deceptively conventional-sounding today but contrary to and transcending the dogma of how to succeed in business during the 1970s:

- Market-driven innovation underpins business success—and creates value to the customer.
- This value, not low price alone, wins.
- Unrelated diversification is a mortal enemy of winning performance.
- Bureaucracy and business success are irreconcilable.
- The bottom line is much more than profit.
- The leaders somehow transform personal obsession with the business into enduring institutional values and energy.

Innovation: The Best Competitive Edge

Innovation—the applied art of the new and better—underpins the strategies and successes of the winning performers. These companies innovate early and often—creating new markets, new products and services, and new ways of doing business.

Almost by definition, innovation means breaking the rules and overturning conventional wisdom. It's the opposite of imitation and of business-as-usual. For the new competitor who seeks to survive and succeed in a market where established competitors have the advantages of scale, long-standing customer relationships, reputation, and financial staying power, innovation isn't just a nice-to-have. It's a necessity.

Of the companies we studied, 74 percent got their start with an innovative product, service, or way of doing business. In most cases they offered new and better products. Charles River Laboratories, today the world's leading producer of research animals, detected an unmet market for high-quality genetically defined (i.e., "pure") laboratory rats and met it. Cray Research continues to pioneer successive generations of supercomputers, the fast, powerful machines that have become essential in nuclear physics, weather forecasting, oil exploration, and other high forms of number-crunching.

In some instances these companies revolutionized the system of doing business. Lenox China aggressively promoted the bridal registry in America: The bride picks her china pattern, and friends and relatives chip in toward the set, according to their means and disposition. MCI brought the concept of competition to long-distance telecommunications, formerly thought to be a natural as well as legal monopoly.

But for a decade or more—especially during the 1970s, when our winners were achieving their record performances—the sachems of strategy insisted that doing more of the same was the main highway to profit. During World War II, perceptive operations researchers observed the phenomenon of the experience curve—that as more and more aircraft were built, they were produced more quickly and cheaply, because the production skills of the work force improved steadily and management learned how to capitalize on economies of scale.

After those planes helped win the war, the concept of the experience curve began to be applied routinely to business. The thinking was: The way to make money is to be the low-cost producer. The way to become the low-cost producer is to capitalize on the experience curve— producing more, cheaper. The way to move along the experience curve is to gain the largest market share. The way to gain the largest market share is to have the lowest cost and therefore the cheapest price because consumers, as rational economic men and women, will buy the cheapest. And producing greater volume thanks to lower costs enables the low-cost producer to bring costs and prices yet still lower. And then . . . you see how it goes.

Despite the consistency of logic and the appeal of the scientific quantification that undergird this train of economic thought, most of the CEOs we interviewed reject the single-minded pursuit of the pot of gold at the end of the experience curve. Why? Because as entrepreneur after entrepreneur explained, the passionate pursuit of the experience curve has a profoundly disruptive side effect: It rivets the attention of whole organizations on doing the same thing cheaper—often blinding them to quantum-leap innovation.

One of the first chief executives we interviewed told us: "You can do me and my shareholders a big favor if you popularize this experience curve stuff—with my competitors!" Rather than bother with working their way along established experience curves, the entrepreneurs we studied create new ones for others to wrestle with and compete instead on the value of their products and services to the customer.

Value Wins

Oscar Wilde once defined a cynic as someone who knows the price of everything and the value of nothing. The midsize winners are anything but cynical.

Very few of them regard cost, scale, or price as their chief basis of competition. They all watch economy and efficiency with great care, but three in four aren't their industry's low-cost producer. Instead, the new tradition holds that the value the customer receives is much more important than the mere cost of the product or service.

Business success is far more than the science of managing scale and cutting costs. It's the art of leading people, nurturing them, challenging their creativity so they will figure out what customers *really* need and want.

Keeping a close eye on costs is important; no one argues otherwise for a moment. But when the organization's single-minded focus becomes cutting a corner here and there, minimizing production costs through scale, and doing the same thing better and more cheaply, then new ideas—for new products or ways of doing business—become distracting diversions. America's world-scale tire manufacturers rejected the concept of radial tires, in part because radial tires were thought not to be cost- or price-competitive with the mass-produced bias ply tires that then dominated the industry. Radial tires did indeed cost more; they still do. It took the French tire manufacturer Michelin to demonstrate that flocks of American customers would pay the considerable premium because radials last longer and are safer. It took the domestic manufacturers years to catch on and millions of dollars to catch up.

Our successful midsize companies have rediscovered and put back to work the old tradition that used to be known as good old American business sense. They see the role of companies as taking note of customer needs and meeting those needs in a distinctive way by innovating on their behalf. Successful entrepreneurs realize that consumers know they get what they pay for: There are no free lunches in the competitive marketplace. That's why virtually all the winning companies we studied— 97 percent—compete on the basis of value, not price; it's why they often command premium prices in price-sensitive markets.

When some of our friends who are academics and professional strategists first heard about these findings, especially the victory of value over price, they were quick to assert that this phenomenon could surely apply only to specialty products, not to mass-market products or commodities.

A good number of our winning chief executives would respond that there is, in fact, almost no such thing as a commodity. Dermot Dunphy, CEO of Sealed Air Corporation, the company that pioneered plastic bubble-wrap, gives speeches regularly to that effect inside and outside his company. As he told the Sealed Air Corporation sales meeting on March 19, 1984: "The lesson to be learned is that no matter how commonplace a product may appear, it does not have to become a commodity. Every product, every service can be differentiated."

We found powerful and profitable evidence that the true commodity is an exceedingly rare exception.

Anyone who lives on the United States' Eastern seaboard can validate that hypothesis simply by visiting the poultry counter at the local supermarket. Most people think of fresh chicken as a commodity product: a chicken is a chicken is a chicken. Chicken is produced by thousands of farmers; it's common food; its price changes daily. But Frank Perdue's chickens almost always sell for a premium of some 10 cents a pound over the other chickens, and the store manager will affirm that Perdue chickens have commanding market share.

Premium-priced Perdue chicken sells so well because it's *not* a commodity. Maybe chicken used to be, but Perdue chickens aren't. Perdue chickens are *in fact* better than the rest. They cost more to produce because their quality *is* higher. Consumers recognize the difference and pay for it. Through scientific breeding techniques, obsessive quality control, and artful advertising, Frank Perdue has made his chickens a noncommodity.

The evidence is powerful: People can almost always distinguish quality in product and in service, and they are willing to pay for it—as long as someone has the ingenuity to offer it to them.

Diversification: Expansion by Edging Out

Innovation as a way of life and competition on the basis of value to the customer mean the successful midsize growth companies have to know what they're doing—in intimate detail. To that end, they find their growth and their profits by edging out into related businesses—related markets, related products, related services. In some cases they bring existing products to new markets; in others they bring new products to existing markets.

Often, they edge out through selective and careful acquisition. Three quarters of our American Business Conference sample have pursued growth opportunities this way, acquiring an average of six businesses apiece in the decade ending in 1981. For the most part, these acquisitions have been in related businesses. Rather than seek to purchase earnings or sales, the winning performers focus on adding distinctive ideas, skills, and corporate capabilities.

The new tradition of edging out differs fundamentally from the unrelated diversification that became fashionable as conglomerates were assembled in the 1970s. Constructing conglomerates was exciting to the business press and highly profitable to the investment bankers who got to put together and later dissect these corporate Humpty Dumptys.

In the main, however, unrelated diversification didn't work because it was usually based on what might be called the notion of false synergy.

Synergy is the theory that the sum of individual corporate parts, properly managed, can be greater than the whole. Portfolios of businesses would benefit by drawing upon reservoirs of complementary skills and by capitalizing on the opportunity to share common resources such as financing, sales forces, and control and personnel systems. Above all, they would profit from shared leadership—synergistic vision, synergistic experience, synergistic judgment.

Many conglomerates, though, were built on false synergy. For synergy to work, one party has to have something (skills, capital) it can transfer to the other party that the other party needs or can use. If you run a company that distributes home insulation through an effective, widely dispersed sales force, then *maybe* it makes sense to add storm doors to your product line. But common sense says managers who had difficulty making a marginal steel company perform well aren't likely to have better luck with an oil company. And in the business world common sense is an unforgiving master.

Baldwin United, once a leading piano maker, thought it could diversify into insurance, annuities, and other financial services; The Charter Company in Jacksonville, Florida, thought synergy would enable it to add a publishing empire and insurance to its oil business. But pianos, single-payment annuities, newspapers, and oil refineries have little in common—not markets, not production, not technology, not distribution. Both these conglomerates went bankrupt as we were writing this book.

Even Exxon, the world's largest corporation, met its match in its ambitious program of diversification and is shouldering losses that have exceeded $700 million from such nonenergy ventures as electric motors, Chilean copper, and office information and data processing.

The winners diversify, to be sure. Only 2 percent of our sample have remained single-product/single-market companies. But when *they* diversify, they almost always do it by edging out into related products and related markets.

When Charles River Laboratories decided to edge out, it had a sufficiently refined sense of its distinctive skill that it offered laboratory monkeys—not household pets. Safety-Kleen took its existing branch structure into a new market (restaurants). It succeeded because the marketing know-how was transferable and the company had the necessary distribution network already in place.

When it comes to diversification, most of the winning performers don't take giant steps; they take small but sure ones.

Bureaucracy: The Mortal Enemy

It may well be that the gravest threat to American enterprise comes not from unfair foreign competition, government interference, or high labor costs. Rather, it may come from its own bureaucracy—smothering innovation, substituting rules for common sense, stultifying decision-making, and straitjacketing initiative. Sadly, bureaucratic arteriosclerosis is as prevalent in private enterprise as in any of the cartoon-provoking paradigms of government bureaucracy.

No one, of course, defends bureaucracy. But the fast-moving, agile firms we studied do more than bad-mouth it. They contain and combat corporate bureaucracy in at least three classic ways.

They turn their employees into entrepreneurs. No one is more likely to think like an owner than an owner. Instead of imposing systems on their employees, the winners let them earn an actual piece of the action. And they do it not in a token way: Managers and other employees of the American Business Conference member companies hold, on average, more than 30 percent of the stock of the companies—about six times the employee ownership levels among the country's largest companies. More than one receptionist told us that she worked hard because she owned part of the place.

They shun traditional management overhead functions. These companies have some of the most creative and practical business strategies we've encountered—but 40 percent of them don't have corporate planning departments. And those that do have a small staff whose job is to coordinate and perform devil's advocacy, not to design or approve final plans. Similarly, these companies achieved 38 percent annual compound growth in market value during the five-year period we tracked it, but 80 percent don't have an investor relations department.

The winning performers are convinced that planning, personnel, communications, and similar "staff" tasks are too important to delegate to staff specialists. These companies frequently regard such functions as an explicit responsibility of every line manager—who is, accordingly, a personnel director, a corporate strategist, and a company representative to employees, shareholders, and government. The winners let general managers be general managers.

Top management signals clearly that it will not tolerate bureaucratic behavior. Bill McGowan, chief executive of MCI, the "other" long-distance telephone company, dropped in at a meeting of MCI's management group to ask about a report he had heard that somebody in the company was compiling a personnel practices manual. As it turned out, the work was indeed under way, because (as the explanation went) a burgeoning enterprise like MCI, with operations throughout the world, can't do without some consistency in titles, hiring practices, application forms, and so forth. McGowan's reaction: "Find out who's doing this and fire him!" It was typical flamboyant McGowan symbolism; although no one was fired, the message was clear. MCI doesn't tolerate bloated corporate staffs to think up, enforce, and adjudicate rules and policies. MCI doesn't tolerate procedures manuals. Those that exist are typically underground—created and used only by managers who are incapable of operating without them. MCI hires its managers to exercise business judgment and common sense—not to create or follow rules and regulations.

The Bottom Line: It Isn't Only Profit

Everybody except the successful entrepreneur knows that making a lot of money is the successful entrepreneur's sole driving obsession. The men and women we observed seem as interested in making a difference as in making a fortune. They are builders, not bankers.

The tipoff came at the outset of our research when we arranged a series of meetings with the CEOs of our winning companies—sometimes one-on-one, sometimes in small groups—to help us understand their companies. We expected the CEOs to talk about themselves, bring samples of their products, refer to plans and financial records, give us organization charts and annual reports, even show press clippings about their companies.

Instead, most of the business leaders talked about corporate credos and philosophies—literate, concise statements of values. In each case, these credos set forth vividly the company's guiding principles—defining the ways value is to be created for customers, the rights and responsibilities of employees, and, most important, an overall affirmation of "what we stand for." These mission statements often dominated our discussions with the leaders of midsize growth companies. And we have become convinced that the cultures reflected in these credos, codes, and philosophies—indeed, the credos themselves—constitute one of the winning performer's most powerful weapons. Philosophy and values are hard to measure—but their value can't be overstated.

A statement of beliefs alone will not, of course, make a successful enterprise. Credos are an articulation of culture—not a substitute for it. In fact, the concept of "corporate culture" that has enthralled some business writers, academics, consultants, and executives has in some quarters taken on the trappings of a fad.

But culture doesn't get installed overnight by committees and consultants. Culture is the articulation of well-thought-out, passionately felt values that give meanings to institutions. Among the winners we studied, cultures are deeply rooted and widely shared. Generally, the culture began to take shape in the company's early growth stage.

We distilled four general themes that run through the culture in most of the winning performers. The first is *earned respect*—a sense that the enterprise is special in what it stands for, what it does, and how it does it, and demands and deserves uncommon effort and contribution from those who work there.

The second is an almost *evangelical zeal*—an honest enthusiasm that spills over on those with whom the enterprise does business, from employees and prospective employees through customers, suppliers, distributors, even to competitors.

The third is a *habit of dealing people in*—the tradition of communicating just about everything to everybody in the organization and enfranchising them as partners in the crusade. Strategies, plans, ambitions, and problems are not the secrets of the palace guard; they are known and appreciated throughout the company.

The fourth is *a view of profit and wealth-creation as inevitable by-products of doing other things well*. Money is a useful yardstick for measuring quantitative performance and profit and an obligation to investors. But even though most of the CEOs we interviewed came from backgrounds of modest means, making money as an end in itself ranks low.

Those corporate value systems eliminate the need for much of the bureaucratic baggage that burdens many organizations. Rules, regulations, policies, procedures, instructions, and the like aren't so necessary when powerful and widely comprehended guiding principles are in place. By contrast, in companies that lack well-understood, well-followed guiding principles, formal systems and processes proliferate and grow ever more explicit, detailed, and universal. They direct people on what, where, how, when, and to whom—whereas guiding principles instill an understanding of *why*.

Instead of creating and enforcing new rules and regulations, the winning performers reinforce their philosophies and creeds by word and deed. The majority of the winners we studied do not simply develop a credo and then hope it will work its way through the organization. Top management takes the lead in promulgating it. Because the midsize company is so much the personification of its CEO, it's not surprising that the winner CEO believes fervently in the statement of mission. Reinforcing it constantly, in ways both substantive and symbolic, is one of the CEO's chief functions—and, because of the strength of his faith in it, one of the easiest.

We heard about and sat in on training sessions, for new employees and veterans alike, devoted to discussing and reinforcing values. Chief executives like Dee d'Arbeloff at Millipore and Bill McGowan at MCI explain in videotape programs "what we stand for." Many CEOs meet with every employee at least annually.

And the philosophies breathe. Groups of managers regularly revisit these mission statements to ensure that they remain valid, vibrant guides for day-to-day business.

Leadership: Building an Institution

There are at least two stereotypes of the kind of men and women who lead the winning midsize growth companies. Both are wrong.

On one hand, some subscribe to the popular image of the entrepreneur as a creative genius, soul-driven by the need to achieve, but personally disorganized, hopelessly short-term in his perspective, and undisciplined in direction. Alternatively, other people conjure up the image of a cool, rational professional manager who, by dint of training and expertise in sophisticated scientific methods and theory, can run just about anything.

The men and women who have established the new tradition of management fit neither of these stereotypes perfectly; but in some ways they fit both.

Foremost, the entrepreneurial executive shows extraordinary commitment to the business, often to the point of obsession. That they work long hours is demonstrable: 64 hours a week on average for the winners, as compared with the 56.9 hours the Robert Half organization found in a 1984 survey of senior executives of one hundred of the largest companies in the United States.*

More revealing and important, though, is the intensity of the effort. The CEOs with whom we talked were genuinely excited—even about the mundane details of the business. They cited market share shifts, individual customer relationships, costs, competitor actions, yields, rates— without referring to notes, printouts, reports, assistants-to, or other aides-mémoire. When we sent them a detailed eighty-two-question survey, most of the CEOs completed it themselves. And among their co-workers, their obsession is legendary—Jim Macaleer, the CEO of SMS (Shared Medical Systems), working in his company's computer room for seventy-two unrelieved hours to fix a problem during the firm's early years; Bill McGowan meeting regularly with his top staff on Saturday mornings during one of MCI's darkest periods, not to throw in the towel

---

*"Executives' Work Week Found to Be 56.9 Hours," *The Wall Street Journal* (January 2, 1985, p. 2.

or even announce belt-tightening, but rather to begin making plans for international expansion.

Individual obsession without a following is frustration. Without perspective, it is fanaticism. The CEOs whom we came to know have mastered the balancing act to avoid those fates without diminishing the fervor of their commitment. They know how to transform their personal zeal into institutional commitment and energy.

The winner CEOs are highly selective in what they do themselves— appearances of omnipresence to the contrary. They're conspicuous in the attention they pay to the comparatively few factors that are most critical to the success of the business. While they monitor some handful of measures with intense interest and care, they leave the bulk of monitoring and decision-making responsibility to the judgment of trusted lieutenants.

Among the CEOs we observed, Management by Exception—the practice of dealing with something only when it stops running smoothly, long a foundation of scientific management—is a dirty phrase. Their attitude is the opposite of the old saw "If it ain't broke, don't fix it." They say instead, "If it ain't been fixed, it'll break." Their habit of immersing themselves in the business is combined with a constitutional contempt for business as usual. If things work well, they can work better, and if you don't figure out how, the competition will.

Management by Exception requires formal information and control systems, of course, to help managers keep abreast of things. And while the companies we studied generally have strong financial and operating control systems, the CEOs and other top managers take imaginative steps to sample straight information about important matters themselves.

That's part of the reason they spend lots of time with customers—10 percent, on average—solving problems, getting ideas, learning about the competition, and just listening.* They use their own and their competitors' products, occasionally spend time on the firing line (as salesmen, engineers, or complaint-takers), and even call themselves up.†

And they get their hands dirty. Spending time in the trenches is an easier way to find out what's going on and to monitor key functions, after all, than having to listen to formal reports (or, worse, having to read elaborate memoranda), and it minimizes the possibility of distortion.

---

*The rest of their top management, 20 percent.

†We often advise chief executives to call their main switchboard and ask to speak with the boss about a service problem. It's always useful and frequently interesting to find out how complaints are handled—how customers are treated, how well organized the enterprise is, and the extent to which the incident is handled with common courtesy.

THE TEN COMMANDMENTS OF
HOW TO SUCCEED IN BUSINESS

The Wisdom of the Seventies	The New Tradition
To outpace the economy in sales and profit growth, you'd better find the most fashionable and rapidly expanding industries.	It doesn't matter. There are winners in every sector—doughnuts, glue, and textiles as well as software, health care, and telecommunications.
Size is just as important as sector. Find and penetrate the biggest markets.	You're better off if you create and develop niches.
Achieve economies of scale by moving down the experience curve.	Create new experience curves through innovation. Let competitors work their way down the ones you just made obsolete.
Low price yields high share.	Value wins.
A. Find a good business and stay with it. B. Diversify. Become a conglomerate.	Don't stay where you are but don't go everywhere, either. Edge out—into related products or related markets or both.
Your employees are bureaucrats, waiting to be told what to do—so tell them.	Give your employees values and a vision. Make them shareholders: They will behave like owners because they *are* owners.
The company's mission is to create wealth for shareholders.	The company's mission is to create an institution, leave a legacy, make a difference. Well managed, the company will create wealth as a by-product.
If it ain't broke, don't fix it.	Fix it or it will break.
Successful executives are cool, rational, professional managers.	Successful leaders are obsessed with the business. Justifiably, they have at least as much faith in their own instinct and intuition as they do in facts and analyses.
Successful companies are run by quirky entrepreneurs who are disorganized and undisciplined.	Successful companies are run by people who have their priorities straight, their values clear, their direction tight, and a strong grasp of the culture.

Shelly Weinig, founder and chief executive of Materials Research Corporation, says one of his most important jobs is eating with down-the-line people—and not just lunch, but breakfast and dinner, too. Bob Rosenberg and Tom Schwarz, chairman and president, respectively, of Dunkin' Donuts, dropped in on 113 stores in 1983 (they had the figure in their heads) for coffee, doughnuts, and ideas. MCI's Bill McGowan answers his own telephone.

In sum, the winning chief executives (and their management teams) have their priorities straight. Their aspirations are limited only by the CEO's vision and ability to inspire others to share it; at the same time, they are solidly anchored in reality. The winner CEOs calculate the payoff from risk-taking over the long haul, not to be short-circuited by quarterly earnings trajectories. They forsake some opportunities that appear on the surface to be extremely attractive if they don't fit with real skills. But most important, they never blink from the recognition that innovation is the only sustainable basis of competition—and they never lose the voracious appetite for change that defines a winner.

Chapter II

The Will to Grow and the Skill to Win

The achievements of the winner companies are particularly impressive because they are accomplished in the face of heavy odds. It is easy to start a company, but fewer than one in a thousand reaches the midsize threshold, $25 million in sales. Having achieved this initial success, midsize companies face a whole new set of obstacles to growth. The ultimate winners anticipate these threats and deal with them effectively while continuing to manage their businesses skillfully day-to-day. Most important, the winning performers want to win and know how to do it. They have both the will and the skill.

THE ODDS AGAINST REACHING MIDSIZE

The United States has never lacked for entrepreneurs ready to start their own businesses. Some 600,000 corporations were launched in 1983 alone, a continuation of the steady upsurge in corporate formation that saw new ventures jump from 234,000 just fifteen years earlier. Recessions make scant difference; the biggest decline in business formations over that fifteen-year period came in 1982, during the worst business downturn since the Great Depression. Start-ups in that year fell to only 567,000 companies, compared with 582,000 in 1981—hardly a ripple in the wave of new-business creation. And it's happening everywhere—more than 50,000 new corporations in 1983 in New York, Florida, and California, and 1,000 annually in less-populated states such as the Dakotas.

Beyond corporate formations lies a much larger but literally un-countable number of new partnerships, proprietorships, and individuals launching new ventures every year. And, theoretically, at least, every one of these companies is a potential winner.

Meanwhile, businesses are disappearing in droves. In 1983, more than 95,000 businesses declared formal bankruptcy, and tens—probably hundreds—of thousands more simply close their doors or sell out every year.

With rare exceptions, then, "business" in the United States means very small business. In fact, if just 1 percent of the companies in exis-tence today had had the will *and* the skill to reach midsize—$25 million in sales—the American economy would be *more than double* its current size. Yet the fact remains that more than 999 of every 1,000 companies stay small.

THE WILL TO GROW

While conventional wisdom holds that growth is a top priority for any business, the facts say otherwise. To illustrate what the American business economy most frequently looks like, let's take the handy exam-ple of Tupper Lake, a picturesque village in the Adirondacks of upstate New York, some sixty miles from the Canadian border, where much of this book was first drafted.*

Tupper Lake got its start late in the nineteenth century with the area's then-burgeoning forest products industry. The arrival of the rail-road in 1890 became its major impetus for growth. Today it is one of the few communities in the area to have survived the disappearance of the lumberman. A few surviving forest products businesses, several other small manufacturing operations, tourism, and a state school are the community's major sources of income.

Over the years, industry has come and gone. Mills operated by Norwood Manufacturing, the A. Sherman Lumber Company, and the Santa Clara Lumber Company all disappeared well before World War II. A plant opened in 1949 by the Draper Corporation (later a division of Rockwell International) to turn out rough bobbin blanks that were ulti-mately destined for use in textile mill looms closed down in the late 1970s as rising transportation and labor costs made its operations uneconomic. As best we can determine, few if any of these or other

*Thanks to Louis J. Simmons, *Mostly Spruce and Hemlock* (Binghamton, N.Y.: Vail-Ballou Press, 1976), for many of the early dates and events.

forest-products-based businesses that were centered in Tupper Lake over the years ever did $1 million annually in volume.

Yet, in a village of six thousand people, the Tupper Lake Chamber of Commerce business directory lists more than two hundred businesses in eighty-two classifications, from antiques and auto dealers to suppliers of wedding gowns and wholesale distributors.

The greatest number of businesses in Tupper Lake are in the service sector—restaurants, motels, hardware, department and sporting-goods stores, electricians, plumbers, gasoline service stations, and so on. The turnover is substantial; shops and restaurants we visited a year or two ago have changed hands or have disappeared.

Even some of the longtime mainstays have been sold in recent years:

- Ginsberg's Department Store was founded nearly ninety years ago by Mose Ginsberg, who went from lumber camp to lumber camp on foot, purveying dry goods in the remote Adirondack wilderness. A landmark in the community as well as its largest and most highly regarded department store, Ginsberg's was for years managed by Muriel Ginsberg, Mose's daughter. But a few years ago, wearied by the increasing complexity of the retailing industry, the trend to discounting, and the rising emphasis on volume rather than individual service, not to mention the advancing years, Miss Ginsberg sold the store to a Michigan couple.
- The Tip Top Sport Shop, founded after World War II by Bert and Roland Richer, has long been the place to buy sports equipment— and it was an important village barbershop as well. Then the two founders decided that they had worked hard enough and long enough, and they sold out to Dick Parent, a former employee. The barbershop is closed, but the sports shop continues to thrive under its new management.
- In 1931, the principal of Tupper Lake High School, L. P. Quinn, founded the Tupper Lake *Free Press*. He had the foresight to hire Louis Simmons early the following year after his original editor quit, and Simmons led the paper as editor until 1977. By then, the *Free Press*, which was still printing by the old-fashioned hot metal process, was under economic pressure to follow the trend among other small local papers and convert to offset. Rather than undertake the expensive and demanding transition to the new technology, and because the three corporate owners (Simmons, Mary Quinn, and Ben Schryver) were all over seventy, they chose to sell the paper to a small but very successful Canadian newspaper chain, which carried out the conversion but otherwise continues to operate the *Free Press* in much the old style.

Other Tupper Lake enterprises continue to be managed by their founding families. Time will tell whether succeeding generations will maintain the tradition. For example:

• Frenette Brothers began in 1925 to manufacture and distribute ice cream and soft drinks, and after the repeal of Prohibition added beer as well. Throughout the years, the Frenettes have been prominent in the community not only because of their business, but also because of their intense involvement in North Country sports. The current head of the business, Bill Frenette, was head coach for the United States Deaf Olympic ski team and a frequent winner of cross-country skiing and canoeing races; his wife, Ginny, has been head ski instructor at the local Big Tupper ski area. Clearly, they prefer their style of life and Tupper Lake's environment to the alternative of trying to make an empire out of the business.

• Perhaps the retail store under the longest-standing family management in Tupper Lake is Fortune's Hardware, founded by Tom Fortune in 1920. While he sold the business to his son "young Tom" in 1959, and a grandson is now active in it as well, the founder still comes in most days. When we visited him late in 1984, Tom Fortune was ninety-one— and proud to be the village's oldest active merchant.

Rapid, sustained growth simply isn't among the objectives that drive the world of Tupper Lake commerce. One proprietor told us: "I make a decent living here, and I like the community. Who needs to grow? Who needs the headaches? If I start trying to do business over in Saranac Lake, they'll just start competing against me here. It doesn't make any sense."

Lou Simmons summed it up well in a recent letter he knocked out on his ancient Remington typewriting machine: "We're satisfied to make enough to take care of our obligations, live comfortably, and put away enough for the inevitable rainy day—and have enough leisure time to do a little fishing, empty a few steins, and enjoy a lot of friendships."

The point is: Tupper Lake's business establishment is an accurate reflection of the 999 out of 1,000. It's a slice of all-American life. The overwhelming majority agrees with Lou Simmons, not with the high-growth companies. Almost none of the companies that open their hopeful doors every year have any intention of becoming big businesses. Aspiring to the *Fortune* 500 never crosses the mind of the typical founder-owner—whose purpose is simply to make a living for the family, to contribute something to the community, and to enjoy the many advantages of manageable pace and strong, lasting relationships that can be the envy of hassled employees in large corporations.

But what about that other tenth of 1 percent?

The tiny handful of founder-owners who do aim for growth are in no way lacking for opportunities. It is hard to think of any business that doesn't have tremendous growth potential. There is no institutional or economic reason why any corner retailer or local service organization cannot open more outlets and eventually create a national chain—as Dunkin' Donuts (doughnuts and coffee), Levitz Furniture, Standard Brands Paint (home decorating products), and California Plant Protection (security guards) demonstrate.

Most consumer credit reporting services, for example, are local, though there is no reason why they have to be. Chilton Corporation proves it, having extended its reach from its base in Dallas to scores of other cities from Boston to Denver. Automatic Data Processing has achieved unusual growth by bringing its computing services into one new territory after another, even while many other computer service companies remained local. Virtually any business can broaden its geographic horizons if it chooses. The constraint on growth is not lack of opportunity. As the Tupper Lake story shows, it is lack of desire—lack of will.

THE SKILL TO WIN

But even companies that do aspire to grow usually fail. The reason, of course, is that while the will to grow is necessary, it is not sufficient by itself. Most of the companies that have the will lack the skill.

Up to midsize, this inability to grow usually comes down to one or more of three factors:

1. *Faulty design.* Sometimes a successful small business fails when it tries to expand because the business isn't designed to be operated on a broad scale. Plenty of chain restaurant marketers who didn't develop standardized menu items and operating guidelines (to ensure consistent quality-control, food-preparation, and service policies in all locations) have gone out of business. Still other companies have been stopped because their products were designed for too narrow a market, as with high-priced electric automobiles. Others failed to provide for a stream of new products to replace an initial success that had a short life cycle—as many companies have learned with products as diverse as clothes and video games. And some never

developed the marketing programs to substitute for the founder's personal relationships in his local community—the frequent cause of collapse among personal-service firms that try to expand geographically.

2. *Financial overextension.* Most small companies that fail financially do so because they lack the fundamental disciplines and controls to manage growth. Some hire staff and build inventory too far in advance of revenues, which drives them broke. Others take on too much business too fast and find themselves unable to keep up with demand without running out of cash. Either way, growth must stop or the company fails.

3. *Human frailty.* In at least as many instances, small companies that seek to grow seem to snatch defeat from the jaws of victory because they cannot achieve the cooperative climate or sustain the personal motivation to continue the journey toward midsize. Sometimes the problem is that the owner himself loses his driving interest in the business; sometimes he doesn't sense the importance early enough of dedicated personal follow-through; sometimes egos get in the way and lead to family or employee squabbles; sometimes the problem is downright dishonesty. Perhaps most frequently, the founder-owner finds that he really wants to do it all himself rather than manage others, and so the growth potential of the business is strictly limited by his personal energy and capability.

The winning companies have overcome all three of these obstacles in reaching midsize. They do it by learning (or sensing) how to cope with the stringent business, financial, and human requirements of a small growing company.

But with growing size and scope, once a company reaches midsize, a whole new set of challenges emerges. The winners have to run the gauntlet of these obstacles to midsize growth by combining their will to grow with the skills necessary to win—skills that are explored in later chapters of this book.

THE RISKS AND CHALLENGES OF GROWTH

Three distinctive challenges of midsize success typically show up by the time a company reaches $25 million in revenues, although some businesses experience them earlier or later. Whenever the time comes, the midsize business must demonstrate a level of ability to meet these challenges that goes well beyond the desire to grow, the development of business and financial disciplines, and the ability to cope with basic human frailties. They must:

1. Cope with tougher financial requirements in a more hostile business environment.
2. Respond to explosive growth in product and market complexity by mobilizing new organizational capabilities.
3. Fundamentally adapt the leadership role of the CEO to shifting demands that come with growth.

The winning performers do better than most in understanding the many facets of these challenges and conquering them.

FINANCIAL STRESSES

Once a company reaches midsize, a number of forces create an environment with higher financial risk and stress. A threshold company almost always covers a lot more territory than it did when it was small— out of the personal line of sight of the founder, leading to far greater risk of things going wrong. If it operates in international markets, it faces the currency risks that have so severely affected the balance sheets and profits of many large U.S. corporations in the past few years. The midsize company is almost bound to have a larger product line or offer a broader range of services than it had before it reached the threshold. If the company makes things and sells them, it has to design, engineer, manufacture, distribute, and service its products, and take back or fix products that don't work right. If it provides a service, the challenges are parallel and no less difficult. Among other things, all this takes time, and usually demands financial outlays well before the money comes back in the form of sales revenues.

More threatening still, more people are now spending the company's money. In the early days, the entrepreneur could sign every check and oversee every commitment personally. Now there are salespeople and servicepeople making commitments, and perhaps division managers spending money without day-to-day supervision or approval. Money can easily be spent in ways and on things that simply don't mesh with the founder-owner's values. Money can disappear.

Meanwhile, the company's success in achieving greater size invites competition. No company that bites off $25 million of any market, even if it created the market and monopolized it initially, is going to go unnoticed either by established corporations or by other entrepreneurs.

(Think, for example, of the game "Trivial Pursuit" and the number of imitators that have swarmed into the market it created.) Larger competitors who scarcely noticed the company when it was small begin to see it as a significant threat. Furthermore, to maintain a growth rate of 15 percent, a $25 million company has to add new revenues of $4 million or more every year—revenue potential that is tempting to big players in the market and compelling to smaller ones.

Competitive pressure comes not only from new entrants; it may come through price competition, from competitors' improvements to their own products, or intensification of competitive service levels—to name just a few sources. And the midsize company is likely to find that its larger, better-financed competitors have more resources than they do, while its smaller competitors may be even hungrier.

As a result, it probably should come as no surprise that the financial condition and performance of typical threshold companies are less robust than that of their larger competitors in terms of volatility and risk, and levels of debt as well.

Greater Volatility and Risk

The typical midsize company is less stable in sales and earnings than its larger competitors. We examined the financial performance characteristics of all midsize companies (not only the high-growth winners), and compared them with the giant corporations at a number of points in time over the past twenty years. Our earliest research compared the performance of companies in the $20 million to $200 million sales range with the *Fortune* 500 from 1965 to 1970.* That analysis showed that a substantial majority of the *Fortune* companies had unexciting but stable earnings growth—close to the average rate of growth in the economy itself—and that very few lost money.

But the midsize companies as a group were all over the lot. Of them, the great majority had earnings that grew very rapidly, declined seriously, or were negative. A similar analysis for 1978–83 showed a comparable pattern.

Even the winning performers we studied—the best of the midsize group—are not immune from instability. At the extreme, about half of the ABC chief executives told us that at some point in their history their companies had been "broke" or "near broke." Between 1964 and 1983, 85 percent of the ABC companies experienced at least one decline in sales or earnings, and most had more than one down year. More than a

---

*Donald K. Clifford, Jr., *Managing the Threshold Company* (A McKinsey Report to Management, McKinsey & Company, Inc., 1973), pp. 9ff.

third showed a loss in at least one year. (That these companies managed to learn, profit, and recover from these vicissitudes is one characteristic that distinguishes these winners from the rest of the pack. Chapter VI describes how they deal with adversity and turn it to their advantage.)

Greater Indebtedness

Companies live on money. If people are the brains and muscle of the corporation, money is its lifeblood. It is an economic truism that the more money a company has to borrow, the more it risks financial trouble. And over the years, the midsize companies have had to borrow more.

Financially, midsize is a tough stage of corporate life. Until now, after all, the company was local—a protected and personal operation, with short lines of supply and communication and with, for example, little need for field inventories. Its capital needs were understandably modest.

In contrast, growth typically means geographic expansion, which calls for lengthened supply and communication lines, multiple inventories, several factories, offices in several locations, and bigger transportation systems—all of which require capital. Overall, midsize companies carry 15 to 25 percent more debt relative to their equity capital than do the giants, and on average they pay interest rates that run a full percentage point higher.

THE CHALLENGE OF COMPLEXITY

Success brings complexity, and complexity makes management much tougher.

In 1970, Pandick, Inc. (then Pandick Press), pounded out all of its work in a single location on a handful of traditional Linotype machines. Now Pandick operates ten plants in the United States and soon will initiate operations in Europe and the Far East. Pandick operates today with computerized typesetting and offset press equipment, and all its locations are connected by a telecommunications linkup that allows virtually instantaneous changes to financial documents being produced in any number of its locations. This proliferation of locations and modernization of equipment and communications have greatly expanded Pandick's capacity and flexibility—but have also increased enormously the management complexity of the company.

From 1970 to 1980, Pall Corporation, a company marketing a wide range of filters used in aircraft, hospitals, industrial plants, and just about everywhere else, showed the highest total return to shareholders of any *Fortune* 1000 industrial company.* Through the first half of that period, new products were substantially the creation of one man, Dr. David Pall, and decisions about launching new products were reached in weekly meetings of the top three or four executives. Today the company turns out new applications and new products at vastly higher rates, reflecting a far broader range of market sectors served, as well as new filter systems and new technologies. Its management approach has had to change dramatically: In order to cover all the necessary disciplines, the research group now consists of some 125 scientists in 9 separate groups (4 working on basic materials, 5 on equipment). Periodically, 40 top line and functional executives meet to select the new products to be put on the market.

In simplest terms, *small companies are driven by individuals*. The initial growth of a small company is based on personal achievement. While success may spring from the efforts of a small group of people who know one another well, most often the mainspring of early success is a single individual—usually the founder and owner, always the entrepreneur—who knows his business in microscopic detail and runs it personally.

In contrast, *the large company is institutionally driven*. Complexity dictates that success must be achieved through a broad range of strengths that extend throughout the organization—institutional strengths exerted through many leaders responsible for an array of diverse businesses, territories, and functions.

If the midsize high-growth company—in transition between these two phases of corporate life—is to continue growing, it must institutionalize the skills and functions of the entrepreneur in a larger organization while continuing to operate the business successfully day-to-day. To do both, the managers involved have to understand the nature of the various challenges that have resulted from the company's growth *and* they have to recognize which ones are most pressing so they can know where to focus their attention.

In helping threshold companies identify those challenges and prepare to meet them, we sometimes find it useful to illustrate the complexity of the business in a simplified fashion that separates the central complexity of a business into ten components, grouped into three broad classifications: *products* (number; design complexity; degree of integration; rate of technological/product innovation), *market complexity* (geographic scope of production; geographic scope of marketing; number of

---

*In 1984, sales of exactly $1 billion would have placed a company 302nd on the *Fortune* list.

distribution channels; number of end user groups), and *environmental* complexity (competitive intensity; other external pressures). The framework assigns a fixed weight—one, two, three, or four—to each component according to its complexity in the actual company under study (see Exhibit II-1).

Exhibit II-1
Product/market complexity of a business depends on 10 major variables

DEGREE OF COMPLEXITY

Product complexity	Low (1)	Moderate (2)	Substantial (3)	High (4)
1. Number of products	Single line	Several related	Several related, some unrelated	Diverse and complex
2. Complexity of technology/ individual products	Simple design	Multiple components	Highly intricate, technically sensitive	Complex systems
3. Degree of forward/ backward integration	None	Partial, one step	Extensive, more than one step	Highly integrated
4. Rate of innovation - technology, product, process	Slow	Slow to moderate	Moderate to rapid	Rapid
Market/operating complexity				
5. Geographic scope - Production	Single location	2-3 locations	Many domestic, some overseas	International
6. Geographic scope - Marketing	Regional	National	National, significant export	International
7. Distribution channels	Single	2-3	Several	Multiple, complex
8. End-user groups	Single, well defined	2-3	Several, distinct	Multiple, diverse
Environmental complexity				
9. Competitive intensity (price, product, marketing)	Low	Low to moderate	Moderate to intense	Very intense
10. External pressures (economic, governmental, societal)	Stable	Stable to moderate	Moderate to heavy	Volatile: major threats, rapid changes, major penalties

Assigning each critical variable to a complexity column can highlight the scope and magnitude of the tasks senior managers face and help them arrange their priorities for tackling them. It also identifies specific issues that remain to be resolved, enabling managers to evaluate their comparative urgency.

When a company is new and small, it is likely to have a limited product line; it is unlikely to be integrated either forward into distribution or backward into raw materials or components; the rate at which it introduces new products or technology is typically slow. The scope of marketing and production is generally limited; there isn't likely to be formidable competition or pressure from trade unions or the government. The company's people are busy exploiting the initial idea. Such simplicity allows one individual or a small founding team to operate a company informally through personal knowledge and intensive individual involvement. The complexity is low.

But growth inevitably complicates this attractive profile. The number of decisions that must be made, the activities that must be carried out, and the consequent need for coordination and control expand many times.

Consider Millipore Corporation, which competes in such esoteric technologies as microporous membranes, high-pressure liquid chromatography, and supporting systems to separate substances from one another in high-sensitivity applications (for instance, in chemical analysis and in ensuring the purity of intravenous fluids and pharmaceuticals). In 1973, Millipore had a single line of moderately complicated products, all of which were manufactured at its plants in Bedford, Massachusetts, and Jaffrey, New Hampshire. The company had a single direct sales force and some distributors, selling into about a dozen market segments in the United States. Manufacturing was significantly integrated—that is, Millipore had its own machine shops and could fabricate stainless-steel equipment around its membranes. It had a strong flow of new products. Competitive and regulatory pressures were manageable. Sales were $31 million.

Today, Millipore has many more separations technologies, products, and systems and is adding new products at a far faster rate than it did before. It has entered well in excess of a hundred distinct niches to meet the diverse, demanding needs of many different customers. Millipore manufactures and markets products in most major countries around the world and has three direct sales forces and a major distribution organization. Competition is far more intense, the impact of product regulation by the federal Food and Drug Administration and the Environmental Protection Agency is substantial, and international currency dislocations have proved expensive. Millipore's management complexity is far greater now than it was in 1973.

Companies such as Millipore have used the complexity grid to evaluate their growth in complexity and to highlight issues that need attention. In Millipore's case, that growth has been explosive. In 1973, Millipore's complexity was $1 \times 2^6 \times 3^3$, or 1,728. By 1984, complexity had increased to $3^4 \times 4^6$, or 331,776—almost two hundred times greater (see Exhibit II-2).

Exhibit II-2
The Millipore move toward complexity: 1973 $\bigcirc\!\longrightarrow\!\bullet$ 1984

DEGREE OF COMPLEXITY

	Low	Moderate	Substantial	High
Product complexity				
1. Number	$\bigcirc$		$\longrightarrow\bullet$	
2. Complexity		$\bigcirc$		$\longrightarrow\bullet$
3. Integration			$\bigcirc\!\rightarrow\!\bullet$	
4. Innovation			$\bigcirc$	$\longrightarrow\bullet$
Market complexity				
5. Production		$\bigcirc$		$\longrightarrow\bullet$
6. Marketing		$\bigcirc$		$\longrightarrow\bullet$
7. Distribution		$\bigcirc$	$\longrightarrow\bullet$	
8. End-users			$\bigcirc$	$\longrightarrow\bullet$
Environmental complexity				
9. Competition		$\bigcirc$		$\longrightarrow\bullet$
10. External pressures		$\bigcirc$	$\longrightarrow\bullet$	

Such a calculation is simply directional—it demonstrates an exponential increase in Millipore's complexity and, as a result, in the nature of the challenges facing senior management. The number of decisions that must be made, the activities that must be carried out, and the consequent need for techniques of coordination and control have expanded many times. And it suggests some issues—such as product development, global production and marketing, and competitive monitoring—that now need particular management attention.

At its simplest, such an explosion of complexity calls for running the business in very different ways. The entrepreneur can no longer make all the decisions. Specialists have to be put in place; complex communications channels to tap their skills must be created. For the first time there has to be formality—a formal structure, formal management systems, formal mechanisms for communicating objectives and values—because informal personal contacts no longer are enough. And the way the company is managed is never the same again. It's a new ball game. It's unfamiliar. And because companies are only human, it's natural that this encounter with the unknown makes them uneasy and vulnerable to human problems. The demands on corporate leaders are unusually tough as a result.

CHANGING DEMANDS ON LEADERSHIP

The ultimate task in providing leadership in dealing with financial stringency and exploding complexity ultimately falls to a single person—the CEO. Almost without exception, the American Business Conference CEOs told us that complexity in the midsize range demanded they shift their primary attention from running the business to building an organization.

Dee d'Arbeloff, chairman of Millipore, is a good example. From his earliest years, d'Arbeloff was no stranger to rapid change in his world. He was born in 1929 in Paris, the city to which his parents had escaped after being driven out of Russia by the Bolshevik Revolution. He moved to the United States seven years later and got his M.B.A. from Harvard in 1955. An entrepreneur early in his career, d'Arbeloff founded United Research, a Boston-based consulting firm, in the late 1950s. He headed that firm until joining Millipore in 1962, when Millipore's sales were only $2 million. At the time, he intended to spend no more than five years at Millipore to gain manufacturing experience and then move on to found another company.

But it didn't work out that way. After becoming executive vice president of Millipore in 1967 (sales were then $11 million), he became president and CEO in 1971 and chairman in 1980 and led that company's growth to nearly $300 million in 1983. D'Arbeloff comments this way on the changing leadership job at Millipore: "Suddenly, you find yourself facing the need to change everything about the way you run the business except the basic values. You have a fundamental dilemma: The company has become complex and you've got to hire specialists and create divisions to keep it all together. But the very process of imposing formality on an organization tends to create bureaucracy and parochialism. These forces in turn can cause people to lose their business judgment and to focus on the more particular needs and agendas of their own division, department, or function. At that very time, you yourself are no longer as close to the details of the business as you once were. I used to run customer seminars and I used to be out there selling, so I knew firsthand what was going on. I can't do as much of these things anymore. And you have to adapt, or else the vitality of the business—the innovativeness, the responsiveness to changing external events—will fall between the cracks. The CEO simply can't have his finger any longer on the day-to-day pulse of the organization to the extent he used to—there are just too many pulses. The job becomes one of somehow helping each employee think like and behave like a founding owner-entrepreneur. But there's one thing you can't delegate, and that's the job of maintaining the critical balance between innovation and control."

Changing Leadership Roles

The CEO has to play at least four identifiable roles in the growth of a company from inception to giant corporation. First, there is the *founder/start-up CEO,* who knows each detail, does most of the work, and makes every decision himself. He must be followed by the *hands-on operator,* who has many people working under him but still operates the business personally. The *organization builder* puts together a team of managers and creates a management culture, while the *organization leader's* task is to chart a broad direction while maintaining an environment that attracts and motivates people who have the capacity to be builders and leaders themselves.

While some skills are common across all these roles—for example, understanding the economics and dynamics of the business, and the ability to persuade and motivate other people—still other requirements of these distinct phases are highly diverse. In Chapter V, we will examine in detail the characteristics and practices of CEOs who succeed and the ways they have coped with the challenges posed by these changing growth requirements.

In fact, it is rare that one person carries an organization through all four phases of CEO leadership. Few individuals have the personal capability, flexibility, and energy to evolve through two phases, let alone all four. Few CEOs of *Fortune* 500 companies were in management positions with those companies when they were small, and fewer still were founders. Yet if the company is to continue to grow and prosper, the transitions must take place. *That* they occur is much more important than whether they occur in the persona of one individual or several.

The obstacles in the path of reaching midsize, let alone moving through it successfully, are formidable. The first step is the will to grow. The second—an even more difficult step—is developing and exercising the skills needed to win. Financial volatility and risk, explosive growth in management complexity, and the need for a transition in leadership style—all at the same time the company is attempting to develop new businesses and compete effectively with larger competitors—define the magnitude of the task.

Yet a small group of companies confronts these obstacles, negotiates successfully over and around them, and outperforms the best of the nation's and the world's largest companies. The rest of this book takes a close look at the anatomy and dynamics of these winners and tells how they took the classic challenges of transition and turned them to their own advantage.

CHAPTER III

Guerrilla Strategies

In many important ways, what we think of as business strategy finds its roots in military strategy.* One tenet of military strategy, of course, is that the successful warrior finds his adversary's weak spot and takes him off guard—guerrilla warfare. Midsize growth companies, lacking the advantages of scale and resources, have become masters of guerrilla warfare. Like the American revolutionaries two centuries ago, they base their strategies on selection of the battlefield, speed and surprise, fanatical spirit, concentration of effort, and the triumph of ingenuity and common sense over heavy odds.

Our McKinsey colleagues have defined a successful business strategy as one that provides *a sustainable competitive advantage based upon delivering superior value to the customer.* When a business has it in place, the world becomes its oyster. Everything desirable can follow. Shareholders are rewarded, suppliers and distributors are gratified, growth provides pride and enviable opportunity for employees, and wealth is created. It is a concept easy to describe but excruciatingly difficult to implement.

In recent years the theory of business strategy has received too

---

*The analogy between military and business strategy is a useful one, but like all, it has limits. Military encounters by definition must have losers: They are win/lose games—with victors and vanquished—or lose/lose games—where there are no winners, only losers. While many competitive business endeavors also have win/lose or lose/lose outcomes, others have win/win outcomes when new markets and industries are created.

much attention and its practice too little. During the decade of the seventies, American managers became fascinated by fashionable tools and technical theories. Business-school graduates were trained to think through the frameworks of growth/share matrixes. They talked in barnyard portfolio-management analogies that featured cash cows to be milked, dogs to be taken to the economic pound, and wildcats to be domesticated. They conceptualized about experience and cost curves.

Often, the high priests of strategy, the corporate planners, employed those and the rest of the contents of their strategic tool kits to create technically correct, analytically elegant, sophisticated strategic theories— which, when followed blindly (as they sometimes were), just didn't mesh with the workaday world of customers, competitors, and employees. In extreme cases the sideshow ran off with the circus—planners *made* the promises of performance and line managers were left to *keep* them.

The winning midsize companies we examined are exceptions to those abuses. Most are superior strategists; some are superb.

From our discussions with entrepreneurs, our comparison of their performance compared with that of their competitors, and extensive statistical analysis of their strategic practices, we've discerned that the great majority of winning performers combine five strategic traits:

- a focus on *how* to compete, less so on where
- emphasis on innovation
- skill at creating and serving niches defined by customers' needs
- ability to identify and build on distinctive strengths
- recognition that the value of product or service, not just its price, spells success.

WHERE VS. HOW TO COMPETE

Glue, industrial hardware, credit reports, furniture, packaging materials, and prospectus-printing have, apart from an almost absolute lack of allure, very little in common. It would take some effort and imagination for most of us to think of six more unexciting, mature sectors of the economy, or six more apparently marginal, sleepy businesses with modest promise of profit, or six lines of work in which we'd rather a son or daughter promise not to plan a career. A mutual fund that specialized in these industries, competing against other funds in communications, high technology, and health care, would probably appeal to as many people as ask their dentists for elective root-canal work.

Yet in all six of those industries—no matter how unfashionable and unexciting they seem at first blush—some companies have grown explosively and profitably enough to be included among our winning performers. Some of these companies have been identified as the best places to work in America. And an investor who put his funds into these companies a decade ago would have done very, very well:

Glue. Ever since man's clumsiness led him to break things, he has sought to stick them together again. In 1956, Vernon Krieble, a chemistry professor at Trinity College in Hartford, Connecticut, discovered a way to make pieces of metal, like nuts and bolts, lock together. With his family and friends he started a business of making and selling his revolutionary anaerobic adhesive drop by drop. In its first year the Loctite Corporation sold about $300 worth of the glue a month. Today, Loctite is a $240-million business that holds about 85 percent of the worldwide anaerobic adhesive market. Loctite's sales have grown fivefold since 1974—from $48 million to $242 million in 1984—and the company has expanded into the consumer market as well.

Widgets. During the past two decades (1964 to 1983), Harvey Hubbell—a Connecticut-based manufacturer of plugs, switches, outlets, fuse boxes, and other electrical gear—has grown in profits every year and in sales for nineteen of those twenty years—a record few enterprises in America can match.* In 1983 a $422-million enterprise, whose profits had tripled during the preceding ten years, Hubbell employed some fifty-seven hundred people who produced more than four thousand electrical products, outdoor lights, rebuilt air-conditioning compressors, and controls.

Even in widgets, there are more than a few topflight achievers. According to the understandably popular book *The 100 Best Companies to Work For in America,*† the Kollmorgen Company should be high on the list for anyone seeking a rewarding career. Kollmorgen makes top-quality circuit boards, interconnection systems, specialty motors, and periscopes—$326 million worth of them in 1984. Both Augat, a New England producer of interconnection devices, and Thomas & Betts, a New Jersey manufacturer of electrical and electronic connectors and accessories, have achieved substantial long-term sales and earning growth records as well.

---

*Sales were down in the recession year of 1982 by 4 percent.
†Robert Levering, Milton Moskowitz, and Michael Katz, *The 100 Best Companies to Work For in America* (Reading, Mass.: Addison-Wesley, 1984).

Maybe Benjamin Braddock's uncle in *The Graduate* should have whispered, "Widgets—think about it."

Credit Reports. In 1983, the Chilton Corporation had the greatest increase in the market value of its shares of any of the American Stock Exchange's member companies. An old-line family-operated credit reporting business begun in Dallas decades ago, Chilton has one business —it collects, files, and retrieves credit reports on individuals. In 1965, when it was a $4.5-million company, its current chief executive, Bob Chilton, decided that the future lay in computerizing what had been a fragmented, manually executed, paper-dominated service business. Investing $8.5 million in software and computers—more than the company had made during its entire history—made Chilton the pioneer. By early 1985, Chilton's market value had risen to $155 million.

Furniture. If you want to find another of those hundred best companies to work for, you might go to Zeeland, Michigan, to the headquarters of one of the few companies in America where 100 percent of the full-time regular employees own stock. Herman Miller, Inc., has been making office furniture there since 1930. By sticking to office and factory furnishings and doing it well, Herman Miller's sales grew tenfold (from $40 million to more than $400 million) between 1974 and 1984, while profits increased eleven times (from $2.5 million to $29 million) during the same decade.

Plastic Bubbles. Sealed Air Corporation makes plastic bubbles—the ones that come stuffed into boxes shipped through the mail. These sheets of plastic bubbles are high-tech excelsior, the successor to yesteryear's shredded newspaper and wood shavings. Plastic bubbles are good business: By 1984 Sealed Air was a $166-million business whose sales grew from $19 million in 1974 and whose profits shot up eight times, from $1.5 million to $11.9 million. Plastic bubbles aren't used only for packaging fragile goods, either. Great big sheets of them can keep the heat in—and the bugs and leaves out of—the swimming pool you can afford if you invested in a winning performer.

Printing. A rite of passage for newly minted associates of Wall Street law firms and investment banks is showing up in the wee hours of the morning at the printer's to deliver, inspect, and make last-minute changes in offering statements, prospectuses, shareholder notices, and the like. The printer these tired but well-paid men and women visit most often is Pandick, the nation's leading printer of fast-turnaround financial documents we looked at in Chapter II. Although printing in general is neither a growth industry nor particularly profitable, Pandick's niche strategy has been lucrative. It's now a $158 million business that has grown seven times in sales and thirteen times in earnings since 1975.

* * *

These winning performers in unexciting industries are not the rare exceptions. Our sample of American Business Conference companies is in fact broadly representative of both midsize companies and of the American economy as a whole. But beyond our sample, the evidence that business success is essentially independent of the industrial sector is overwhelming.

Our examination of all the 6,117 nonfinancial midsize companies whose performance is recorded in the Dun & Bradstreet data base was especially revealing. When we looked to see in which industries those companies with sales growth in excess of 25 percent a year operated, we found winners in *all fifty-eight* two-digit Standard Industrial Classification codes, encompassing the major profit-seeking segments of the Gross National Product.* In fact, in fifty of these fifty-eight sectors, at least 10 percent of companies enjoyed sales growth rates at this level. For readers who enjoy bell curves and statistical distributions, Exhibits III-1 and III-2 display the data and analysis.

Exhibit III-1
**DISTRIBUTION OF INDUSTRIES BY PERCENTAGE
OF INDUSTRY PARTICIPANTS EXPERIENCING "HIGH GROWTH"***

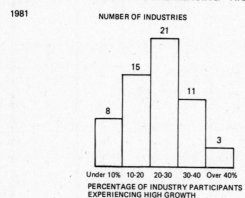

1981   NUMBER OF INDUSTRIES

PERCENTAGE OF INDUSTRY PARTICIPANTS
EXPERIENCING HIGH GROWTH

* Achieving sufficient growth to be in the top quartile of all midsize companies in terms of sales growth

Note: 58 (2-digit primary SIC) industries representing 6,117 companies analyzed; excludes finance, insurance, and real estate

Sources: Dun & Bradstreet; McKinsey analysis

A further analysis of the twenty SIC manufacturing sectors confirmed that profit performance is also independent of industry type. In nineteen of the twenty, at least 10 percent of all participants earned returns on equity in excess of 18 percent.

*See footnote, page 5 for a brief explanation of the SIC system.

Exhibit III-2
**DISTRIBUTION OF MANUFACTURING INDUSTRIES BY PERCENTAGE
OF INDUSTRY PARTICIPANTS EARNING A HIGH RETURN ON EQUITY***

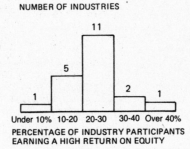

NUMBER OF INDUSTRIES

PERCENTAGE OF INDUSTRY PARTICIPANTS
EARNING A HIGH RETURN ON EQUITY

* Sufficient to place a company in the top quartile of all midsize companies in terms of return on equity

Note: 20 (2-digit primary SIC) manufacturing industries representing 1,157 midsize companies analyzed

Sources: Compustat; McKinsey analysis

Nor is it only in the midsize economy that companies can achieve superior performance in drab industries. Among the excellent giants—the companies chronicled by Peters and Waterman in *In Search of Excellence*—there are, in addition to high-tech stars such as Hewlett-Packard and IBM, a textile company (Blue Bell), a candy maker (Mars), an auto-parts company (Dana), an engineering and construction company (Bechtel), and an electrical-appliance manufacturer (Maytag).

A look at smaller emerging companies tells the same story. Peter Drucker noted in *The Wall Street Journal* that an examination of *Inc.* magazine's list of the fastest-growing publicly owned companies younger than fifteen years showed that "80 of 100 companies on the 1982 list were decidedly low-tech or no-tech—women's-wear makers, restaurant chains and the like."*

The 1984 *Forbes* 300 Up & Comers list—publicly held high-growth, high-profit companies no larger than $250 million—tells the same tale. Half the top twenty companies it identifies are in nonglamor industries such as footware, fibers, clothing, and ice cream. But the five-year average return on equity these companies have achieved ranges from 51

*"Why America's Got So Many Jobs," *The Wall Street Journal* (January 24, 1984), p. 32.

percent to 713 percent, and their five-year annual sales growth rates range from 67 percent to 810 percent.*

And the new entrepreneurs are well aware that business success is not limited to fashionable, exciting sectors, but can be found in some of the economy's seemingly more mundane sectors as well. In addition to our conversations with young men and women starting businesses, the December 1984 issue of *Esquire* magazine—entitled "The Best of the New Generation: Men and Women Under Forty Who Are Changing America"—offers interesting evidence. Of forty-two leaders in business and industry the magazine profiled, about half were entrepreneurs who had started and were still managing new, highly successful businesses. (The others were in endeavors like investment banking and venture capital or were with established corporations.) Some of the entrepreneurs, like Steven Jobs and Stephen Wosniak, who founded Apple Computers, or Mitch Kapor, who started Lotus Development, are clearly associated with high-technology enterprises in computers, biotechnology, and medicine—but at least as many made their mark in less fashionable fields—chocolate chip cookies, garden tools, auto parts, seafood, tea, and toys, among others.

We also discovered that high profitability and fast overall market growth don't necessarily go hand-in-hand. The theory that fast-growing markets are the place to be is intuitively appealing: growth should connote opportunity. But our analysis of 525 midsize businesses and business units, drawn from the PIMS program of the Strategic Planning Institute in Cambridge, Massachusetts,† shows virtually no relationship between the two. We traced raw profitability (return on investment before interest and overhead) over four years. In markets with real growth of less than 5 percent, the average return on investment was 21 percent. In markets where real growth exceeded 20 percent, the average was 19 percent. Between these two extremes, returns varied as well (see Exhibit III-3).

All this is to say that fashionable, growing markets don't necessarily mean success nor do unfashionable, mature industries necessarily portend failure. There are notable success stories in each. But how they compete, rather than in which broad industry, holds more useful lessons about business success.

---

*"The Up & Comer 300," *Forbes* (November 5, 1984), pp. 128–74.
†See Appendix II for a description of the PIMS data base.

Exhibit III-3
REAL MARKET GROWTH RATE AND BUSINESS PERFORMANCE
Four year average return on investment*

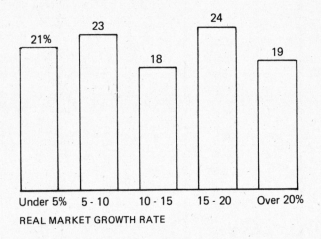

* Before interest expense and corporate overhead; 525 midsize businesses
Source: PIMS Program

INNOVATION: THE WINNING COMPETITIVE EDGE

"If you want to succeed," John D. Rockefeller, Sr., said, "you should strike out on new paths rather than travel the worn paths of accepted success." The winning performers agree—and prove the point. Innovation—the purposeful application of new ideas—underpins the success of the winning performers. These companies innovate early and often. As noted in Chapter I, among the American Business Conference companies we surveyed, three quarters reported that it was a unique product or way of doing business that brought the company its initial success.

Our analysis of the PIMS program, with its information about a wide range of business units with varying records of success, also shows the importance of innovation. Companies that characterized themselves as "pioneers"—innovators—fared substantially better than followers even as markets mature (see Exhibit III-4).

Winning companies innovate continuously. Among our survey participants, 84 percent characterize themselves as frequent innovators. In

Exhibit III-4
TIMING OF MARKET ENTRY AND BUSINESS PERFORMANCE
Four year average return on investment*

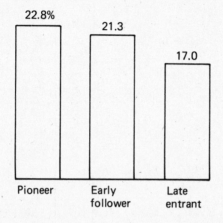

* Before interest expense and corporate overhead; 525 midsize businesses
Source: PIMS Program

addition, the survey respondents report that, on average, more than a quarter of their sales come from products that didn't exist five years ago; of these, 40 percent did not exist a decade ago. They said further that, on average, their companies account for 40 percent to 60 percent of all the major innovations in their industries.

Practical pioneering in business can take many forms. In some instances the innovator creates and offers a product or service that simply didn't exist before. In others, new products are developed by refining or redesigning old ones. In still others, innovators envision and devise new ways of doing business. And in many cases they create a new market. Let's examine each of these forms of innovation in turn.

New Products

At the high-tech end, Seymour Cray pioneered the creation of the supercomputer—first at Control Data Corporation and later with three generations of supercomputers at Cray Research. In low and medium tech, Safety-Kleen developed the product and service system to clean greasy machine parts and tools, and Sealed Air introduced plastic bubble protective packaging.

In the high-technology companies, innovation as a bedrock of strategy is a necessity, not a luxury. J. P. Barger, a founder and now president of Dynatech Corporation, a Massachusetts producer of communications electronics, explained it to us this way: "In 1962 I attended the American Management Association president's course where we discussed major discontinuities in Western society—things like the population trends, the information explosion, technological advances, and the like. One of my observations was that product cycles would grow shorter and shorter—meaning that any company in a single product would not be in business long. And to survive in the era of shorter product cycles—especially in the really fast-changing high-technology areas—it's necessary to have lots of new products in the works, to smooth out the cycles."

Barger's observation proved both prophetic and profitable for Dynatech, which has posted thirteen years of increases in sales, earnings, and earnings per share. In the decade since 1973, Dynatech achieved compound annual growth rates of 32 percent in sales, and 33 percent in earnings. About two thirds of that growth has been internally generated; the rest has resulted from an aggressive program of related acquisitions.

In 1965, Ray Stata and his MIT roommate, Matthew Lorber, founded Analog Devices, the Route 128 producer of electronic components and systems whose return on equity in 1983 was more than twice the industry average. Stata has focused this fast-growing company (30 percent a year since 1978) intensively on innovation. And innovate Analog Devices does: In 1983 it introduced thirty-five new products—twenty-nine of them unique in the field.

Stata's obsession with innovation—he is coauthor of a book, *The Innovators**—is founded on his view of marketplace economics. As he told us in his Norwood, Massachusetts, office one winter afternoon: "You know, a lot of people seek market leadership so they can become the low-cost producer. That's hogwash. The reason to seek market leadership is to attract the top talent and have the resources to clear the brush and trailblaze the new frontiers."

In an industry plagued by price wars, oversupply, and recent deficits at leading companies like National Semiconductor and Texas Instruments, the Analog strategy has been to compete at the leading edge of technology—the high-performance, state-of-the-art (or -science) applica-

---

*James Botkin, Dan Dimanescu, and Ray Stata, *The Innovators: Re-discovering America's Creative Energy* (New York: Harper & Row, 1984).

tions, where precision and reliability are more important than price. As Gerald Fishman, an Analog vice president, explained in *Electronic Business* magazine, "We avoid the semiconductor commodity business, preferring to sell into market niches with what I call proprietary products, meaning they have no second sources."* Analog markets more than two hundred proprietary products that help computers recognize and interpret real-world signals—be they human heartbeats, airline cabin pressures, or radio signals. *The New York Times* reported, "Analog Devices is the market leader over all and often the only source of supply for particular models."†

To Stata, the key to innovation is creating and sustaining a working environment that serves as a "magnet" to attract top talent. "Most management processes inhibit rather than facilitate innovation." So Stata and his management team devote inordinate attention to finding the "ready-made" innovators who feel inhibited by the corporate climates of other companies and to stressing and rewarding practices like mentorship, "empowerment," and idea championship to help develop "latent innovators." (See Chapter IV.)

New products are not the exclusive domain of high-technology businesses; witness the Perdue Oven Stuffer Roaster, the Thomas & Betts Ty-Rap wire fastener, or the Dunkin' Donuts Munchkin doughnut hole snack.

New "Old" Products

Some of the successful innovators we studied focus their effort on improving existing products so radically that they become new ones in the eyes of their customers. One of the best illustrations is Key Pharmaceuticals' development of new ways to administer old medicine. Miami-based Key Pharmaceuticals ranks among the top performers in the American Business Conference and the nation. In the five-year period 1979–83 it increased its sales and its profits almost tenfold, posting a return on equity that constantly exceeded 25 percent.

Pharmaceuticals is a tough business for a new competitor. And Key is one of a select few new pharmaceutical companies founded since World War II.‡ The conventional way to succeed in the business is to plow heavy investment into research and development, spend years testing new drugs and navigating government safety requirements, and then take these new drugs to the medical profession

---

*"Niche Chips: A Three-Pronged Plan to Boost Productivity," *Electronic Business* (September 1983), pp. 178–82.

†Robert Metz, "Semiconductor Maker's Goals," *The New York Times* (February 25, 1982), p. D8.

‡Marion Laboratories is another very successful midsize growth company that entered the industry in 1950.

via armies of "detail men." In this high-technology, highly regulated, research-oriented industry, Key innovates in a far different way.

Key's product called Theo-Dur is a good example. The most frequently prescribed drug for the treatment of asthma in the United States, it's made from theophylline, now a commodity drug that has been known and prescribed for decades. Key's innovation was to figure out how to administer it more effectively. In Theo-Dur's case, Key made it time-released so that a steady dose enters the bloodstream over a twelve-hour period. The U.S. Food and Drug Administration gave Theo-Dur a rarely awarded "zero-order release" claim, in essence verifying that the time-release system is the effective equivalent of intravenous delivery systems. Key's time-release concept and technology are so successful—and potentially applicable to other medicines—that giant international drug companies have signed agreements with little Key to develop versions of their products jointly with this once-upstart company.

Nitroglycerin provides another Key example. It has been prescribed to patients with angina pectoris since the 1800s. It used to be that someone with angina would pop a pill under the tongue when an attack threatened and could count on a short period of relief. Key, however, developed a bandage treated with nitroglycerin that can be applied to the patient's chest. It not only works faster, but also provides a steadier dose that prevents attacks over a longer time than a pill can. Another old drug—another new treatment.

Michael Jaharis, Key's chief executive (son of an immigrant from the Greek island of Lesbos—which enables him jokingly to introduce himself as a "Lesbian drug dealer from Miami"), got his start in drugs in the army. On the day he showed up at the induction center, everyone with a last name in the first half of the alphabet was assigned to be trained as a medic. After Korea, Jaharis made ends meet in law school by working as a drug detail man for Miles Laboratories, and upon graduation he became a lawyer and later a manager for the company.

In 1971 Key was struggling, having lost more than $600,000. Jaharis and his partner, a physician named Phillip Frost, took control of the company and turned it around.

Key's strategy for innovation was an act of necessity, not choice. Because of Key's financial situation, Jaharis set out to innovate. His challenge was to figure out what the company could do with no money—perhaps the quintessential challenge to innovation. The Food and Drug Administration, which regulates the pharmaceutical industry, demands that new drugs be both safe and efficacious—that is, they must do no harm and indeed must do good. And proving safety and efficacy is an arduous and expensive process. By necessity Jaharis focused on accepted drugs about which there was no question as to efficacy or safety and put full effort into improving their delivery. By 1984 Key Pharmaceuticals had become a $150-million enterprise.

New Ways of Doing Business

Innovation is not limited to new and better products; sometimes the way the business is conducted can be changed to bring real value to customers. Consider the case of Bergen Brunswig, a health-products distributor whose success has now pulled it past our billion-dollar upper limit.

One of the toughest, slug-it-out businesses in America is wholesaling. Traditionally, local, intensely price-competitive wholesalers kept the loyalty of their customers from one order to the next only as long as they could guarantee the lowest price, together with reliable delivery. And within wholesaling, one of the most intensely competitive fields is the drug business. That competitive intensity grew as drug chains across the nation began to increase their share of the overall drugstore market following World War II.

In the old days, the wholesaler's representative would call on the pharmacist, write down the orders for hundreds or even thousands of items on a pad of paper, and carry it back to the warehouse, where the myriad items would be pulled from shelves and delivered to the customer's store. It was a tough, local, hand-to-mouth business, not one in which you would especially expect to find an especially dramatic success story. Retailers did business with numerous wholesalers, which added to the wholesalers' costs, and it was difficult to compete with direct-selling manufacturers.

In 1956, when Emil Martini took over as head of a family wholesaling business, the company was doing about $16 million in annual volume. In debt up to the then-Bergen Drug Company's corporate eyeballs, Emil and his management team decided that agility and inventiveness were indispensable to their survival. They were among the first to use extensive sale and leaseback of "everything that was not nailed down," as he put it, to raise the money to keep going. He also recognized early that strict inventory control was the fastest way to keep financial requirements to a manageable level, and so Bergen became one of the first companies to employ punch-card machines in inventory control.

Most important, however, Martini was looking for ways to link his business inextricably with that of his customers'; to get away from the high customer turnover and uncertainty of a business that operated solely on the basis of day-to-day pricing. Though Martini gave customer service top priority from the start, his critical breakthrough innovation came in 1974, when the company designed a hand-held computer terminal "scanner" that allowed pharmacies to control their inventories and order merchandise with great speed and accuracy while using about one quarter the labor and time required by conventional systems. Since labor and inventory are the major costs of running a drugstore, Bergen Brunswig's customers welcomed the new system enthusiastically. Customers relied on Bergen as their primary source, which increased efficiency and competitiveness. Martini's program to build a "partnership" with his retail customers was launched on the basis of that scanner and became the driving force behind Bergen Brunswig's march to $1.7 billion in 1984 revenues.

Bergen Brunswig's innovations did not stop with the original terminal and the related system. The company developed price stickers that Bergen Brunswig prints for its customers, showing not only the product's customized price as determined by each retailer but also coded to provide precise data on turnover. The company also supplies shelf labels with computer-readable codes that pharmacies use to establish permanent shelf positions for thousands of items. And Bergen has developed advanced computer-based systems that allow drugstores to reduce inventories further and achieve seven-day-a-week, twenty-four-hour-a-day communication with their local warehouses.

Beyond these product ordering and inventory control systems, Bergen Brunswig has been an innovator in providing management control data and promotional programs extensively to customers. As Bergen Brunswig grew, it developed the capability to provide outstanding merchandising programs for its customers that go well beyond what the drugstores could do on their own. As a result, Bergen Brunswig continues to take an increasing share of the business of regional and even national drug chains. Furthermore, while cementing the partnership with its customers, Bergen Brunswig has achieved far more predictability in its business. Its innovativeness has helped revolutionize its industry and has contributed to a rise in Bergen Brunswig's common stock of 44 percent, compounded annually, since 1975.

MCI's tradition of questioning authority and reversing the conventional wisdom has brought profound change to the once-stable monopolistic long-distance telephone business. Begun as a private-line service between Chicago and St. Louis using microwave technology rather than embedded twisted copper wire lines, MCI found itself in serious financial difficulty in the late 1960s and turned to Bill McGowan, an entrepreneur and consultant who had earned a reputation as a turnaround specialist. McGowan saw four forces at work. *First,* he saw that government regulation of the telephone system was the critical determinant of any communications company's degree of strategic freedom. *Second,* he sensed that the Bell System's long-standing monopoly position had bred some economic inefficiencies. *Third,* he realized that Bell's own advances in technology provided opportunities for competition. *Fourth,* he knew that Bell set its long-distance rates high so as to keep the cost of basic telephone rental and local service low—a virtual invitation to somebody not in the local service business to take advantage of the high long-distance rates.

McGowan decided there was room—that in fact there was a need—for another phone company. After months of reviewing documents in the Federal Communications Commission's public reading room, McGowan discerned the forest where others had seen only trees. Although local telephone systems across the land were legal monopolies, long-distance service connecting the local monopolies had never been granted exclusively to a single provider. Most everyone else assumed it had, but nowhere in the law, congressional committee reports, or FCC rulings and regulations had it in fact happened.

McGowan also observed the FCC's practice of ruling on service requests within sixty days of receipt. In essence, if no one objected to a request (for instance, to be allowed to inaugurate private-line service between—say—Cheektowaga, New York, and Perth Amboy, New Jersey), the FCC routinely granted the license. Thousands of such requests, usually highly technical in nature, flowed through the FCC bureaucracy each year. McGowan's plan of attack was simple. Simultaneously, he submitted hundreds of operating license requests for private-line service between major telephone markets. And no one noticed until he had created a second long-distance telephone network.

Lots of court cases, lawyers' bills, congressional hearings, and FCC rulings later, McGowan's vision of competition in the telephone industry is the law of the land, and MCI has become a $1.9-billion company whose sales and profits grew by as much as 100 percent a year between 1978 and 1983. Although profits suffered in 1984 (a topic we cover in Chapter VI), MCI continues to expand. Its innovation was to bring competition to what had previously been regarded as a natural and legal monopoly. McGowan knew not to take anything, especially the status quo, for granted.

Of course, business system innovations are not limited to medical supply distributors or long-distance telephone companies. Dunkin' Donuts brought the franchising concept to coffee and doughnuts. Levitz brought mass merchandising to furniture. Frank Perdue decided to advertise chickens on television. In fact, among the most innovative companies, we observe a *shift over time from competition on the basis of new products to competition through distinctive ways of doing business*. As Exhibit III-5 depicts, of the innovators we surveyed, 72 percent attributed their early success to product or service innovation—but only 44 percent rely on it now to sustain their momentum. And though 52 percent said distinctive ways of doing business led to their initial success, 72 percent say that's how they maintain it today.

Exhibit III-5
CONTINUING INNOVATORS*:
THE SHIFTING NATURE OF INNOVATION

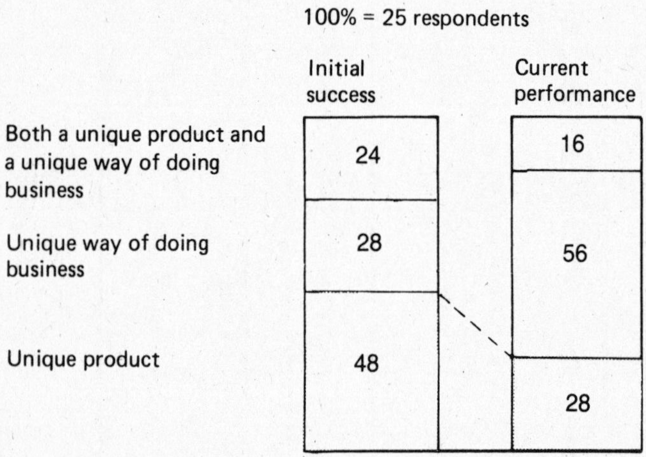

100% = 25 respondents

	Initial success	Current performance
Both a unique product and a unique way of doing business	24	16
Unique way of doing business	28	56
Unique product	48	28

* Continuing innovators are defined as those companies that attribute both their initial success and current performance to innovation

Source: Survey of ABC membership

Whatever its character, innovation becomes increasingly difficult to maintain as businesses become bigger and more complex—as 59 percent of the CEOs we surveyed told us. The 61 percent of our survey respondents who say it still provides them with their competitive advantage represent a significant dropoff from the 74 percent who attributed their initial success to innovation (see Exhibit III-6). Furthermore, among a broader base of less successful midsize companies we have encountered professionally, a high proportion recognize that their innovative drive has diminished and are deeply concerned that their people may be resting on their laurels.

Exhibit III-6
**IMPORTANCE OF UNIQUE FACTORS TO INITIAL SUCCESS AND
CURRENT PERFORMANCE FROM SURVEY**

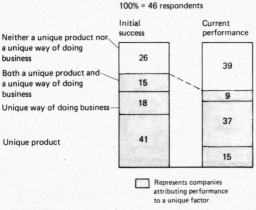

100% = 46 respondents

	Initial success	Current performance
Neither a unique product nor a unique way of doing business	26	39
Both a unique product and a unique way of doing business	15	9
Unique way of doing business	18	37
Unique product	41	15

☐ Represents companies attributing performance to a unique factor

Source: Survey of ABC membership

The message is clear. The more successful a company becomes, the more difficulty it encounters in maintaining its innovativeness—and the harder the winning performer knows he has to try.

New Markets

In many cases, the innovative entrepreneurs create markets that didn't exist before. This chapter is being written with a Cross pen, for example. While pens have been around since paper was invented, the A. T. Cross Company created the high-quality, upscale pen market (yes, the pen in hand was a gift). Once this manuscript is typed on an IBM text-editing system and proofread, it will be photocopied on a Xerox machine. (Xerox literally created a new market by making it easy and inexpensive to copy documents.) It then will be sent to our publisher via Federal Express. Before Federal Express was created in 1973, there was no mass market in guaranteed overnight delivery of packages and documents. Aside from the paper, every product or service we used to produce this manuscript is an example of a new or better product—gift pens, electronic text-editing, Xerography, and overnight document delivery.

There are new markets other than those associated with writing a book. Sometimes creating a market simply means finding new customers for old products. The early tribulations of John Cullinane—the founder and now chief executive of Cullinet, a leading software company—illustrate the process.

In the spring of 1968, Cullinane, a strapping Boston Irishman, figured he had paid his dues in learning about computer software working for other people and decided it was time to do business a different way.

His concept of the new business was clear. First, he believed that people make the difference in a knowledge-intensive business like software and that his new company would do everything to attract and keep people who could make that difference. His second belief was that computer software, at the time a custom one-of-a-kind art, could be more like a product—that basic software could be developed and then would be customized, instead of starting each new assignment with a clean sheet of paper. Cullinet's president, Bob Goldman, described the concept to us as a "set of tools to make businesses more productive—not a finished good." Third, Cullinet sought to acquire software products and designs from leading-edge customers who had developed software themselves to meet their own needs but who were not in the "software business." Two business values—"integrity and customer service"—pervaded his concept.

To this end, John Cullinane opened shop with a handful of compatriots who sought to reorder the world of software in America. Their first product, developed internally rather than acquired from the outside, was called "CULPRIT"—an easy way to produce reports from computers programmed in the Cobol language. Unfortunately, CULPRIT attracted few customers, and with $500 in the bank, an $8,500 payroll due in two days, and no means of visible support, Cullinane took his single unsuccessful product and repositioned it in the marketplace—renaming CULPRIT the "EDP Auditor." Rather than try to sell it to programming and electronic data processing departments, where "not-invented-here" was the kiss of death, Cullinane saw a new market—not the staff people who ran the computers, but the internal (and later external) auditors who now had to deal with computers, programs, and tapes as well as with the bookkeepers, adding machines, and paper records they were so familiar with. In essence Cullinane created a new market—with special training, new features and audit routines, separate support services—and even the creation of an EDP Auditor Users Group, who could commiserate on the changing times and collaborate with Cullinane on how to meet them with Cullinane products.

The EDP Auditor—an old product for a new market—was Cullinane's first commercial success, the one that gave the fledgling company a base upon which to build. In 1973 Cullinet acquired from B. F. Goodrich the rights to the Integrated Database Management System (IDMS) that the tire manufacturer had developed for its own use. After numerous refinements, improvements, and revisions, IDMS became the basic product line for Cullinane's data-base management offerings. By 1975 Cullinane had applied the "dictionary" concept to data bases—but applied it in such a way that both EDP professionals as well as generalist end users could use it to manipulate, access, and generally unlock the full potential of the computer. The result was a single set of software programs that could be used by everyone—saving customers the expense of having to create duplicate software for various users of the data. Cullinet's longtime employees call its history of building on strength "creeping integration."

Having mastered data-base management, the company turned to developing or acquiring and then offering functional software products—aimed at helping clients find and use data they already had to solve problems in manufacturing, sales, personnel, finance, and the like. Having created this Chinese menu of software tools for corporate clients, Cullinet then moved to what it calls "decision support"—integrating the micro and personal computers used by that client's managers at remote locations with the client's mainframe machine, its overall data base, and its various management and analysis applications.

In short, Cullinet's big innovation was putting it all together so that corporate clients can do one-stop shopping for data and analysis. Putting it all together seems to work. Cullinet counts among its current clients such leading-edge customers as the Strategic Air Command, Harvard University, Citicorp, Lloyds of London, General Electric, AT&T, ITT, and DuPont. With some twenty thousand installations under its belt, Cullinet counts twenty-eight consecutive quarters of growth in sales and profits—56 percent and 51 percent, respectively, at this writing.

CREATING AND LEADING IN NICHE MARKETS

Midsize high-growth companies succeed by identifying and meeting the needs of certain kinds of customers, not all customers, for special kinds of products and services, not all products or all services. Business academics call this market segmentation. Entrepreneurs call it common sense.

Comprehensive analysis as well as our own interviews and survey underscore the importance not only of competing in targeted segments—market niches—but also of leading in them. PIMS data on the performance of 525 midsize business units show clearly that participation in smaller markets is more likely to be profitable than participation in larger ones (see Exhibit III-7) and that return on investment is generally

Exhibit III-7
SIZE OF MARKET AND BUSINESS PERFORMANCE
Four year average return on investment*

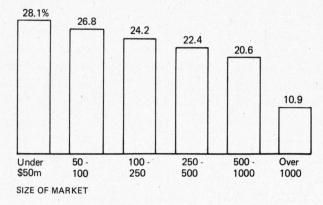

SIZE OF MARKET

* Before interest expense and corporate overhead; 525 midsize businesses

Source: PIMS Program

Exhibit III-8
MARKET SHARE RANK AND BUSINESS PERFORMANCE
Four year average return on investment*

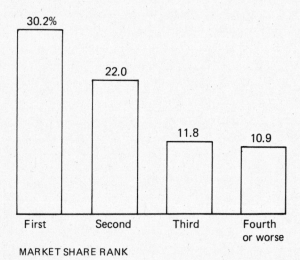

MARKET SHARE RANK

* Before interest expense and corporate overhead; 525 midsize businesses

Source: PIMS Program

higher if one has the largest market share (see Exhibit III-8). In our American Business Conference survey, nearly four out of five respondents told us that they compete in niches, and two thirds reported that more than half their revenues come from niches in which they are the leader.

For the midsize company, the niche strategy is born of necessity but cultivated by design. Small and midsize companies simply don't have the resources or staying power to fight head-to-head battles across the board against large, entrenched competition. Instead, they seek out niches that initially are either unknown to larger potential competitors or too small to attract them. Through sheer perseverance and dedication to serving their customers better than anyone else—which to them means knowing the customers and their needs better than anyone else—the midsize companies capture niches and protect them from even the biggest and most formidable companies.

FINDING THE RIGHT NICHE

Finding the right niche isn't always love at first sight; it's often a matter of trial and error or plain serendipity. The stories of three successful niche players might be illuminating: Charter Medical Corporation, the leading investor-owned provider of mental health services in the nation; ASK Computer Systems, Inc., a fast-growing Silicon Valley producer of software; and Millipore Corporation, one of New England's high-tech leaders.

From Real Estate to Psychiatric Care

Charter Medical Corporation is the largest employer in Macon, the seat of Bibb County in central Georgia. Bibb County is named after a physician, Dr. William Wyatt Bibb, so it's fitting that Macon's best-known business is a medical enterprise.

But Charter Medical began as a family real-estate enterprise. As Bill Fickling, Charter's chairman and chief executive, tells the story, his father, a pillar of the Macon community, ran a successful commercial and residential real-estate company that eventually moved into the property development business. At first it developed shopping centers and the like. Later it began to develop nursing homes. Building the homes led to owning and managing them. Nursing homes led to hospitals, and that in turn led to hospital management contracts around the United States.

Along the way Charter purchased two or three psychiatric hospitals—not by design but because they were good opportunities in their own right. During the late 1970s, Charter's management group decided it was time to become a leader in its industry. This noble resolve was hampered, however, by the fact that Charter didn't know exactly what its industry was, except that it probably had something to do with the broadly defined field of health-care services. So Charter launched what it called an "internal strategy audit." First it looked inward, an activity facilitated by the fact that it was a veritable Noah's ark of health-care activities, in order to discover what it did best and most profitably: It ran its psychiatric hospitals well. Charter then looked outward, examining health-care trends, needs, and competition. It discovered an attractive opportunity to take advantage of a neglected market.

Mental health care was the right niche for Charter for two reasons. First, the business (it *is* a business) was in transition, and a participant who got in on the ground floor as the industry restructured itself stood a better than average chance of succeeding. Until not so long ago, psychiatric care consisted largely of ignoring people who were afflicted with chronic, incurable conditions as long as possible, then putting them out of sight and mind. Most who were admitted (or committed) to mental hospitals were sent there to be "put away" for the rest of their lives; they were regarded as inmates more than as patients.

The development of psychiatric drugs that could treat emotional problems effectively and enable the mentally ill to return to productive lives was a technology invented by others but capitalized upon by Charter. The treatment for many illnesses no longer was chronic institutionalization in remote asylums. Instead, the new technology allowed shorter, rehabilitative stays in the local community—and Charter made the most of the trend by building and managing small, specially designed hospitals to provide intensive short-term treatment near home.

The second industry phenomenon that Charter recognized and capitalized upon was the stigma associated with psychiatric treatment. Very few people—in either medicine or business—were very interested in it. Except for one other firm that specialized in community mental-health-care facilities, the field was open. By and large, the other proprietary (investor-owned, profit-seeking) chains avoided psychiatric hospitals as an unglamorous, unappealing, unfashionable field. Just as important, Charter recognized that general hospitals often accorded low priority to their small and troublesome psychiatric wards. At most general hospitals, psychiatry fell low in the pecking order, partly because it is not a large consumer of high-revenue ancillary services (for example, diagnostic tests and X rays) associated with practices such as surgery, and partly because psychiatric care connoted patients who caused problems. As a result, psychiatry did not have the stature in most general hospitals to receive the priority it takes to get the kind of care their patients needed.

Charter's specialty psychiatric hospitals changed that. The psychiatrist and psychologist reigned supreme—like the surgeons in general hospitals. Moreover, specially designed programs and facilities for treatment and therapy provided a competitive advantage not matched by traditional wards. In fact, Charter began to develop niches within its niche—special programs and facilities for alcoholism; drug abuse; and adolescent, child, and adult populations.

By turning around the stigma of psychiatric treatment, Charter grew explosively to become a half-billion-dollar business in 1984 with thirty-eight psychiatric hospitals across the nation. It's a profitable business as well; Charter's earnings increased from $1 million in 1974 to $35.1 million in 1984, and its return on equity has fallen below 25 percent only once* since 1978.

From Diapers to Diskettes

The drive for improved manufacturing productivity in the United States has at last become a national obsession. In industry after industry, America's once preeminent position in manufacturing efficiency is challenged—and too often the challenge uncovers high costs that arise from obsolete processes and antiquated logistics.

At the company level, manufacturing effectiveness can be a matter of survival. In a typical small company, the sales, engineering, purchasing, and production functions operate independently; each keeps its own records, often (even nowadays) by hand, in card files and folders.

As long as the company remains small, there's modest harm in the arrangement. But as the small manufacturer grows, the number of parts involved in turning out a rapidly expanding product line can explode into the thousands. The complexity of managing such a parts inventory—ensuring the right numbers of the right parts at the right time—begins to boggle the mind. If engineering design and production requirements aren't coordinated, products don't get made when they're supposed to be. Increasingly, the company has to have integrated systems and control information, because the alternative is likely to be soaring inventories, missed shipment dates, lost customers, and plunging profit margins—in the worst cases, putting the company's existence in jeopardy.

The problem (and therefore the opportunity) was that nobody was meeting the smaller manufacturer's need for exactly such a set of reliable systems to coordinate and control inventories, purchasing, engi-

*To 24.7 percent (1979).

neering, and production—in other words, systems to lower manufacturing costs with growth, rather than to increase them; to ensure that products are available when the customers want them; and to advance the odds of corporate survival.

ASK Computer Systems filled that void by accident. It's now a leader in specialized computer software for manufacturing information systems, but its founder never intended it to exist. Sandra Kurtzig left her job at General Electric in the early 1970s to raise a family. Having an extra bedroom and a computer terminal, she wrote programs for a few small companies to help them improve their manufacturing efficiency.

Because she designed her software for a Hewlett-Packard computer, HP saw in Kurtzig's product an exciting opportunity to increase the demand for its computers. So HP became Kurtzig's first sales force.* Coupling free computer time that she cajoled from HP with her own ability and drive, Kurtzig built a series of integrated software products for manufacturing management that took the company past the $65-million sales mark in 1984. The business simply took off. And so it is that Sandy Kurtzig balances both careers—as a mother and as owner of a controlling share of one of the fastest-growing midsize companies in the United States.

"What Is It and How Do We Sell It?"

Millipore's success in what has come to be known as "separations technology" traces from a series of creative niche entries, frequently into tiny segments in which its products created advantages that were valuable to the customer and frequently unique. Millipore got its start with the 1954 acquisition of German technology for making microporous membranes out of cellulose. That technological coup gave the fledgling company a monopoly position in what founder Jack Bush described to us only half jokingly as "a product for which there was no known market."

The microporous membrane has a broad range of capabilities. By varying the structure of the membrane, Millipore could separate just about any size of microscopic particle it wanted from just about any liquid. But at the outset, it was a laboratory curiosity—the early challenge was figuring out how to use the stuff.

Initially, Millipore tried to identify the most economic and high-potential applications on its own. It developed a system to analyze contaminants in municipal water supplies, and still other systems to

---

*HP simply updated an old strategy for creating demand for equipment. Before people will buy hardware, there has to be something they can *do* with it. Sixty years ago, RCA began broadcasting radio programs to induce people to buy radios.

analyze jet aircraft fuel and the hydraulic fluids used in missiles. Yet Millipore was convinced that these internal efforts were not turning up new applications and potential growth markets fast enough. They needed a new approach to creating new niches.

The key to developing the array of niche markets Millipore has subsequently built was, it turned out, to encourage future customers to define the markets themselves. Jack Bush and his colleagues of the 1950s and 1960s, Walt Kenyon and D. V. d'Arbeloff, couldn't afford to mount a nationwide sales campaign to talk person-to-person with potential customers. Instead, they invested heavily in mass mailings to microbiologists all over the country and made a movie about the range of uses of their unique material.

Most important, they developed a series of field seminars for prospective customers. "We took to the road and presented our product to anybody who would listen," Bush says. Dee d'Arbeloff believes Millipore to have been the first industrial company ever to put on seminars for the technical staffs of prospective customers, as well as the first to computerize their extensive mailing lists.

This customer-oriented strategy worked. Ideas poured in. One potential customer suggested using Millipore membranes to control contamination in fluids used in manufacturing sensitive electronic semiconductors. Millipore's customers saw uses for the membranes in solving water- and oil-contamination problems, in food processing, and in sterilizing polio vaccine.

In each application, Millipore custom-tailored the membrane and the system containing it, creating subniches in which the company grew. As a result, Millipore today caters to more than a hundred identifiable product or customer centers.

BUILDING ON STRENGTH

Leading in niche markets means that the midsize high-growth companies know their customers—not only intellectually but viscerally. As important, these enterprises meet the difficult challenge of knowing themselves—their skills, potential, and limitations. The best know what they are good at—and can get better at—as they introduce new products, enter new but related markets, and evolve strategically to anticipate and capitalize upon the changing marketplace.

There are as many strengths to build on as there are factors that matter to customers in the products and services a company delivers.

Among those potential strengths are distinctive products and technologies, reputation and brand franchise, and entrenched distribution channels. Companies can build on functional skills as well, such as research and development, manufacturing, or distribution. Organizational strengths can provide yet another basis on which to build. A company's competitive advantage might lie in its innovativeness, in its customer orientation—for instance, expertise in (and aptitude for) solving customer problems, fast response time, and flexibility—or in plain old energy and perseverance. While the easiest to describe, these kinds of skills are the most difficult to develop and, once developed, to sustain.

Whatever the company's strengths, building on them becomes critical as the demands of growth force it to look beyond its original niches. While it's impossible to predict when a midsize growth company will discover that its original niche no longer offers sufficient growth opportunity, it's a fact that most of them do discover it sooner or later. Only 2 percent of our survey respondents still rely on a single product in a single market.

Successful midsize high-growth companies do not abandon the notion of targeted niches that led to their original success. Rather they most often move into related areas where they can build on their strengths—the niche next door. The superior performers in the American Business Conference provide compelling evidence that building on strength through related niche competition is more likely to yield sustained success than unrelated diversification. Three quarters of the CEOs who took part in our ABC survey reported that they edged out into adjacent niches. A surprising number told us of diversification moves that proved to be ill advised or premature. (Their general response was early recognition that diversification had been a mistake and cutting their losses quickly.)

It stands to reason that acquisitions, too, will mesh more effectively if they complement and build on a company's core strengths. In addition to internally driven expansion, three quarters of the ABC members have pursued growth opportunities through acquisitions, and most of those acquisitions were in related segments rather than in unrelated businesses.

The Augat Circles

Roger Wellington, the chairman and chief executive of Augat—a Mansfield, Massachusetts-based producer of precision components for the electronics industry—explains how edging out and building on strength shaped his company. Augat, which began as an old-line jewelry parts company, has achieved sales and profit increases over the past decade, growing from $38 million in sales in 1974 to $257 million in 1984 (restated) by producing electromechanical and electronic widgets—connectors, clamps, sockets, accessories, panels, switches, knobs, and fixtures. These products, which interconnect and package electronic systems, find their uses on telephone poles, on the Space Shuttle, in satellites, and in pacemakers.

When we first visited Wellington, he took out a piece of paper and drew concentric circles. (Subsequently this graphic exercise became the organizing motif for Augat's 1983 annual report—"a portrait of a corporation's strategy.")

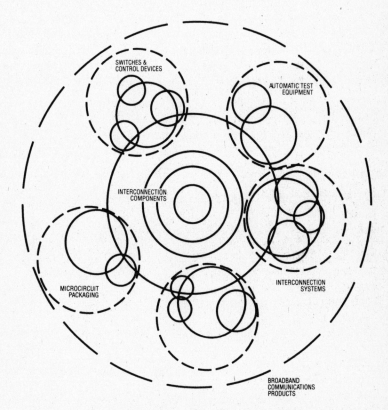

After Augat sold its jewelry business in 1958, it began in the innermost circle of the diagram, producing clips and clamps to hold and connect electromechanical parts. The company then moved into a related business—the second circle—inventing and patenting a socket for crystals and relays. In 1964 Augat had developed sockets for transistors; it later added sockets for integrated circuits. All these new applications were based on interconnection technology—but through innovation and Augat's willingness to customize its products for customers, the company became a world leader in the field.

Not content to be merely the leading producer of integrated circuit sockets, Augat created four more big circles, building on its technical strengths and customer franchise in each instance. These include broadband communications products, interconnection systems, automatic test equipment, and switches and control devices. And these four circles of enterprise in turn begat other related circles.

Today Augat produces approximately thirty thousand different products—all related to one another and all built logically upon existing involvements in markets and technologies. And as the first slide of the presentation Wellington makes to every employee every year proclaims, *quality* and *innovation* remain the bases of Augat's competitive advantage.

Although the tiny parts Augat produces might strike some as a cost- or price-driven commodity, Wellington does everything in his power to make sure that his company and his customers don't view Augat as a commodity producer. One of the company's practices is to avoid second-source opportunities—the situation in which a customer seeks a second vendor to ensure a supply of the good (in the event the first supplier has a problem) and price competition is engendered. In such cases the customer usually gives the second source specifications for the product (perhaps drawings or an actual sample) and asks for a price quote. Wellington disdains such business because "if you spend the money to copy somebody else's product, you'll spend as much time and money as if you were designing a new and better one. It's just better business to establish quality and performance in your products and let competitors get out their pencils and erasers and try to copy it."

This is not to say that Augat doesn't watch its costs—in fact in some product lines it has created unique proprietary machinery and manufacturing processes that reduce costs dramatically. But the primary bases of Augat's competitive strategy are quality and innovation: improving precision, ensuring reliability, and delivering on its promises. And delivery is important. As Wellington recalls a recent conversation with a major customer, he was told, "Your competitor sells a similar component for twenty percent less, but he sometimes has problems delivering enough at the right time." Wellington's response: "I'll also sell it to you for twenty percent less if I don't have to deliver it."

The Analog Answer

Analog Devices, a geographic and industry neighbor of Augat, has also mastered the art of edging out.

Analog's 1983 annual report opened with this message:

> Analog Devices has pursued a single, consistent strategy since its
> founding: the development, manufacture and marketing of products
> used to process real-world signals. . . .

And, as we saw earlier in this chapter, Analog's devotion to innovation has been a critical element in the company's success. True to its
name, its first offerings were devices used to amplify and process analogue signals. It later mastered the science of converting analogue signals to digital form—and subsequently digital signals to analogue form.
This mission—products that process real-world signals so computers
can understand and use them—has taken Analog into many related
technologies and into a diverse set of market segments: laboratory automation, industrial automation, health care, energy conservation, defense
weaponry, aviation and avionics, and telecommunications. But the diversification in markets served has never left the skill base of the
company—real-world signals.

Analog's passion to lead in technologies central to its mission has
put it in the venture-capital business—a seemingly unrelated endeavor
that many other companies have entered only to be disappointed. But
for Analog, corporate venture capital is a way to secure access to future
technological capability rather than a purely financial investment game.
Its first experience, in 1969, was a $1-million investment in a small
company that made integrated circuits, Nova Devices. Subsequently,
Analog bought control of Nova and today that division has grown to be
Analog's most profitable and successful group—a $60 million business.

On a broader scale, Analog Devices Enterprises (a group financed
by Standard Oil of Indiana, a major and long-standing Analog shareholder) has invested in twelve new high-technology ventures in fields
such as medical imaging and high-speed integrated circuitry. Unlike
conventional venture capitalists who seek a good deal in whatever field
of endeavor, Analog Devices invests in companies that are developing
technologies that may prove central to its own future innovations. And
rather than accept the prospect of a future public offering, Analog structures many of the investments so that someday Analog Devices has the
opportunity to buy the enterprise it has financed.

In addition to providing financing, Analog Devices brings management experience, technical assistance, and marketing know-how to its
affiliated ventures. When we asked Ray Stata *why* Analog had under-
taken this exciting but unconventional way of edging out, he gave us

three reasons. First, he said, in some cases Analog Devices would have been unable to attract the technical talent and entrepreneurial spirit in any other way—that even with Analog's well-deserved reputation for celebrating technical contributions and encouraging entrepreneurship internally, some of these ventures demanded independent gestation. Second, in cases where the technology is truly speculative today (but perhaps not tomorrow), Stata doesn't want to distract his existing organization from core projects and efforts that already stretch its management and technical skills. Third, as a successful entrepreneur himself, Stata understands the need for new enterprises to develop their own cultures and management styles—in some cases done best in isolation.

High-Profit Manufacturing

Xidex Corporation was formed in 1969 by five men who had left Memorex, the magnetic tape and microfilm company. Xidex had used up most of its three initial financings, nearly $6 million, and was in poor financial shape when the board of directors brought in Lester Colbert as president in early 1972.

Colbert was hardly a high-technocrat: His education had been in history and business administration, and he arrived fresh from a career in accounting and general management at Reichhold Chemicals, Inc. But high tech wasn't the only thing Xidex needed. Unlike most ABC companies, its core strength lay in manufacturing capability, and Xidex became the low-cost producer of duplicate computer output microfilm and, later, floppy disks. Colbert brought managerial discipline that turned Xidex profitable within eighteen months and laid the foundation for dramatic, highly profitable growth ever since.

Duplicate microfilm was Xidex's first product, and at the end of 1984 the company had more than 70 percent of the market. The company edged out first by building on its market leadership and on the strength of its relationships with microfilm users. By 1980, it introduced a microfilm reader (and is now number two in that market), and shortly thereafter added silver origination film, reader printers, dry silver paper for micrographic reproduction, and microfilm printing to its product line.

As the microfilm market matured and growth slowed, Xidex next edged out into flexible "floppy" computer disks—floppies. Though the market was highly competitive, Xidex chose it confidently because it knew the technology: coating polyester film with chemicals. In taking on entrenched floppy manufacturers such as Verbatim and 3M, Xidex built on its manufacturing strengths—among them the capability to treat a wider roll of polyester film than most others (giving Xidex a 50 to 100 percent advantage in production speed) and the ability to apply thinner but more consistent chemical coatings, leading to yet another substantial cost advantage.

Xidex soon prospered—in contrast to the floppy industry in general. By mid-1984 it was well enough positioned to take over Dysan—older and bigger, but ill equipped to compete in a market increasingly characterized by price erosion and lack of brand loyalty, and therefore a money loser in 1984.

Xidex's strengths in technology and manufacturing enabled it to move into an extraordinarily fast-growing market and within two years become arguably the most formidable participant.

Socrates and the Doughnut

Recognizing what's a real strength and what isn't is obviously crucial, and sometimes the answer is elusive. A good example of this is the Dunkin' Donuts story, a good illustration of the Socratic adage, "Know thyself."

Dunkin' Donuts was founded by William Rosenberg, a child of the Depression with an eighth-grade education. He launched his business with a food truck he wheeled in and out of factories and offices, selling coffee, sandwiches, and snacks at lunch and coffee breaks.

William Rosenberg's food-service business blossomed. By 1955 he had six doughnut stores and began franchising them throughout New England. Bob Rosenberg, the founder's son, finished his studies in 1963—at the Cornell University School of Hotel Management Administration and the Harvard Business School. Most important, Bob Rosenberg had been born to the business—working in the kitchen when he was nine years old.

For the first five years of the younger Rosenberg's reign, everything seemed to work. Dunkin' Donuts expanded rapidly. It reached out to new locations with its successful doughnut shops. It expanded its institutional feeding and vending machine business. Dunkin' started a drive-in hamburger chain called Howdy Beefburgers. It went into fish 'n' chips. Bob Rosenberg and his team began to believe that the company's skill was franchising, and they even considered pursuing opportunities to franchise hat shops and educational programs.

Within five years this seemingly related—but in truth unrelated—diversification caught up with Dunkin' Donuts. In their rush for growth and new businesses, Rosenberg and his team had neglected the old ones—some of them were "out of control." Profits suffered, franchisees began to complain. In short, things were going wrong. Rosenberg recalls that the downturn in his business coincided with his reading David

Halberstam's *The Best and the Brightest*—a book whose message included the lesson of hubris among the Harvard-trained technocrats who thought they could run a war about which they knew little firsthand.

Rosenberg and Tom Schwarz (Dunkin's president and Bob's long-term work partner) realized they needed to get back to basics—to figure out what they were really good at, and concentrate on it. They sold the vending machines, closed down scores of unproductive stores, abandoned the hamburger and fish 'n' chips businesses, and stopped thinking about unrelated deals. Dunkin' Donuts decided it would be the best in serving coffee and doughnuts—and forty-four consecutive quarters of increased sales and profits from coffee and doughnuts suggest the decision was a wise one. In 1984, worldwide sales were $532 million in some 1,350 shops throughout the United States and thirteen foreign countries.

Building on strength for Dunkin' Donuts means creative, obsessive, and commonsense attention to the basics. Take coffee—one of the staples of the doughnut shop menu. In the five years from 1979 to 1983, coffee consumption in America declined by 10 percent. But during the same five years, the typical Dunkin' Donuts shop has increased its sales of cups of coffee by 20 percent.

Dunkin' Donuts really cares about the quality of its coffee. Its goal is to serve the "best cup of coffee in the world," and if you spend any time with Bob Rosenberg, he'll tell you why. Dunkin' Donuts has a twenty-three-page specification of what it requires in a coffee bean. But buying high-quality, specially blended coffee beans is just the beginning. Dunkin' Donuts franchisees have to make sure their coffee is fresh. Beans are to be used within ten days of their delivery; if they are not, they are returned on the next Dunkin' Donuts supply truck. Once the coffee is brewed, it can be served for only eighteen minutes; after that it must be thrown out. And the coffee must be brewed between 196 and 198 degrees Fahrenheit exactly. Dunkin' is one of the few chains that still use real cream—not half and half, not milk, not the sugar-based powder. No wonder the company sold 350 million cups of coffee in 1984.

Gold Medal Guardians

On the other side of the continent, California Plant Protection* provides another good example of a successful company that got singed when it edged out in a direction that coincided only superficially with its core strength.

---

*California Plant Protection is considering changing its corporate name to "CPP Security Service"—as it is already known in its one hundred offices outside California.

Tom Wathen bought CPP, now a $215 million guard service, in 1964 when it was a tiny company. Wathen's notion from the outset was that CPP should be a leader in the field of security. His organization spent all its time understanding the protection and security needs of its commercial customers.

These explorations led CPP in its earlier days into a series of new ventures in security-related businesses: fire extinguishers, central alarm stations, detective services, executive protection (read: bodyguards), and mobile patrols (guards who travel from one store or customer site to another in much the way the old town watchman did many years ago). A few years of profitless growth demonstrated to Wathen and his key people that these other supposedly related businesses were very different from the core business of providing guards to watch over individual plants. Fire extinguishers meant dealing with manufacturers and maintaining an inventory. Central station alarm systems require heavy capital investment in secure central offices and communications equipment. Investigators and bodyguards proved to be very different people from the stationary guard of CPP's central business. Each of the new businesses demanded very different management skills.

Reacting quickly, Wathen sold or discontinued all but the old reliable plant-guard business. Now all of CPP's energy goes into extending and improving on that business through better recruiting and training of guards, closer relationships with key clients, and carefully targeted geographic extension from city to city and state to state. By building on the strengths of its highly disciplined guard management system, CPP has achieved one of its industry's highest retention rates both for customers and for guards.

CPP never had a better showcase to display its organizational strengths than during the 1984 Summer Olympics in Los Angeles, at which CPP provided the lion's share of the security. For the assignment, CPP screened eleven thousand new guards and hired and managed more than seven thousand. The impressive Olympian orderliness testifies to the effectiveness with which this winning firm has built on a highly specialized capability.

VALUE, NOT PRICE

Everyone knows how to succeed in business: Buy low, sell high. But many of the most successful high-growth businesses buy high and sell higher. The winners almost always compete by delivering products and services that provide superior value to customers rather than ones that just cost less. In fact, 97 percent of our survey respondents reported that value rather than just price competition was a basis for their success.

Loctite's anaerobic adhesives—which cost more by the ounce than Château Lafite-Rothschild or Chanel No. 5—hold metal assemblies together better than fasteners and washers. The result is a dramatic decrease in plant maintenance expense and repair costs. Customers pay Loctite's premium price because the adhesive works—and often yields savings that far outweigh the price.

Cray Research produces and sells the most expensive computers in the world, often to not-for-profit buyers such as governments, universities, and research laboratories—all known for their price sensitivity. They buy Cray because nobody does it better. In fact, Cray has become the yardstick by which supercomputers are measured. One government agency even expresses its computer needs in "units of Cray."

Thomas & Betts, the electrical and electronic accessories company, has built its business by saving its customers time and money in two ways. First, T&B provides products that outperform the competitive products they replace. Some of them generate labor economies that exceed the actual price of the product. Second, by maintaining parts inventories close to customers' production sites, T&B makes sure that customer operations are never shut down long for lack of a part.

Another remarkably high-value niche is financial printing, a highly specialized service to corporations and Wall Street underwriters that is estimated at some $600 million to $700 million annually. As we've seen previously, Pandick, Inc., is the leader in that specialty field, with an estimated share of the market that approaches 25 percent, having displacing a previously larger competitor in 1983. Pandick's success has been based solely on providing unusual value to its customers.

Whenever new securities are offered to the public, they must be registered with the Securities and Exchange Commission in the form of a prospectus that is 100-percent error free. In a world of leveraged buyouts, takeovers, initial public offerings, and new types of security issues, the number of such prospectuses is staggering. More significant still, however, since market conditions can change overnight, and since shifts of just hundredths of a percent can make a colossal difference when hundreds of millions of dollars are involved, speed and accuracy are worth a bundle. But speed and accuracy are not easily arrived at. Most "deals" are negotiated up to the eleventh hour, often in all-night sessions involving lawyers, accountants, financial wizards, and general management. Prospectuses and related documentation may be rewritten a score of times, with changes up to the very last minute—and so the ability to meet these incredibly time-sensitive demands is at the core of Pandick's success.

As Pandick puts it, printing is the easy part. The real key is typesetting—the ability to make changes up to the very last minute, to create flawless offset printing plates, and to have those plates running on a press wherever in the country it's necessary in a matter of hours, often minutes. To achieve top capability in its industry, Pandick was the first to computerize its entire typesetting process, and it did so in the early 1970s, when computer capabilities were still suspect to most business people. As a result, it gained a half-decade lead on all of its competitors.

Pandick's service to customers goes far beyond typesetting and printing itself. The company provides eighteen fully equipped, well-appointed conference rooms in New York alone, where its clients can thrash out the details of a deal, make final changes, and work directly with Pandick's customer representatives on a twenty-four-hour basis—and often these sessions last all night, with a need to have initial approval copies of a prospectus in the office of the SEC the following day.

Thanks to the value it creates for customers, Pandick's annual earnings growth has averaged 35 percent from 1978 through 1983, with return on equity averaging 23 percent during the same five-year period. The company runs a round-the-clock, high-value service in a field where it makes a tremendous difference to the customer, and Pandick has been well rewarded for an outstanding job of consistently meeting those customer needs.

Even companies that sell to the U.S. government (that epitome of multiple-bid price competitions) find that value can overwhelm price—if the service or product is demonstrably better than the competition's. Cullinet's software and data management tools generally cost more at the outset than those of others, including IBM's. Yet Cullinet's clients include the U.S. Treasury and Department of Justice. More to the point, John Cullinane likes to tell the story of a visit he made to the Strategic Air Command in Omaha to try to sell Cullinane tools to manage the nation's arsenal of bombers, missiles, and radar. As Cullinane entered a room full of highly decorated generals and colonels to make his pitch, one of them announced, "If your software doesn't work, now's the time to get the hell out of here." For the Strategic Air Command, working right all the time is the key value—price comes second.

BDM International—one of America's fastest-growing technical service firms, focusing its energies on helping the U.S. Defense establish-

ment resolve technical, policy, and strategic issues—forms its name
from the initials of three Fordham Ph.D.'s in physics who decided to go
into business for themselves in the early 1960s. During the decade 1974–83,
BDM's revenues and profits grew more than tenfold: It is now a $191-
million enterprise that worked on almost seven hundred assignments in
1984.

As one might expect of a technically based enterprise that prides
itself on making a difference in solving tough and important problems,
BDM has distilled the key factors for its success down to a formula:
RQ^2TC^2—customer satisfaction through the *requisite quality* and *quantity*
of work, done on *time,* and with *costs controlled.* In the fiercely competitive marketplace of selling professional services to the government, BDM
wins about 50 percent of the proposals it submits.

BDM recruits highly educated and motivated professionals—engineers, systems analysts, social scientists—who are dedicated to working on national security and other complex problems. But aside from
creating teams of highly talented men and women, the BDM corporate
culture values hard work that helps meet the quantity and timeliness
components of its corporate charge. For example, the Friday evening we
visited with Earle Williams—the chief executive the original BDM founders elected in 1972 so they could focus on their technical specialties—we
noted that at 7 P.M. the BDM parking lot was about half full (starkly
contrasted with sparsely populated adjacent parking facilities at the company next door, which two days later was to declare near-record losses).

While BDM people celebrate hard work and long hours, the company encourages its professionals to achieve expert status through writing and research. A recent example was an article written by Philip
Karber—one of BDM's fifty-four vice presidents—about European forward defense, which initially appeared in the *Armed Forces Journal.*
More than ten thousand reprints of the article were requested, and the
West German minister of defense wrote to BDM to say it was "by far the
best I have read about our defense situation in Europe for a very long
time."*

BDM's projects demand quality first because of their complexity
and import. They have included engineering laser systems and artificial-
intelligence applications, testing command post aircraft, and helping
design intelligence systems. Although technically based, not all solutions are high tech. For example, the company helped accelerate a
military target analysis capability for the army by modifying Apple Computers with new software and operating systems.

*Letter from Dr. Manfred Worner, Bundeminister der Vertedigung (June 10, 1984).

Although cost is always an important constraint in government contracting, BDM's strategy is to win and deliver on the quality of its analysis—whose total cost pales by comparison with the massive investments and resources the decisions it advises on. In Williams's words: "Our mission is to give objective advice on issues where good advice makes a difference." And good advice, by definition, is measured by its value.

This emphasis on product quality and customer service is clearly evident in the priority it receives from the CEO. Of our ABC survey respondents, 58 percent said their companies spend "considerably more" on customer service support (technical services, repair hotlines, and engineering aid, for instance) than their competitors do. Four out of five said their products were "superior in quality to the industry average," and 56 percent reported that their products represented the highest quality available in the marketplace. Their opinions are biased, of course— but the statistics aren't what is important. Rather, it's the fact of consensus on value as the basis of competition.

The 525 midsize business units whose statistical profiles are maintained in the PIMS data base show clearly the relationship between profitability and quality. Companies whose competitors view them as being the high-quality providers earned returns on investment (measured over four years) that were 60 percent greater than the returns earned by lowest-value producers, as shown in Exhibit III-9.

Exhibit III-9
RELATIVE PRODUCT QUALITY AND BUSINESS PERFORMANCE
Four year average return on investment*

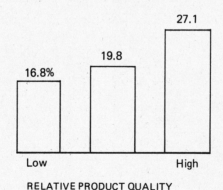

RELATIVE PRODUCT QUALITY

* Before interest expense and corporate overhead; 525 midsize businesses
Source: PIMS Program

The same is true of price: Premium-priced products yield higher returns on investment than do lower-priced products (see Exhibit III-10). And the relationship holds even in price-sensitive markets. Only one respondent in our American Business Conference survey told us price is relatively unimportant in his industry, yet our ABC findings are fully consistent with our findings from the larger PIMS sample.

Exhibit III-10
RELATIVE PRICE OF PRODUCTS AND BUSINESS PERFORMANCE
Four year average return on investment*

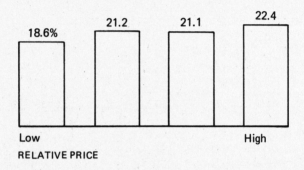

* Before interest expense and corporate overhead; 525 midsize businesses
Source: PIMS Program

But high value does not necessarily mean high production costs; in fact, winning companies that compete on the basis of value rather than price are sometimes still the low-cost producers (27 percent of our survey sample). Several of the CEOs we interviewed, in fact, said their companies have both the highest-quality product on the market *and* the lowest cost of production.

It is the combination of the strategic characteristics discussed in this chapter—innovation as a way of life, leadership in niche markets, growth by edging out into adjacent niches, and value-based competition— that underlies the winning performers' success.

Exhibit III-11
**NUMBER OF STRATEGIC TRAIT INDICATORS
AND BUSINESS PERFORMANCE**
Four year average return on investment*

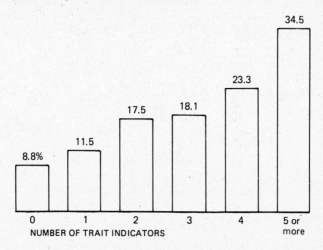

* Before interest expense and corporate overhead; 525 midsize businesses

Note: Six variables were used as indicators of a company exhibiting a strategic trait; e.g., having a market share rank of one or two was considered an indicator of a market leader

Source: PIMS Program

As Exhibit III-11 demonstrates, drawing again on PIMS data from 525 businesses, companies that employ all of the strategic practices enjoy *four times* the profitability of those that apply none. Having just some of the traits isn't enough. Doing all of them positions a company to shape its own future.

Just as any element of strategy by itself cannot ensure success, merely having a sound strategy is not enough. That strategy must be adapted, executed, and renewed through effective organization—the subject of the next chapter.

CHAPTER IV

Winning Organization: The Eternal Conflict

Organization is people with a purpose working together. *Good* organization is effective people working constructively together toward a common goal. The distinctions are monumental.

As Bob Waterman points out,* organization does not mean structure alone. As we address organization in this book, we refer as well to the essential elements of corporate culture—style and shared values; management systems, both formal and informal; and, most important, people and the institutional skills that derive from those people, their capabilities and priorities.

Good small companies have some of the best organizations you'll find anywhere because they have so little structure and formality. There are only two things that matter: the quality and motivation of the people, and the validity and power of their common goal. Communication is clear and simple; it can occur in hallways or around a table, and it does. Everyone knows what's to be done, who's to do it, and how. And perhaps most important, they know each other, can interpret each other, support each other.

The driving force in the growth of every small company ever launched is the entrepreneur, typically the founder. His information system is personal involvement in the business, complete immersion. He is intimately involved in its technologies, products, manufacturing processes,

*Robert H. Waterman, Jr., "Structure Is Not Organization," (A McKinsey staff paper, June 1979).

distribution channels, and—first, last, and always—its customers and its people. It's clear to him (if only intuitively) that if he's not fully dedicated and fully informed, his business will fail. If the product is outstanding or the business area is growing fast, it may take a while longer to fail, but fail it inevitably will unless he (or she) is fully on top of it, because the entrepreneur is the brains, heart, and soul of every small enterprise.

Not so the large, complex business. There, power and knowledge are ordinarily diffused throughout the organization rather than centered in one individual. Instances in which a single heroic figure dominates a large organization and drives it to success by sheer force of personality—for example, a Lee Iacocca at Chrysler—are the exceptions that dramatize the rule.

The trick of bigness is to keep a diverse, often dispersed group of personalities working together productively so they can succeed in the infinitely varied activities that make for corporate success. Formalization and specialization are necessary evils of bigness—in structure, in communication systems, in development and exercise of specific management skills, in support functions. Just keeping a big company running demands budgets, job descriptions, central systems, and group meetings to keep together what specialization and the limits of span of control have split asunder. Formality is necessary but no less evil: With it inevitably come politics, internal competition, red tape. These are degenerative diseases, and controlling them is one of the central challenges facing any company. It is an art whose demands are greatest among companies on the threshold of bigness, during their midsize growth.

The staggering task of the midsize high-growth company is to transplant the intuitive skill of the founder-entrepreneur into a large, changing organization. The key to meeting that challenge lies in *combining* the *discipline* necessary to execute the day-to-day activities of the business with the *freedom* to adapt to a changing world and to innovate rapidly by coming up with new products and novel ways of doing things. The winning performers know that these qualities are essential and that they are inherently in conflict; the ways they live with that conflict and put it to work for their benefit hold important lessons for anyone attempting to build or live within a successful organization.

The intrinsic conflict between those indispensable needs—for militaristic discipline and for creative freedom—is one that no company can afford to resolve. It is a dilemma winning performers learn to understand and live with. In the best of all possible worlds, the outcome is a managed stalemate that generates reliability, quality, and efficiency on the one hand, and notable invention, resourcefulness, and creativity on the other.

To manage this paradox, a company—somehow—must:

1. Attract and motivate people of rare competence and character whose capabilities fit the needs of the business and whose personalities fit its culture and thereby lend themselves to collaboration;
2. Communicate a consistent message of corporate values, objectives, and ways of doing things across growing geographic, personality, and functional gaps;
3. Nurture a deep-felt ambition and determination to be outstanding—even while the connection between individual tasks and the overriding mission of the corporation becomes harder to comprehend; and
4. Keep changing things, often dramatically, in anticipation of and in response to developments in the outside world and to new ideas generated inside.

The winning company's response to these challenges is, essentially, single-minded dedication to the proposition "If it ain't been fixed, it's gonna break." They earn their organizational victories through restless, unrelenting attention to even the most microscopic details.

The discovery of that attitude is, in a superficial sense, yesterday's news. Lots of companies these days have learned to sing the right words, make the right pronouncements. The problem is that most of them do it by rote. The winning performers, in contrast, instead of just talking about it like the weather, actually *do* something. There are at least five identifiable patterns to their behavior.

The Ripple Factor

First, the winning performer focuses relentlessly on every facet of the organization and on the ways the facets work together. Winners know that when strategy changes, structure may well have to change, too—and that when structure is changed, everything else is liable to need changing, from management-information systems and control processes through the way meetings are conducted. The new structure and the new systems supporting it demand new, different skills that have to be brought into place through inside training or outside hiring. The whole process of introducing the structural changes—and of course the structural changes themselves—have to be related explicitly and conspicuously to the underlying objectives and values of the company as well as to its style and culture.

The Comfort-with-Conflict Factor

Consciously or intuitively, the best companies maintain an implausible balance between the array of apparently contradictory, seemingly conflicting organizational needs they encounter. They provide for careful, methodical execution as well as for innovation; they can live by the numbers and still allow people to break the rules, try new things, even fail. They know the importance of continuity, particularly in the underlying values and mission of the organization, and they balance this with the need for change. They reinforce unshakable values while simultaneously upholding the freedom of the individual, even the freedom to be wrong. They change managers who consistently perform poorly, but they work exceptionally hard to help their people succeed. Many companies—probably most companies—find it difficult to comprehend the elusive balance between opposing attitudes and patterns of behavior, much less to strike it. But achieving it lies at the core of building an organization that can carry a company through the growth pains of midsize.

The "Us" Factor

The high-growth companies also understand fully that people are the source of lasting success. Products can't achieve it; technology can't; reputation and financial strength can't. Market shifts and competitors' weaknesses aren't the fountainhead of success, either. They are opportunities, and they can sometimes lead to short-term wins—but success is long-term, enduring. In dealing with people, winning companies emphasize strengths and not weaknesses. They recognize human needs and aspirations, and they create a sense of excitement, commitment, and personal obligation that extends to all levels. They avoid the sense that there are individuals called "us" and a corporate superpower called "them." There is only "us." It is "our" company.

The Missionary Factor

Winning companies create meanings for people. They create transcending values that attach to their products and services, and transmit them to their customers, employees, and anyone else they do business with. They know how important it is for people to lead lives of significance, to sense that they make a difference, because, after all, work takes up the largest part of the waking lives of their people. Many of the qualities that have made the leading organized religions strong over thousands of years have their analogies in the winning companies.

The Communication Factor

Winning companies know that there just ain't no such thing as overcommunication. Communication ought to increase exponentially as any company's size and complexity increase; but that almost never actually happens. The winning performers understand that actions speak louder than words—but they also understand that the words may have to be repeated endlessly. They recognize and respect the power of consistency and reassurance, and they're fearful of the disruption that springs from surprise and miscommunication. So they never stop communicating. The leaders spend prodigious hours writing, speaking, visiting the troops in the outposts, doing whatever's necessary to get the essential messages across.

DYNAMICS OF CHANGE

The sheer extent of organizational change in high-growth companies, the skill with which it is brought about in the best cases, and the consequences of ineptitude offer compelling lessons.

Turning Grime Into Gold

The product that became Safety-Kleen was invented in a Wisconsin gravel pit for the purpose of cleaning grimy truck wheel bearings. It was, and basically still is, a metal sink on top of an ordinary metal drum with a submersible pump that draws solvent from the drum through a gooseneck faucet into the sink. The user puts dirty mechanical parts or tools under the faucet, and the grease and grime go down the drain. As part of the service, the dirty solvent is periodically exchanged for a clean drum by a Safety-Kleen representative and the dirty solvent is returned to a Safety-Kleen recycling plant for processing. True to its eventual name, the process was simple to use and safe both to the people who used it and to the environment. Thus are industries born.

Chicago Rawhide bought Safety-Kleen in October 1968 for the not-so-grand sum of $25,000, and at the time some believed it was too much. But the connection was less farfetched than it sounds at first. Chicago Rawhide had been serving the transportation industry since the days of the horse and buggy. When the world, in another of its relentless progressions, moved to the horseless carriage, Chicago Rawhide forsook making buggy whips and became the world's largest manufacturer of oil seals for all types of motor vehicles. That's why Chicago Rawhide had a sales force assigned to serving the automotive repair market. And so it was natural that Safety-Kleen, then a sleepy little Milwaukee-area business going nowhere in particular, would be interesting to Chicago Rawhide when it stumbled across the product in a Wisconsin garage.

Eventually recognizing the dissimilarities of the new business from its own, however, Chicago Rawhide spun Safety-Kleen off to its shareholders in 1974. Ten years later, Safety-Kleen had sales that approached $200 million, and had never turned in a return on equity of less than 24 percent. (By contrast, the top ten *Fortune* companies earned less than 15 percent ROE, on average, in 1983.)

In the fall of 1968, Safety-Kleen's organization had consisted of Don Brinckman, now president and chief executive officer, and W. Gordon Wood, now vice president of marketing. Shortly thereafter, it also adopted a business plan that defined 130 routes along which each of 130 salesmen would periodically call on approximately 400 automotive repair outlets.

Brinckman later said that this plan was the critical organizational ingredient in Safety-Kleen's early success, because if Chicago Rawhide had encountered many big surprises during the start-up years, it might understandably have pulled the plug after investing up to $3 million with no profits to show for it. The discipline of drawing up a realistic, achievable business plan enabled Brinckman to lay out clearly for Chicago Rawhide where he intended the new company to go, what it would cost to get there, and how the cash-flow and profit pictures would look during the multi-year, nationwide rollout.

Then, in November 1968, a SWAT team consisting of Brinckman, Wood, seven regional managers, and two salesmen launched an all-out blitz to put five hundred machines into five hundred repair outlets in the Minneapolis–St. Paul area. The strategy was to put a machine into each outlet at no cost to the owner; they left a supply of solvent for trial, promising to return for the used solvent and leave a fresh supply for a fixed time interval for a service fee if the station proprietor liked it.

In a month, this Gang of Eleven had not only reached the five-hundred-station installation objective, but were generating a confirmation rate from the introductory free service offer of more than 90 percent—well above their highest expectations. They discovered that the stations valued the service not only because it gave them an easy way to clean dirty tools and parts, but because it did away with the headaches connected with cleaning dirty parts cleaners and with dumping dirty solvents even in an era when the nation's concern for the environment was not a major issue.

The seven regional sales managers immediately swept out and applied the Twin Cities success formula across the country. Success demanded a fast launch, because the process wasn't patentable. Safety-Kleen had to establish itself securely before anybody else realized "Hey—I can do that." They solidified their position by building a series of strategically located recycling plants that recovered 90 percent of the solvent and gave Safety-Kleen cost economies that no follower could afford to match.

Safety-Kleen succeeded largely because Brinckman managed to establish an enviable balance between strong discipline and personal freedom in the organizational system he built. The company generates information in detail on every four-week cycle within five days. The "war room" at headquarters in Elgin, Illinois, is impressive in the amount and the detail of data it makes available on markets, share, revenue, and profit results compared with goals, cash management, and inventory controls. Quotas and budgets apply to new-customer expectations as well as to service levels and retention of existing customers. Invoices are prepared and mailed centrally; cash is managed worldwide from headquarters as well.

On the face of it, it's hard to think of a system more regimented. But the truth is that there is little feel of regimentation in the Safety-Kleen organization. Balancing the discipline of the performance-monitoring systems and short-term focus are three facets of organization practice that generate enormous drive and energy in the company down to the route salesmen:

1. *The branch manager feels like an owner.* Safety-Kleen's branches are set up as though they were franchise units, contributing to the sense on the part of the branch manager that he is an owner rather than an employee. He is paid on straight commission, but there are additional cash incentives for timeliness in billing, maintaining solvent inventories, and other important contributions to performance. The local salesmen are paid salaries, much as though they worked for the branch manager, and the manager receives a commission of his own on the salesmen's production—a major incentive to develop and encourage the local sales representatives.

2. *A clear set of values.* Safety-Kleen builds pride and a clear sense of direction among its employees by nurturing not only the feeling that they are creating their own businesses, but that in so doing they are contributing to the conservation of America's resources as part of an outstanding company. The message the leadership carries to the organization was nicely summarized on the cover of the 1983 annual

report: "A commitment to excellence—marketing concepts—service to the customer—organization—recycling technology—concern for the environment—innovation." Safety-Kleen emphasizes these themes consistently in all its communications.

3. *The pervasive presence of the CEO.* Don Brinckman travels extensively, meeting with members of the organization in small groups at every level of the organization. He bridges the gap personally between discipline and the softer, more human side of management. Gordon Wood says: "Don knows the numbers better than anyone in this company. He personally spends time in our computer center, and nothing escapes his attention." On the other hand, Mike DeAngelis, a branch manager in the Chicago area, sees the other side of Don Brinckman: "When Don walks in here, he knows all of my guys by name, and how they are doing." Brinckman is also Safety-Kleen's head cheerleader, consistently promoting his theme of "unlimited opportunity" for everyone in the company. He meets with an advisory council of top performers; he initiated a series of regular sales promotions for salesmen and branch managers with prizes that reward them with plaques, TV sets, and trips to exotic places.

This emphasis on balance in the organization has transformed what might have been a mundane, regimented, and functionally organized business into an enthusiastic partnership of businessmen who, in fifteen years, have earned themselves a reputation for winning and their shareholders more than $400 million in market value.

A Family of Entrepreneurs

Before World War I, Kollmorgen was a tiny company supplying periscopes to the U.S. Navy. By 1984, it had become a highly successful complex of technology-based businesses with an impressive growth record and sales of $326 million. The transition began after World War II, when Kollmorgen decided to face up to the wild fluctuations in revenues and employment that came from being a single-product, single-customer company. Today's Kollmorgen resembles the Kollmorgen of 1914 in only two respects: It still makes periscopes, and its business is still run by entrepreneurs—lots of them now.

Over the years, Kollmorgen has become as thoughtful and innovative in its approach to management and organization as it is in technology and marketing. The result is a distinctive culture that creates unusual enthusiasm among its employees. In brief, Kollmorgen has learned to manage itself well in the face of four basic "givens":

1. *Its product and market diversity are extraordinarily broad.* Kollmorgen competes in some sixty high-tech product and market niches—all linked by their dependence on electrical and electronic technology—grouped under the broad fields of electronic interconnections, motors and controls, and electro-optical instruments. Markets range from the U.S. and foreign governments and major defense contractors, to manufacturers of computers, machine tools, robotics, test equipment, process controls, and automotive electronics, to papermaking, textiles, plastics manufacturing, and electrical utilities—to name just a few. Kollmorgen continues to search for new avenues of growth, and at the time of our research it was examining several new businesses that involved, for example, a French joint venture in magnetic bearings, growing crystals, and high-energy lasers.

2. *The markets in which it competes are volatile.* It knows that at almost any time some of its markets will unexpectedly go into sharp decline—as did some computer peripherals and numerically controlled machine tools in the early 1980s—and that others may virtually disappear overnight, as happened with videogames, for which Kollmorgen once supplied the great majority of printed circuits. As a result, the aggressive introduction of new products and businesses and the phase-out of the old is a continuing Kollmorgen requirement.

3. *The competitive environment in which it competes is highly combative.* Kollmorgen tries always to anticipate its competition, knowing that within even its strongest markets, other companies will introduce new products and fight for market share through lower prices, resulting in a tremendous premium on technological leadership as well as on cost competitiveness.

4. *Kollmorgen itself still has a strong appetite for growth.* Having quadrupled sales and tripled earnings in the decade ending in 1984 and achieving returns on equity of about 18 percent, Kollmorgen aspires to improve on that performance even further. (The company was hit by lower earnings in 1982 and 1983, joining many companies in cyclical industries, but recovered in 1984, with earnings increasing 21 percent over 1983.)

To compete in the world it has chosen, Kollmorgen needs an unusually responsive, inventive, and capable organization that can cover sixty bases simultaneously—and do it in a way that avoids the confusion, quality problems, and breakdowns in customer service that threaten to accompany high complexity. The approach Kollmorgen has chosen is to put people in charge of each little piece, encouraging them as much as the company can and interfering as little as possible. In brief, Kollmorgen is a family of entrepreneurs with strong views about organizational success:

They keep divisions small. Since 1980, Kollmorgen has split its Photocircuits Division (printed circuit boards and related interconnection products) into five separate units; Inland Motor (electric motors) into three units; and MacBeth (electro-optical products) into two. Generally, the company considers any division greater than $30 million in annual revenues to be a candidate for splitting up—because Kollmorgen is convinced that small companies can outperform big companies.

They break divisions into profit centers. Reflecting its dedication to "putting people in charge and letting them run their business," Kollmorgen assigns small teams under the leadership of a product or market manager to each of the businesses that make up its divisions—businesses defined by customer group, product line, or market segment. Each is responsible for profits as well as for the balance sheet, and for those things that generate superior performance: customer contact and service, product innovation and design, order processing and manufacturing (usually contracting with shared facilities), and inventories. Kollmorgen refers to this profit-center approach as "productizing" the business.

They drive toward clear financial objectives. Kollmorgen is convinced that people running a business do better if the goals are clear. Says Bob Swiggett, former CEO* and architect of Kollmorgen's organization: "People like to play hard and bet on the score of the games they play. The people who know what score it takes to win will always outperform those who don't." Kollmorgen's management group meets periodically to reaffirm the company's growth objective—to double sales and earnings every four years, coupled with a return on equity of 20 percent.

They pay for business success. Business teams and divisions are paid based on profit growth and pretax return on net assets ("RONA," which is, essentially, inventory, receivables, and net fixed assets less accounts payable). Prebonus profits in each division are shared equally three ways once the division reaches its financial goals: one third for the employees, one third for the government, and one third for the shareholders. Even the lowest-level workers can earn a hefty bonus in a good year, and upper-level managers can become substantial stockholders

*In late December 1984, Kollmorgen announced the election of James Swiggett, Bob's younger brother, as president and CEO. Bob Swiggett remains chairman.

over time with bonuses paid partly in cash, partly in Kollmorgen shares. The pretax RONA objective is the same for all businesses—30 percent; Kollmorgen has found, as we have, that the best competitors, the ones that are sufficiently agile and innovative, can earn that kind of return in any business.

They foster values that support innovation and individual freedom. A company with sixty independent business managers has to have faith in its people—and Kollmorgen carries its faith far beyond what you'd find in most decentralized corporations. Senior management's monthly window into the businesses is a one-page profit-and-loss statement for each and a few balance sheet figures, together with a phone conversation. Kollmorgen looks on its managers as a group of partners, with responsibility for helping each other as well as for Kollmorgen's results.

Bob Swiggett and other top corporate executives spend a good deal of time in the field preaching respect for the individual and personal responsibility for results. Several years ago, Swiggett and his senior management team put together a statement of corporate philosophy that Kollmorgen people believe really reflects the way things work in that organization. The front cover sets the tone: "Freedom and respect for the individual are the best motivators of man, especially when innovation and growth are the objectives." These values support another of Kollmorgen's nonquantitative but strongly held goals: to earn the right to the number-one position in each of its market segments by gaining and maintaining technological leadership.

They define a supportive but limited corporate role. Kollmorgen's corporate team consists of fewer than ten people on a single floor in a small building in Stamford, Connecticut, plus fifteen in an office in Hartford. The attitude of these ten is that if there were more of them, the urge to meddle in division affairs might become irresistible—which would undermine the company's fundamental commitment to putting people in charge of their businesses. As described by Bob Swiggett, however, the corporate office has three corporate leadership responsibilities, as well as a role to play in support of the divisions:

1. The corporate office ensures that each division has a clear *vision* of where it will position itself in the marketplace and how it will beat competition.
2. The corporate office helps create a *structure* that will foster business success, innovation, and growth. "We look for structural causes of trouble and then for the solutions. Sometimes this means spinning out a product line or even a new division; on rare occasions it may mean replacing key people," says Bob Swiggett.

3. And the corporate office is charged to protect the Kollmorgen *culture.* Senior management spends a major portion of its time communicating fundamental values—respect for people and commitment to corporate objectives. "Because we respect the individual, we have nothing to hide around here," Bob Swiggett says. "We bring our problems to each other. Everyone knows it is permissible to have problems, even to fail—and so we can look openly to each other for help. Protecting the culture also means ensuring that compensation is based on performance and competence, not power and position."

In support of the divisions, Kollmorgen provides pure staff services as well: "We act as the bankers to the divisions. Just like an outside bank, we provide them with capital if they can sell us on their ideas. We help the divisions recruit outstanding higher-level people. And we give them advice and legal help—we are a cheap source of good counsel."

One of the distinctive characteristics of Kollmorgen's corporate structure is that there are neither a chief operating officer nor group presidents; all the divisions report directly to divisional boards whose relationship to the division resembles that of a board of directors to a corporation. Each board consists of two presidents of other Kollmorgen divisions and two or three corporate staff officers, one of the latter as chairman. The board reviews all major strategic and investment questions as a sounding board to the division president, and on major customer commitments will probably participate in the decision. It also evaluates the division president and decides whether or not he is doing his job adequately. Kollmorgen thinks it's a great advantage to substitute group consensus for the potential veto power of an individual group president. In general, however, the board is there to offer suggestions and ideas, to raise questions, but not to command—in keeping with Kollmorgen's deeply held conviction that no one can understand any business as well as the management team charged with making it a success.

They operate with simple systems. Consistent with Kollmorgen's overall philosophy, corporate-level systems are few. It's one of the few companies we have found whose corporate officers do not approve annual budgets but rather are given frequent volume and profit forecasts by the divisions. Divisions can spend funds as they see fit, and corporate management receives simply that one piece of paper for each profit center each month, letting them know how things are going. Each division has a five-year strategic plan that includes capital spending forecasts that are updated at least twice a year, sometimes more frequently.

And—to be sure—there is a good deal of personal communication and interaction beyond the monthly telephone review. Kollmorgen's overriding discipline is its clear financial goals and philosophy, and the teeth lie in the fact that a division which underperforms for too long, even with all the help that its board and corporate management can give it, is likely to be sold or have its senior executives replaced. What's particularly impressive is how infrequently these actions have had to be taken.

It can be difficult for a casual observer to understand the difference between the Kollmorgen approach to organization and management and the average decentralized corporation. Our sense is that the distinction is a matter of emphasis, of intensity, and particularly of genuine commitment to succeeding as a large family of independent entrepreneurs, all of whom are motivated and allowed to operate as though they were running their own small businesses.

In fact, the Kollmorgen approach had its genesis in a small business—in the problems that Bob Swiggett and his brother Jim encountered in their own company prior to its acquisition by Kollmorgen in 1970. The Swiggetts were self-taught winners: They had lived through explosive growth at Photocircuits Company. There, heavy emphasis on new technology (research and development expenditures exceeded 10 percent) led to many new product lines as well as to growth in complexity. As a result, Photocircuits found itself in the late 1960s with five hundred employees in a single factory trying to make good on some one thousand orders at the same time. The result followed as night follows day: product problems, falling plant yields, deteriorating profit performance and morale.

The Swiggetts first tried to attack these problems of growth through rational management—the installation of formal, computer-based production planning and control systems. But things got worse until they installed a notion called "team manufacturing," the forerunner of their later concept of truly independent business entrepreneurs. Having learned to make the concept work in the $15 million Photocircuits business—output per employee doubled, and delays in deliveries to customers were cut 75 percent in a matter of months—Bob Swiggett was later ready to extend the concept to Kollmorgen's other businesses when that company encountered severe problems in the early 1970s.

In the view of Bob Swiggett, Kollmorgen's organizational concept will continue to work at least until the company doubles its present size and achieves $600 million in annual revenues. What modifications might then have to be made are yet to be determined: Perhaps Kollmorgen will have to "productize" itself and split into two separate corporations.

THE ALSO-RANS

Most companies, however, are neither Safety-Kleens nor Kollmorgens. Success in building an effective organization once a company hits midsize is the exception, not the rule. Let's look at some of the typical problems mediocre companies encounter, drawing from real-life examples whose identities have been changed to protect the innocent.

Inability to leave things alone. The CEO of a midsize automotive equipment company with which we were familiar decided one evening the time had come to restructure the company. He elevated his long-time senior division general manager to the presidency and made him chief operating officer as well, specifically responsible for all domestic activities, leaving the CEO to focus his full attention on international development and finance. We were skeptical that the CEO would be able to keep from interfering in day-to-day domestic operations but couldn't dissuade him from forging ahead. When the CEO announced the changes the next morning, everybody responded enthusiastically.

The new structure survived while times were flush. But the fundamentals—the supporting systems, the CEO's ability to discipline himself to monitor but not manage operations, and the depth of competent, responsive down-the-line people—were inadequate to withstand the combination of a stressful market downturn and the inherent indisposition of the CEO to give up control even when he knew the company had grown too big for him to run by himself. Sure enough, at the first glimmer of a market downturn, the CEO seized back the operating reins, and the president departed for another company.

Recklessness. A small manufacturer of housewares grew meteorically: Fifteen years after it was founded, its sales exceeded $300 million. So great were its success, its preoccupation with increasing sales, and its confidence in its own ability that it failed to develop the basic accounting and operational disciplines required to understand product profitability and control cash flow. All decisions remained the intuitive province of the owner, who, together with his chief operating officer, entered into major, long-term contracts in domestic and foreign markets without any apparent consideration of the impact competition or a downturn in the market would have. Lacking management depth and discipline, the company was in bankruptcy proceedings before the end of its second decade.

Long-distance management. The CEO of one well-known midsize consumer goods company decided he wanted to live in a different part of the country from the company's headquarters. Worse, he continued to dominate decision-making, showed little trust in the judgment of his own people, and limited his communication to telephone conversations that very much followed his penchant for hierarchical rigor. Market share eroded steadily until eventually the company had to be sold.

The Pollyanna syndrome. A computer services company was the leader in its field, and undertook a major project to determine how it should organize itself to prepare for doubling its revenues. When outside consultants looked at the facts of its business for the first time, they found that dramatic technological change was rapidly rendering the company's core business obsolete. Meanwhile, prices had been increased to a premium above competitors' in the belief that the company provided superior service, when in fact the perception of major customers was precisely the contrary. In addition, the company had no idea whether, much less how regularly, its salespeople were calling on the most important customers and prospects; there simply were no records. A massive strategic and organizational shift, coupled with major personnel changes, appears to have bailed the company out, at least for the immediate future, though the jury is still out as to whether the company will adopt the organizational disciplines and incentives it still needs.

Focus on the wrong disciplines. A manufacturer of industrial equipment in the South had long been a leader in innovation. But as the company grew into midsize, it launched a misguided effort to control new-product development by adopting a review and evaluation process so cumbersome that innovation ceased entirely for a year and a half. At the same time, the company didn't have (and didn't worry about putting) the kind of systems in place that would allow it to assess profitability by specific product. As it turned out, the company was selling many of its products at a loss and didn't even know it—yet from a competitive standpoint, price increases could often have been justified. Meanwhile, sales of low-profit and even unprofitable products increased because the sales force was allowed to give price discounts and to alter trade terms (allowing customers to put off payments for as long as six months, for instance)—and salespeople were paid a commission based on revenue, not profit. The company's growth has slowed, profits have declined, and its market position has deteriorated against two better-managed competitors.

Corporate neuroses. Yet another machinery manufacturer allowed its margins on its core product line to fall in half because of fear over competition—though there was no competitive equipment available anywhere in the market, and though its primary customers would have to pay about fifty times the price of the machines to retool their plants to use alternative technology. At the same time, management imposed growth and profit objectives so severe as to drive several of the best, most creative managers out of the company.

In short, the widespread tendency of Unwinners is to overdo the fundamental disciplines or neglect them entirely; to overcontrol their people or abandon them entirely; to fool themselves into believing they are stronger than they are without benefit of facts on competitors, markets, and technologies; to communicate poorly to their people and act inconsistently. The failure of leadership in these companies lies in a managerial inability or unwillingness to create an organization that balances freedom and discipline, then to manage its evolution—an absence, in other words, of the energy and emotional commitment that characterize the winning performers.

HOW THE WINNING PERFORMERS DO IT

Our examination of the ways the American Business Conference companies organize themselves turned up evidence that high-growth companies do, in fact, focus on the search for ways to revitalize their people and renew businesses. Their most important practices center on the cultures they create rather than the structures they erect and the systems they impose.

As we explored the patterns of behavior the ABC companies exhibited in making the transition from small to midsize, we encountered one theme time after time: *the need to institutionalize the qualities that were intuitive and informal when they were small—the qualities that led to their initial success.*

To do this, they exhibit six distinctive traits of organizational behavior:

1. They instill a strong sense of mission and shared values—and work constantly to reinforce a deeply ingrained set of beliefs.
2. They pay relentless attention to business fundamentals.
3. They treat bureaucracy as an archenemy.
4. They encourage experimentation.
5. They think like their customers and work hard on behalf of them.
6. They count on people, and put development and motivation of their people at the top of their list of priorities.

Successful companies have and maintain all six attributes. We observed it ourselves, and we found that the CEOs of high-performance companies are well aware of it, too: More than 90 percent of our ABC survey respondents believe these attributes are important to their success. By contrast, "shooting star" companies—those whose success was meteoric but momentary—almost always have major gaps in at least one of these practices.

As is the case with the strategic traits we observed earlier in Chapter III, these organization practices are not pursued in isolation, but rather build upon one another. Their common element is *people*—be those people customers or associates who work in the enterprise.

Thus, shared values help set the ambitions, expectations, and focuses of those who make it happen. Attention to business fundamentals is the disciplining of the enterprise's most critical human acts—whether acts of intellect or energy. Preventing and containing bureaucracy and encouraging experimentation are both really ways to unlock the imagination, creativity, and energy of men and women. Thinking like customers, and enlisting them as partners in innovation, is predicated upon understanding what people want and need. And placing development and motivation of people at the top of the priority list speaks for itself.

It is also clear that the best companies work deliberately to sustain these six qualities over time, despite (or because of) tremendous changes in the internal and external conditions that affect their businesses. The best companies seem to contain a special renewal ingredient we call *dynamic adaptability*—a restless drive that permeates the organization and asserts that the job is never done; that no product, service, or function is ever good enough; that the search for more, new, and better must go on.

While perhaps less important than the cultural elements of organization, structure is highly visible, affects human motivation and relationships, and is the focus of extensive experimentation among high-growth companies. Among the ABC companies, 36 percent reorganized themselves at least three times in the ten years up to the time of our survey; 80 percent had reorganized at least once in the most recent five years. The lesson we draw is that a company can make almost any structure effective if it has the six attributes of midsize organizational effectiveness in place.

AN EVANGELICAL SENSE OF MISSION

Winners almost universally live by a clear sense of mission; they are value-driven. They have an unusually clear vision of their distinctive roles and (as important) their limitations—the markets in which they will (and will not) compete, the kinds of products and services they will (and will not) offer, the level of quality they expect. In other words, they have an acute sense of the basis of their competitive advantage. Similarly, they work hard to maintain a common set of company values, spelling out the nature of the company's commitment to serving its customers and the way people are to behave and be treated (and the way they are not).

This definition of mission does more than simply ensure quality-oriented consistency and common focus, though it would be indispensable even if that were all it did. The mission instills a sense that "this company is a special place that deserves more from me than a routine effort." Typically among the winning performers, the mission and its supporting rituals are almost religious in nature, and the commitment the mission generates pervades the company from the most senior officers to the entry-level worker. In the best companies, the mission serves several functions.

It Distills the Articles of Faith

A valid mission is, virtually by definition, durable and adaptable. Like most things of real worth, it outlasts trends but recognizes fundamental change early (often anticipating it, in fact) and accommodates it easily. One of the impressive accomplishments of the winning performers is their ability to sustain a sense of mission and shared values over time. They do this through a variety of communication vehicles—almost always transmitting the sense of values as though by osmosis, but usually articulating it explicitly as well. Twenty-five percent of the ABC companies have written creeds explaining their fundamental beliefs, and more than three quarters have formal programs of one kind or another to communicate values.

Of the ABC high-growth companies we investigated, 84 percent said their entire employee corps "share values that provide substantive guidance and direction." Eighty-six percent said they believe managers three levels removed from the top would "substantively agree" on the organization's three most important strengths and its three greatest challenges. Our follow-up interviews and other experience in working with winning companies confirm the impression that fundamental values are typically ingrained deep in these organizations.

It Zeroes In on the Long View

Few businesses are more dependent on short-term performance

than ADP, the computer information company that provides daily reports and weekly payrolls to thousands of customers. But ADP's corporate philosophy takes a pronounced long-term view, emphasizing enduring customer relationships and the career-long development of its people.

At Chilton Corporation, which provides consumer credit information on tens of millions of Americans, corporate values are unequivocally focused on long-term performance. The company has been in existence since the late 1800s, and continuity is a high priority. Its philosophy, often stated explicitly to shareholders, allows sacrificing short-term profits for long-term, encouraging people to experiment with new ideas and never to skimp on customer service.

It Beckons the Stumbler Back to the Straight and Narrow

An unusual but important phrase in the Chilton Corporation way of doing things is: "The grass is always browner." What that means is that Chilton people will be tempted to leave the company from time to time, seeking greener pastures, but that when they do, they'll usually find that the Chilton environment was, in fact, much better. The phrase is also shorthand for two other related values: Chilton is dedicated to maintaining a culture that attracts and motivates outstanding people, and if good people want to return to Chilton after seeking greener pastures, they are welcome back. On six occasions during the past few years, Chilton officers left the company, subsequently returned, and are now doing well—an acid test of Chilton's value system.

Some successful companies also recall times when their values and sense of mission became unclear and had to be restated and reinforced. Several ABC members diversified excessively in the "go-go" years of the 1960s, and lived through periods of diminished performance while getting back on track. Others told us of times when their message became garbled at lower levels, and they had to take corrective action. In one instance, a CEO found on a plant visit that a new product was being shipped despite below-standard quality and yields. When he asked why, he was told that instructions had been given that the quarterly budget was to be met at all costs. The CEO immediately embarked on a program to make it clear that quality and value to the customer were not to be sacrificed for financial objectives. He explained that the company expected both—but that if one had to suffer for a while, it had better be profit. Declining performance in many midsize companies reflects the loss of such fundamental values and sense of direction.

It Establishes the Primacy of the People

A good mission statement focuses directly on the importance of people, too. For years, Materials Research Corporation, widely known as an innovator in ultrapure materials and thin film-coating systems, has maintained a no-layoff policy. As long as employees perform well, their jobs are secure, even when times are tough. CEO Shelley Weinig says this policy is essential to keep a staff of highly talented, inventive people committed to the long-term success of the company. It also serves as an incentive to his people to hire only top talent that will meet long-term corporate expectations and has thus kept the company from hiring people in times of prosperity who would be excess in recessionary periods. During the 1982–83 recession, times were tough indeed for Materials Research, but it stuck to its value system, even at the cost of some red ink. With a strong recovery now in progress, the company's management team remains intact and highly motivated.

When a company genuinely values its people, it shows it in myriad ways. Automatic Data Processing has compiled a record for consecutive years of increased sales and earnings that no listed company in the United States can match. ADP also has no executive dining room; its top executives have to find a table in the company cafeteria along with everyone else. There are no reserved parking lots; the only way to park near the front door is to arrive early. And by arranging for employee stock purchases at a discount from market price, ADP has made two thirds of all employees shareholders.

It Shows How to Beat Goliath

Many of our ABC winning performers credit an intense, widely shared focus on customer service for their ability to beat larger, apparently stronger competitors. Jim Macaleer, CEO of SMS (Shared Medical Systems), which supplies computer-based information systems to the nation's hospitals, says the company's do-or-die commitment to giving customers what they need has enabled it to beat the multibillion-dollar giants that also attempted to enter the hospital information market. "For the big guys, the hospital market is a small piece of business. They budget inadequate funds for sales and service, and corporate management becomes disenchanted when—treating hospitals as an ancillary business—they don't do well in it. They rotate people through the hospital information systems division who can't spell 'hospital,' let alone understand the business.

"Our top priority is caring more. This is our only business. We don't have anywhere else to go. We *have* to care about our customers more than anybody else cares about them. And we do."

SMS's and Macaleer's total commitment to the hospital information market is supported by a driving work ethic that permeates the company from top to bottom. SMS people assume that there will be times they have to work around the clock to meet customer deadlines. And it shows up in little ways as well. When we met Jim Carter, VP for operations, for an August discussion, one of his first remarks was: "Let's take the stairs up to my office—the elevator is too slow!"

It Inspires the Faithful

The winning performers' value systems usually encourage personal initiative and freedom to maneuver as means by which their people can serve customers better. As described earlier, Kollmorgen Corporation puts high priority on technological leadership in order to be first to market with the best. But the way to technical leadership is through people. When he drafted Kollmorgen's formal statement of philosophy, CEO Bob Swiggett included this telling point:

> Management systems and employee motivation may be just as important to a company's success as new technology or fast-growing markets; innovation in this area of "software" may be just as important as innovation in product hardware. These things play a vital part in attracting and holding the good people who make everything happen in a growing business.

Hundred-year-old Harvey Hubbell, the Connecticut-based electrical products company, is one of only two public ABC companies to have increased its earnings from continuing operations every year for more than twenty years (Automatic Data Processing is the other). Bob Dixon, until 1983 Hubbell's CEO, ascribes this success to companywide adherence to a fundamental value: "We meet our commitments, our products do what we say they will do, and we ship them when we say we will ship them, with no excuses."

Linked to this "no excuses" institutional frame of mind is another attitude that has been instilled in Hubbell's people from its earliest days: "Never think you have it made. If we don't keep finding something new and better, someone will catch up to us." The power of these two institutional values, linked together, is the basis for Hubbell's enviable record: The company keeps saying it will be better than before, and it keeps doing what it says it will do.

It Prompts the CEO to Become "Chief Evangelical Officer"

As he does in virtually everything, the chief executive plays a crucial role in communicating the company's message at all levels. Bert Snider, president of Bourns, a manufacturer of electrical and electronic parts, says: "My mission is to communicate who we are, what our dream is, and why it is going to work for us." He assigns top priority to the time he spends with his people—visiting and talking with every one of the company's seven thousand worldwide employees at least twice a year. Jack Bowers, the chief executive at Sanders Associates, a leading supplier of electronic systems to the U.S. government, and Roger Wellington, the Augat chairman and CEO, do the same in their companies, too.

It Supplies Courage in the Face of the Unknown

Some companies have been able to undergo traumatic organizational change, and even to undo mistakes, because of the trust that existed between senior management and the people as a whole.

At Chilton, mistakes are not only accepted but encouraged—if they are "smart" mistakes. The company wants its people to be innovative and take initiative, and is willing to pay a reasonable price for the failures in order to enjoy the benefits of the successes. Chilton has what it calls its "sixty-day rule"—which means managers can generally risk up to sixty days' profit from their business unit trying out a new idea, without negative consequences (although Chilton also expects adherence to the rules of common sense).

Millipore, the materials separations company, provides another example. In the 1970s it experimented with a matrix organization, under which many managers were formally responsible to several others—quite a change from the traditional "one boss" structure. It seemed a rational move, since Millipore had grown to encompass some one hundred distinct product-customer centers, all of which needed to draw on common sources of technical, production, marketing, and other support functions. Despite great effort, the formal matrix system just didn't work. As Chairman Dee d'Arbeloff put it, "Every high-tech company has an informal matrix structure. It's formalizing it that causes trouble. People don't know how to serve several 'bosses' simultaneously and equally without getting into squabbles that slow down decision-making and action." The confusion caused by multiple relationships made it difficult if not impossible to set priorities, sometimes resulting in internal antagonisms. A company that lacked Millipore's underlying values, one with less solid a commitment to solving customer problems, could have paid a dear price in reverting to a divisional system. Millipore, by contrast, survived the two-way transition with minimal discomfort, as we shall see in greater detail in Chapter VI.

RELENTLESS FOCUS ON THE FUNDAMENTALS

While emphasizing initiative, service, and freedom, the successful midsize high-growth companies also pay relentless attention to running the business smoothly and efficiently. Through disciplined, rigorous systems, both formal and informal, they monitor and manage their financial performance, operations, and competitive positions as major sources of competitive advantage.

The First Fundamental—Financial Performance

John Castle, president of the investment banking firm Donaldson, Lufkin & Jenrette, told us, "I began as a venture capitalist, but one of the most important things I've done is to back the development of a strong set of operating statements that we review at divisional manager meetings every month. Those statements incorporate every number that is important to our business. Everyone attends these meetings, even if it means flying back from vacation."

In the mid-1970s, W. L. Lyons (Lee) Brown, chairman and CEO of Brown-Forman Corporation, together with members of his senior management team, created a new financial planning system that deemphasizes earnings growth alone as a target, and instead gives top priority to return on investment above the cost of capital—now recognized as the best way to measure shareholder wealth. (Brown-Forman thus became one of the first companies in the country to adopt this measure.) Lee Brown also emphasized long-range rather than short-term financial performance, noting that "in the liquor business you have to wait years for your product to be ready for the market. We have no choice but to take a long-range view, and that gives us an acute sense of the cost of money." Brown manages to couple this focus on financial performance with heavy emphasis on personal initiative and new ideas, and extensive delegation to create and sustain personal autonomy, freedom, and entrepreneurial spirit.

Financial disciplines were Bob Elliot's most important early contribution to Levitz Furniture when he became CEO in 1974. Levitz, a highly innovative distributor, found itself in trouble when it failed to see a drop in growth on the horizon. Consequently, the company got stuck with too much inventory and surplus staff. Elliot responded quickly by putting a lean, centralized buying organization in place while at the same time decentralizing the marketing organization to ensure local responsiveness and entrepreneurship. Now the company has an information system in place that provides precise details on sales and inventories by product item in every store across the country and a tight budgetary control system. Largely as a result, and supported by a strong economic recovery, Levitz has rebounded impressively from its recessionary lows, and it had record profits in 1984.

With few exceptions, the winning performers' systems are not complicated or "sophisticated"—they are simple and they work. The midsize growth companies' strong financial disciplines are designed not only to energize and concentrate management team efforts but also to generate margin dollars that can be used to develop new products, to support expansion, and to build organizational strength. These superior profit margins, which are crucial to rapidly growing companies, are one of the distinctive signs of the winning performers. In fact, our analysis shows that the high-growth midsize companies consistently achieve pretax profit margins that exceed the margins of average midsize companies by nearly 7 percent of sales.

The Second Fundamental—Operations

The consistently successful midsize high-growth companies know they have to manage *every* element of the business system—not just new products or sales, but sourcing, product design and engineering, manufacturing productivity and cost control, distribution, marketing, and service. Their drive is to be the best, and that demands discipline in all aspects of the business.

On the other hand, the winning companies also recognize that in virtually every business, there are certain critical functions—for example, research in high-technology industries, advertising in consumer packaged goods—that have to receive special nurturing over time if the company is to succeed. Because their larger competitors are more likely to possess expertise in the critical functions (or can add it easily), the winning performers have to work harder at, and do *more* with, these sources of critical strength. And in fact they are, for the most part, leaders in these skills. They pay more attention to them, they put their best people in them, and they spend more dollars than the competition. Furthermore, they do not simply outspend the competition; 59 percent of the CEOs who took part in our survey assert that they spend "considerably more."

It was this drive for a competitive edge in the critical function that led Chilton Corporation to invest millions in computer automation—not once but twice—to put the company at the leading edge of credit information collection, analysis, communication, and retrieval. The same determination to be the best led Xidex Corporation to develop the premier manufacturing capability in duplicate microfilm and floppy disks, giving it a low-cost position in two highly competitive growth markets.

The winning performers tend to have tight operating controls that measure not only manufacturing and cost performance but also such externally oriented activities as customer service and delivery performance. They are also tough negotiators in sourcing and purchasing, and—in contrast to a surprising number of their less successful competitors—many of them require competitive bidding and dual sourcing.

Bob Marbut, CEO of Harte-Hanks Communications, the Texas publishing and broadcasting company, told us: "When I took over in the early seventies, we were growing rapidly enough and had lofty enough ambitions that the old, informal way was on the verge of not working well for us any longer. So the first, most important step was to get organized. We set up a chart of accounts, installed annual planning and budgeting, and began to review performance against the plan. All the while we had to be mindful not to lose the strong innovative values our people already had. We used the planning process to reorient the business from newspapers to supplying information—opening a much broader set of market niches." Jim Macaleer of SMS said: "We must have better operating controls than our giant competitors. Unlike them, we can't afford not to know exactly what our costs are, where every dollar is going, and how rapidly we are improving productivity."

The Third Fundamental—External Focus

Growing introspection is one risk of success. As a company grows, more time inevitably goes to budgets and reports and to the increasingly demanding tasks of keeping people informed, integrating functions, and reaching consensus. The winning performers, however, work hard to keep these internal activities from obscuring or diminishing the intensity of their focus on the outside world.

These companies monitor external forces closely in order to understand competitors' costs, prices, and performance characteristics versus their own. They undertake regular formal competitor reviews, analyzing competitive products, service levels, and marketing programs, based both on regular and structured feedback from their salesmen and on special projects. Some go so far as to reverse-engineer competitive products, buying and dismantling a competitor's machine so as to understand its manufacturing costs, operating characteristics, and maintenance requirements.

At Pandick, Inc., the financial prospectus printer, the CEO, Edward G. Green, and his senior managers have a detailed grasp of the ability of each competitor to meet customer requirements. The fact that one competitor's plants were located in an adjacent state rather than in the same city as Pandick led the CEO to say: "We know it takes them twelve minutes longer to make a correction to a customer's document—and since our business revolves around the ability to manipulate data and redistribute proofs of revised pages within extremely demanding time frames, that is a significant competitive advantage for us." Pall Corporation, Millipore, Automatic Data Processing, and SMS, among others, use formal customer surveys and seminars to evaluate competitive position and performance, and some link the results of customer surveys to annual bonuses.

In the best companies we know, the CEO's first question on any proposal tends to be: "How much would this add to our advantage over competitor X?" This practice enshrines external discipline—making sure that your products and services offer cost or value advantages over your competition's.

Winning companies also track (and seek to influence) environmental, legislative, and regulatory change—positioning the company to take quick advantage by anticipating and capitalizing on changing public policies. It's important to note that they engage in this constant monitoring of the outside world not only in their own industries but in their customers' industries, too—because, after all, in the long run it is their ability to give their customers a competitive advantage that is the winning performers' competitive advantage.

The importance of almost slavish attention to business fundamentals is dramatized by the failure of once-successful companies that ignored them. The internal cost system at a $100 million manufacturer of production-line equipment did not identify major differences in the profitability of its major products, leading ultimately to pricing mistakes that devastated its profits. A searching strategic review finally brought the root problem to the surface, enabling the company to remedy it and get back on a profitable track.

An even larger service firm allowed its marketing information to get out of date; as a result, its salesmen called on high-potential customers sporadically and sometimes not at all. Worse, it also allowed its market research to slide; the company neither measured service performance levels accurately nor compared them with the levels its competitors achieved. As a result, it failed to see that its product had lost its premier position; by maintaining premium prices on an inferior product, the firm experienced an inevitable and costly loss of market share. In this case, too, the problem was eventually identified and corrected, but the profits and market position lost in the meanwhile cost it tens of millions of dollars.

BUREAUCRACY: THE ARCHENEMY

The winning companies recognize that growth in size and complexity bears a potentially mortal risk: bureaucratic behavior. Employees of small companies have a broad perspective on the whole business. Often, they are generalists who operate informally, and find it easy to keep in fairly intimate touch both with the owner-founder and the ultimate customers. As size and complexity increase, however, a shift toward specialization and more formality in structure and management processes is inevitable—changing the nature and reducing the extent of day-to-day contact between senior management, on the one hand, and down-the-line managers and other employees, on the other. Patterns of behavior become increasingly focused on immediate functional or geographic responsibilities. Pressures for short-term performance rise, and the middle manager doesn't dwell on corporate issues the way he did once upon a time. Sometimes he loses sight of them completely. When this happens, there is not only a risk but almost a likelihood that people—thinking like employees—will behave as bureaucrats, not as businessmen or owners.

Bureaucracy is as insidious and stubborn in the business world as crabgrass in a suburban lawn. Once it appears, it's excruciatingly difficult to eradicate. In the advanced state, bureaucracy can cause individuals to work to rule, avoid risk, be afraid of trying new ideas, value their personal positions and prerogatives above corporate achievement, avoid teamwork, and delay action. By themselves, each of those phenomena costs money, which makes them undesirable. In combination, they can be deadly.

Furthermore, although the absence of bureaucracy in a company isn't sufficient to make sure innovation flourishes, the presence of bureaucracy is enough to kill it. Innovation requires champions, unconventional thinking, and willingness to risk failure. Bureaucrats thrive on writing (if not reading) long memoranda, checking all the bases, arranging meetings that are long on agenda and short on substance, and—above all—avoiding decisions and risk-taking. If the multiple forms to be filled out and layers of organization to be persuaded don't kill a new idea, fear of criticism or dismissal in the event of failure will. Stories abound of companies that institute and insist on adhering to elaborate frameworks for developing, screening, testing, and evaluating new products—procedures that prove so time-consuming and frustrating that their streams of new products dry up altogether.

The successful midsize growth companies seem to avoid this peril by fighting bureaucracy aggressively on every front—preventing it when they can, attacking it when they find it has crept in. The winning performers are obsessively dedicated to keeping their systems and structures simple and uncomplicated. They've found that doing so is far easier and more fruitful than trying to cope with cumbersome reporting arrangements and layers of delegation.

Structurally, they strive to keep organizational units small. To accomplish short-term objectives, they establish temporary work groups and ad hoc task forces. They steer away from organization charts, especially charts that highlight differences in the pecking order. They emphasize delegation of decision-making responsibility. They concretely encourage managers to get into the field, to mingle with the employees and customers alike. They refine job descriptions and responsibilities continually.

Companies such as Marketing Corporation of America and Kollmorgen purposely structure themselves to create small units that stress and inspire entrepreneurial thinking on the part of their leaders and employees. And when Donaldson, Lufkin & Jenrette adds a new financial service, it invariably designs it around an individual entrepreneur and sees that he or she operates it as a small, independent business unit.

MCI, now a $1.9-billion telecommunications company, recently split its domestic business into seven operating companies. The reasons: to make the businesses smaller and more manageable, to put business decisions closer to the customers, and to breed and season new generations of general managers. Only relationships with federal regulatory authorities, systems and network planning and design, and finance remain corporate-office functions. Rather than ordain a universal organizational structure for each unit to adopt, even this decision was left to the company managers. Brian Thompson, now the president of one of the new regional companies, explained: "Our sheer success meant that we were getting further away from our customers and our own people. Splitting it up helps resolve that."

The winning companies also deliberately restrict headquarters staff size. Almost all the American Business Conference companies keep their staffs small, and the majority don't even have separate departments such as government relations, investor relations, and public affairs that are routinely found in larger companies (see Exhibit IV-1). Line managers assume these functions, or they are added to the responsibilities of other staff officers.

Exhibit IV-1
SIZE OF STAFF FUNCTIONS IN ABC COMPANIES

	SIZE OF DEPARTMENT			
	Do not have one	Small	Moderate	Large
Government relations	80%	18%	2%	0%
Internal communications	64	24	9	3
Public affairs	58	38	4	0
Investor relations	55	45	0	0
Corporate planning	40	51	9	0
Legal affairs	33	42	22	3
Personnel	7	31	53	9

Sources: Survey of ABC membership; McKinsey analysis

To counteract the innovation-stifling, bureaucracy-cultivating effects of *systems disciplines*—annual budgets, longer-range plans, capital-appropriation processes, formal incentive plans, control reports focusing on performance variances, and the like, ad infinitum—the winning companies come up with such bureaucracy-busting devices as special rewards for collaborators, delegators, and innovators. They tailor their planning processes to the special needs of each business and function, rather than require the units to conform to a single corporate format, or meet the needs of a planning staff. They insist on simplicity. Stuart D. Buchalter, chairman of Standard Brands Paint Company of Torrance, California, a chain of specialty paint and home-decorating products stores whose sales tripled in the ten years 1974–83, has outdone Procter &

Gamble's famous one-page-memo culture: A discussion over lunch is often enough to secure his okay to launch a project. "It isn't always necessary to have a written proposal to get something going," he says. The winning companies accept risk and even failure in experiments or innovations that do not work out; they encourage people who "give it a good try."

As a matter of *style,* the winning performers believe that whenever there are various options for achieving any objective, the simplest is best unless there is overwhelming evidence to the contrary. This also seems to define their attitude toward communication. Their watchwords are *clear, simple,* and *direct.* To find an answer, don't go through a gatekeeper—just ask the person who knows. If doing so means cutting across organizational boundaries (as it usually does with any broad business question), it's fine with them.

The need for new *specialized skills* caused by growth and increasing complexity means specialized functional training; often, it also means bringing in specialists and sometimes general managers from outside the company. Growth also normally means geographic dispersion of people who still share a common goal but now have to work together at long distance, and so formal communications necessarily replaces informal give-and-take. The winning performers balance these disciplines through such devices as frequent job rotation, often across functional and divisional lines; use of multifunctional venture teams; and frequent gatherings—social and professional—within and across functions.

They recognize the value of simple human interaction in keeping everybody marching in the same direction. Memoranda from the CEO are few and brief at Pall Corporation, the leading filter company. As one executive put it: "I rarely see a memorandum from Abe Krasnoff, our chief executive. Sometimes he sends me a handwritten note, but his notes are always hard to read. Fundamentally, I don't think Abe is happy with the written word because he thinks he should be there in person." The primary way Krasnoff maintains a high level of communication within Pall is through constant personal meetings, phone discussion, and group interaction with people throughout the company. He is known for dropping in unannounced. The questions he asks and his upbeat manner are so unthreatening that people at Pall seem to feel free to discuss both their new ideas and their past mistakes—which goes a long way toward busting the most serious negative effects of bureaucracy.

Most American Business Conference companies conduct regular meetings of geographically dispersed executives who share the same functions, simply to exchange ideas and generate enthusiasm. The cash outlay associated with the meetings is often high—but, the winning performers agree, so is the payoff, in terms of bringing new ideas to the surface, reinvigorating everybody's commitment to the corporate mission, renewing personal relationships, and generating overall enthusiasm for the company.

As *shared values* become formalized, they can create a common point of reference and reinforcement. From the moment you arrive in the reception area of ASK Computer Systems' Los Altos headquarters, you can feel the energy generated by the open, youthful atmosphere the company has created. Some people arrive in jogging shoes; another executive is bringing her bicycle into her office. The atmosphere radiates enthusiasm; the employees and the receptionist exchange quips and a few laughs. Then you learn that some of these people had worked through the night twenty-four hours ago—yet here they are back again, loving every minute of it, because they share a commitment to producing the best manufacturing software in the world.

In the best companies, shared values permeate every level. A courier for BDM, the supplier of professional technical services to the defense establishment, arrived once at a government procurement office with a contract bid, only to be told that he was one minute past the deadline. The courier knew he was on time and knew the contract was important to the company, so he wouldn't take no for an answer. He prevailed on the stubborn bureaucrat to call the Time Lady—and won the argument.

Unfortunately, values that are askew can lead to just the opposite—to closed minds (or insufficiently open, unimaginative minds) and a nine-to-five frame of mind that are serious liabilities in times of change. To make sure a corporate value system doesn't have that effect, the winning performers almost always consciously build into the corporate vision a series of notions or concepts that seem simple almost in the extreme (as is true with so much of what they do). The difference is that while everyone nowadays *says* the right words, winning performers actually *behave* the right way—answering their own telephones, for instance, because the organization values accessibility; calling people directly for information, rather than sending a written request, because they value efficiency and loathe paperwork; using first names up and down the entire organization, because hierarchies annoy people and thwart creativity; celebrating initiatives and downplaying good-try mistakes, because a risk-taking organization rarely misses a chance for ballyhoo; reviewing the organization's mission and values every few years "whether we need it or not," as a check on current fit with the business environment.

ENCOURAGE EXPERIMENTATION

Businesses have to try new things all the time unless they want to stagnate. The successful midsize growth companies recognize that initiative, ideas, and innovations are—virtually by definition—the source of their continuing ability to grow. They have the knack for making one man's invention become another's necessity. So they actively encourage experimentation, fostering a climate that encourages people to pursue new product and new market ideas constantly.

Standard Brands Paints, where table talk at lunch can be sufficient to inaugurate a new project, encourages experimentation and ingenuity in an exemplary range of other ways than just eliminating the suffocation of paperwork. Stu Buchalter encourages his store managers always to set aside some space to devote to experiments with new products and merchandising approaches. In one instance, someone asked him about "the new wallpaper shop" one of his managers had opened in an existing store to sell old, damaged, or out-of-style goods rather than return them to the warehouse. He hadn't even heard of it, but he was pleased; his people were upholding the tradition of experimentation and hadn't felt bound to convene committees or distribute new-product-launch flow charts before trying the idea.

One important way the winning performers encourage experimentation and innovation is by sending strong, consistent signals that—as long as experiments meet the test of commonsense reasonableness—failure won't be punished. The greater sin is not trying at all.

Jim McManus is founder and CEO of Marketing Corporation of America (MCA), the fast-growing firm that provides such marketing services to its clients as advertising, promotional design, couponing programs, and market research. McManus spends a good deal of his time encouraging the development of new ideas and new businesses. MCA recognizes success with financial rewards and—just as important—it conspicuously avoids punishing failure. McManus told us: "Most big companies fire or demote their risk-takers who fail. The consequence is that the company loses its ability to learn from failure and to generate better new ideas. Since MCA was founded, we've launched twenty new businesses. Ten were successes and ten were losers—and no one has been fired or demoted as a result of the losers."

In the same vein, Roger Wellington, chairman and CEO of Augat, told us: "We let people who get ideas go ahead and try them, and we've had a lot of big successes as well as a good number of failures. The people who came up with the ideas that succeed are often rewarded with bonuses and stock. The ones whose ideas didn't work are encouraged to keep trying."

Companies like Augat encourage the concept that corporate success is everyone's responsibility, and everyone should be on the lookout for good new ideas.

SMS sometimes experiments on a national scale. For example, early in SMS's history, its salesmen were responsible primarily for finding and making initial arrangements with new customers. As the market grew and became more sophisticated, the tasks of renewing customer relationships and upgrading customer systems took on greater importance, and in order to leave salesmen free to sell, these tasks were transferred from the salesmen to the installation directors. After some time, this arrangement was not yielding adequate results, and a new group was formed to handle renewals and upgrades—hospital systems consultants. Subsequently, responsibility was transferred back to the sales force to put maximum sales power against growing competition. Each step, each change, was in effect a national experiment—one that could be changed on short notice with very little disruption and at comparatively little cost.

GETTING INSIDE THE CUSTOMER'S MIND

The biggest Rolodex we've ever seen is not the property of a talent agent or a Washington lobbyist or high-ranking government official. It resides on the desk outside the office of Bob Goldman, the president and chief operating officer of Cullinet Software. It's filled with the names, addresses, and telephone numbers of Cullinet customers—and it's thoroughly fingerworn because Goldman spends 50 percent of his time calling and seeing customers.

Being "user driven" is a way of life at Cullinet. The day we visited the company's Westwood, Massachusetts, headquarters, two customers were in for meetings, as we learned from the welcome sign in the reception area. Two weeks before, the company had conducted "user week," when more than twenty-two hundred customers had met with Cullinet managers, technicians, and marketing people to describe their needs, problems, and ideas. In a business where companies sign contracts for products that don't yet exist, Cullinet sees its current customers and clients as its most effective sales force. No wonder "having successful customers" was the phrase we heard most often when we asked for the company's most important objectives.

Allen Mebane, the CEO of Unifi, the producer of textured polyester yarn, said: "I have got to know my customer's business and problems as well as I know my own. If I can't show him how much I can help him, I won't keep his business for long." Mebane typifies a central finding of our American Business Conference research: the importance both of gearing an organization to get inside the customer's mind and of the personal identification of the chief executive with this overriding value. Managers in such organizations know that they earn money for their companies by making money for their customers.

Pall Corporation has a lot of customer minds to get inside of. In the process of increasing sales sixfold and profits almost fifteen times (1974–84), Pall has extended its product line from filters and related "fluid clarification" equipment into scores of market niches—from the removal of microscopic particles in the manufacture of wine, electronic parts, and vaccines, to the recapture and recycling of expensive catalysts, to prevention of contamination in the hydraulic and lubricating systems of aircraft, missiles, and manufacturing machinery, to filtration of blood during open-heart surgery, to name several.

Pall swarms all over its customers' filtration needs, aiming to understand them better than anyone else—better than competitors and even the customers themselves. Senior managers are frequently in touch with customers directly, both in person and on the telephone, and are always accessible when a customer has a question or a problem. Beyond this substantive and symbolic involvement by top management, Pall is structured to support the customer in five distinct ways:

- *Local distributors.* As the company puts it: "We find that strong local entrepreneurs with long-standing relationships in their own communities give us a quality and frequency of customer contact that a company of our size could never duplicate with its own employees. We also try to make sure that our business represents at least 25 percent of the distributor's total volume so that he has a vested interest in giving lots of attention to promoting our products."
- *Direct salespeople.* This group spends full time working with the distributors' sales forces, helping them sell and teaching them how to sell better, particularly in the newer and less familiar filtration applications.
- *Applications engineers.* These engineers use their in-depth knowledge of complex application technology to help local distributors and individual customers design filtration systems and solve problems.
- *Industry-oriented market managers.* It is the task of these managers to bring new application ideas to the field organization by transferring

the experience of one geographic area to the others and by developing and communicating creative new ideas.
- *A problem-solving division,* Scientific and Laboratory Services. This group is organized around markets and assists in marketing new systems and applications based on existing and new products out of research, and with providing test facilities for customers who need to solve problems or want to try out new filtration ideas.

CEO Abe Krasnoff expresses Pall's viewpoint this way: "This multi-faceted organization is expensive, but well worth it. It enables us to address customer problems from every conceivable angle. I am intent on giving better service than anyone in the world—I really am—and this organization enables us to do it." The operative acronym around Pall is "EESES," summarizing Pall's commitment to its customers: Ease of use, Economy of use, Safety, Efficacy, and Service.

Loctite's salesmen view themselves as customer problem solvers. CEO Bob Krieble says: "From the start, we have had a sales force with missionary zeal. They get their kicks out of helping customers make better machinery and lower their maintenance costs. We are far and away the leader in this market, but we have only realized ten percent of our potential. And so our salespeople spend most of their working hours in customer plants looking for new applications that will save the customer money or increase performance." When new uses for Loctite's anaerobic adhesives are discovered, they are widely publicized internally— partly to applaud the salesman for his ingenuity, partly to spur his colleagues toward the same kind of imaginative customer-focused thinking, and partly to notify the organization of a newfound opportunity.

Holding a seminar or conducting a survey of customers is one of the best ways to learn what's on the customer's mind, and the practice is common in many of the ABC companies. Some even build the results of customer surveys into their incentive compensation programs for salespeople and servicepeople.

The senior executives of high-growth midsize companies spend substantially more time with their customers than do their counterparts in giant corporations. Our ABC survey found that, on average, midsize high-growth company CEOs devote 10 percent of their time to working directly with customers; one in nine spends a third of his time with customers. Other senior managers in the ABC companies spend an average of 20 percent of their time on customer calls.

Through such devices, the winning companies stay in close step with the needs and inexorable changes taking place in their markets and inside individual customer organizations. This fundamentally market-driven approach is the cornerstone of their ability to identify new niche markets and product opportunities, then to fill those needs; it enables them to anticipate and adapt to new problems and opportunities more quickly, effectively, and successfully than less competent competitors.

In contrast, most companies of all sizes focus too much on their own internal problems and priorities, putting the customer last rather than first. Stores are open when it is convenient for the employees, rather than when the customers choose to shop. Many companies make products that run well in their factories, rather than understand what makes money or creates satisfaction for their customers. For years, package delivery services and freight forwarders provided service based on the transportation schedules that railroads and airlines happened to make available—and they lost ground when Federal Express, a brand-new company now reaching $1.5 billion in sales, designed its own overnight delivery system. Traditional restaurant chains with high fixed costs lost a major share of their market—and a huge opportunity—when more customer-oriented companies created the fast-food business. And the same sort of thing happened when the mass merchandising chains took away the traditional markets of the variety stores and when electronic calculators replaced mechanical adding machines. Time and again, internally oriented companies have lost out in markets they thought they owned because of a competitor's superior understanding of a customer's product or service need, and willingness to meet that need.

COUNTING ON PEOPLE

If we had to single out one overriding theme among winning company organizations, it would be their willingness to count on people to make their companies successful. Since they are at the stage of corporate growth at which neither the CEO nor the senior management team can individually ensure the success of the business, they find various ways of saying to their organizations at large: "Only you can make this company a success—we can't do it all. We have common goals, common values, and we have agreed on our strategic approach and target position in the marketplace. Now it is up to you to make it work—and we know you can do it."

This often unspoken attitude toward people seems to derive from a deep-seated belief that good people—those whom the winning performers would invite into their companies—will consistently rise to the occasion.

They will welcome responsibility and be productive. They want to be winners, and they will show ingenuity in finding ways to succeed. In brief, the winning companies expect the kind of behavior that Chilton Corporation described to us in the following example.

At Chilton, the consumer-credit-reporting company, the computer communications system that linked all its branch centers with Dallas headquarters suddenly went down one day. The head of the data-processing division was determined not to allow this disruption of the company's operations. He couldn't find anything wrong anywhere in the company, though—and that could only mean the problem was in the outside telephone lines. But the telephone company wasn't able to pinpoint the source of the problem. So the DP chief jumped in his car and combed Dallas until *he* found the phone company's problem at a nearby construction site, where a cable had inadvertently been cut.

Whatever their underlying philosophy may be, the winning performers consistently believe in paying lots of attention to helping people develop themselves and their skills. And they believe in providing for financial motivation that will lead people to want to behave more like owners and businessmen and less like employees or bureaucrats.

Counting on people—and recognizing and celebrating their contributions—is a hallmark of management practice at Herman Miller. For the past thirty years, this designer and manufacturer of high-quality office and workplace furniture has made participatory management pay through a Scanlon productivity plan.* In 1984, bonuses averaged 13.7 percent above salary. Every employee is also a stockholder. But even more impressive is the prominence Miller accords individual workers. For example, the company's 1983 annual report contained fifty interviews with Herman Miller people, including a scheduler, a materials-handling lead man, and an assembler—as well as members of the higher reaches of management.

Analog Devices—the manufacturer of devices that enable computers to "talk" to us and to each other—is not just another electronics company, as we saw in Chapter III. Over the past five years, its growth in sales doubled the industry average; growth in earnings per share was 31 percent, while the industry's actually declined.† Sales boomed from $31 million in 1974 to $313 million in 1984—with a jump in profit from $1.6 million to $37.4 million.

---

*Herman Miller was one of the first companies in America to adopt a plan designed by Joseph Scanlon to share with workers the benefits brought by productivity.
†*Forbes*, 37th Annual Report on American Industry (January 14, 1985), pp. 140–41.

What distinguishes Analog in our minds is not so much its business performance but the extent to which the company's focus on people underpins its strategies and operations. Analog produces products that most people don't understand—modular amplifiers, analogue-to-digital and digital-to-analogue converters, and monolithic integrated circuits, to name a few—that, according to founder and chief executive Ray Stata, "allow computers to understand and use 'real world' information." These devices find their way into precision instruments such as those that control radio broadcasting, digital X-ray machines that doctors use for on-the-scene diagnosis, and welding robots in automated factories.

Analog's corporate success derives from a strategy founded on innovation—a strategy that permits the company to charge premium prices for its components and systems. Its unusual level of innovation results in a value-based way of doing business, with Analog positioning itself in the fastest-changing technologies and changing even faster than its competitors.

To pursue this strategy, let alone succeed in it, Analog has had to count on people performing consistently and outstandingly well. The company's focus on people and their development and motivation is not only important but fundamental. In Stata's view, Analog Devices' competitive advantage is based on "acts of intellect"—innovations that come from the minds of its technologists. Quite naturally, the minds of the technologists—whether engineers, marketing professionals, or manufacturing people—are the company's most important asset.

It isn't surprising to find executives in winning companies talking about the importance of people—but Analog's full-court press is notable. It begins with a strategic plan. Like most good strategies, it analyzes the business issues and the strategic environment—trends, challenges, and opportunities in technology, markets, manufacturing processes, economic and social changes, competition, and so forth. But Analog's real distinction is in the heavy emphasis it puts on the internal environment, or culture, and the critical success factors associated with human resources. It outlines, as a central strategic strength, its beliefs about people and organization—describing not only how to unlock the technical potential of engineers, but also how to encourage people across the organization to do their best. For example, Analog's strategy statement includes such articles of faith as:

- "Innovation flourishes in organizations which encourage risk-taking and which value intuition as much as analysis."
- "Better decisions result from power that is based more on knowledge and competence than on position in an organization hierarchy."
- "People want responsibility for their jobs and accountability for results."

About one fifth of Analog's strategic plan is devoted to how to attract, change, motivate, reward, and develop the people necessary for cutting-edge innovation. Issues of turnover, productivity, talent short-ages, and sources—as well as Analog's position in these areas com-pared with competition—are highlighted with the same prominence as technological advances and challenges. The plan articulates strategies with respect to the company's relationships with institutions of higher learning, alternative career paths, and attracting and retaining women and minorities. It lays out training and development programs, ways to strengthen the monitoring process, and the distinct needs and opportu-nities of "early career" and "experienced" groups of professionals.

Analog's intensive focus on people is characteristic of high-performance companies. Attracting and developing good people, and looking to maintain their high motivation and enthusiasm, come at the very top of the list of their critical goals.

Attracting and Developing Good People

When it comes to their people, the winning companies have high standards and reach for the best; they emphasize retention of long-term employees, but they go outside when needed; and they ensure that their focus on people development is embedded in the company's way of life by making their CEOs and senior management team the top "personnel officers" of the company.

- *High standards: Reach for the best.* A theme we found throughout the winning companies is that "to be a winner, we must have people who are winners." Leaders in these companies aim at recruiting people who can be better than they are, who will add value, excitement, and new ideas to the corporate culture as well as its economics. Technical creativity and innovativeness are the staff of life at Pall Corporation. President Abe Krasnoff reaches for the most outstanding chemists and scientists in the country by writing "open letter" advertisements that invite top talent to consider joining Pall's unusual working environ-ment and urging them to contact him directly and personally. It is widely known that Abe Krasnoff not only writes these recruiting ads himself but is involved in the screening process—reemphasizing throughout the organization Pall's commitment to reaching for the very best.
- *Emphasize retention of long-term employees.* The corollary to reach-ing for the best is wanting to keep them. Among our ABC sample, a commanding majority of senior managers were promoted into their

executive positions from lower levels in the same company, and our survey showed that 80 percent of them had been with the company for more than five years. Although there are exceptions, continuity at the senior management level is the rule, not the exception. All but one of the senior managers surrounding CEO Dermot Dunphy at Sealed Air today were with the company when he came on board in 1971. Teradyne, Inc., the high-technology manufacturer of automatic test equipment for the electronics industry, has a dedication to retaining its people that borders on zealotry. In the words of CEO Alex d'Arbeloff (brother of Millipore's chairman, Dee d'Arbeloff): "Well in excess of fifty percent of all the college recruits Teradyne has hired since 1965 are still here—an amazing record for this industry. Everybody around here knows that if you lose good people, you will go nowhere in the company—and so when they think there is a potential loss they get me involved as quickly as they can. As far as I am concerned, when a good person bails out, it is the result of bad management."

In addition to personal attention, communication, planning career progress, and compensation, one notable device used to retain good people is an emphasis on dual career paths. While perhaps not practiced in a majority of the ABC companies, a surprising number, compared with our experience elsewhere, design their organizational practices to encourage individual contributors as well as managers. For example, Analog Devices spends a great deal of time making sure individual contributors get the attention, recognition, and rewards they deserve. While most American businesses heap the lion's share of recognition and financial rewards on line and staff managers, Analog Devices has consciously constructed a parallel career ladder designed to allow—indeed, encourage—"highly competent technical contributors to continue their career growth without the necessity of assuming line management responsibilities." Analog's individual career ladder (illustrated conceptually in Figure 1) designates a succession of positions and titles that run from senior product engineer, to staff and senior staff engineer, to division fellow, and finally to corporate fellow. Those positions parallel the management ladder of engineering supervisor, functional manager, product line manager, director, and vice president.

At the very top, Analog heralds two types of corporate leader: those who manage (influencing and developing others) and those who serve as advocate and strategist (influencing policy and critical corporate decisions). And as a result, Analog's fellows—the handful of top-ranking individual contributors—can and in some cases do

Figure 1
PARALLEL CAREER "LADDERS" AT ANALOG DEVICES

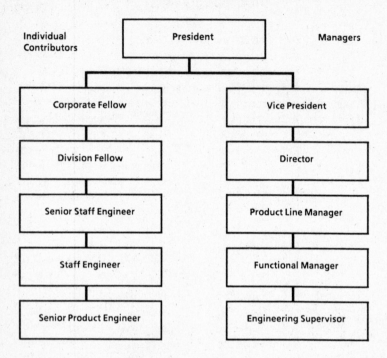

equal or exceed their management peers in compensation. The company also has a "Technology Council" led by the chief executive that includes fellows as well as technical line managers. And top individual contributors are invited to participate at the very highest councils of staff and management executives.

• *Go outside when needed, but emphasize acculturation.* Winning companies, growing at high speed, recognize that promotion and development from within are not always possible. Most have had to recruit for middle and even senior management level positions at one time or another. In fact, in certain specialized areas such as finance, it is the rule rather than the exception for top officers to be brought in from the outside—typically from larger or specialist businesses (for instance, banks are often a source of treasurers for high-growth manufacturing companies).

　　When they do have to turn to the outside, the midsize growth companies work hard at assimilation. The interview process is exhaustive, frequently including meetings of substance (not only courtesy) with potential subordinates as well as coworkers and senior managers. Typically, the winning companies allow outside recruits at higher levels time to travel around, to become acquainted with the company and its people, when they first join—just to promote the process of acculturation.

The same is true of the management team that comes with a company the winner has acquired. The point is to make certain that new executives will fit in well with the old guard, and vice versa. The price of failure in a company dependent on both competence and teamwork is one the winning performers know is too high to pay.

One classic mistake the high-growth companies appear to avoid or find a way to deal with is going outside for a number-two person. The record of threshold companies in the United States over the past twenty years gives strong evidence that one of the highest-risk jobs in America is that of the chief operating officer brought in from outside the company under a strong chief executive—particularly a founder—who is still active in the business. In that position, the newcomer often has little chance to understand and become part of his adopted culture before attracting criticism. The CEO who sought him out is hard to please (or he would have promoted someone from within the company) and probably looking for someone in his own image—a tough specification to meet. And even if the CEO is satisfied, his "family"—all the others who have been working closely with him over the years and have now been separated from the father figure by an outsider—will consciously or unconsciously look for ways to discredit the "foreign body" that has arrived on the scene.

While there are a few notable exceptions, we have tracked more than a score of such situations, and the experience suggests that the typical COO brought in from the outside under these conditions will be gone within fifteen months. To improve the odds that such a transplant will take, many companies follow the course of bringing the outsider into a senior functional position (e.g., chief financial officer) or as a division general manager, where he can earn the respect of his peers and learn the culture of his new company before being tapped as heir apparent. Still others—going the other way—bring him in as CEO, where his senior authority and role are clearly established from the outset. Either approach has proved far more likely to succeed than the "no-man's-land" of the outside COO.

• *The CEO as chief personnel officer.* Most ABC chief executives see recruiting and development activities as a line management task, and themselves as the chief personnel officer of their companies. Fifty percent told us that a decision about people was among the three most important they had made during their careers.

Jim McManus, Marketing Corporation of America's founder and CEO, is one who spends more time on his people and their development than on any other single activity. In MCA's early days, he recognized the need to shift his own emphasis—from personal client work to developing the talents of his people—as requisite to MCA's ability both to grow and to continue meeting the high standards of client service he had established. Several other American Business Conference CEOs said essentially (though in various words): "People are the most important subject I have to deal with. Since our goal is to be the best, we must have outstanding people, and we know that our competitors will always be trying to hire them away. Since our people are spread all over the world, keeping in touch with them often means I have to travel more than I really like, and this is true for the other senior executives as well. But it's essential to keep the team together, and so we do it."

In addition to running Augat, Roger Wellington is chairman of the Massachusetts High Technology Council and has a host of other civic, corporate, and community responsibilities. Even so, Wellington is an approachable guy—the parking garage attendant in Boston calls him Roger. One task Wellington makes time for each year is visiting with all of Augat's four thousand employees, located in thirty-one facilities around the world. Wellington's visits begin with a presentation on the status of the company—the same presentation he uses with financial analysts (appropriate because 50 percent of Augat's employees own stock in the company). This is then supplemented by material on what's going on elsewhere in the company, new products, and strategic thrusts. At each facility Wellington also makes time to meet individually with any employee who wishes to see him. Last year nearly two hundred Augat men and women had one-on-one meetings with Wellington. In some cases the meetings concerned complaints; in others, ideas. But the story we most appreciated about the open environment at Augat concerned a newly hired employee in New Jersey named Josef who had recently emigrated from Poland. In halting English Josef explained his interest in meeting Wellington: He wanted to see if it was true in America that the newest employee of a company could meet with the chairman of the board, so he could report back to his friends and relatives in Poland on just how well the American Dream worked.

Stuart Buchalter of Standard Brands Paint is another who appreciates the importance of CEO contact in developing people. He frequently asks managers from several levels below to come along on trips to evaluate potential acquisitions or to review store performance. This practice has two benefits. The horizon-broadening impact of talking with the CEO on top-level issues helps keep people thinking like corporate citizens rather than narrow, functional specialists. And Buchalter solidifies his understanding of grass-roots operations and the issues that operating people are grappling with.

When California Plant Protection was awarded the security guard contract for the 1984 Summer Olympics in Los Angeles, the company faced the challenge of recruiting more than seven thousand reliable guards within a matter of a few months. Leading the charge in the night-and-day operation that followed was chief executive (and owner) Tom Wathen.

And here is the way CEO Alex d'Arbeloff puts it at Teradyne: "I have always spent lots of time on recruiting. In our business, without the best people, you are dead—and I found out long ago that the best way to get good people is to work at it yourself, not to leave it all to the personnel department."

This is not to say that the winning companies have no personnel departments; 93 percent of them do. But the tasks they expect these departments to carry out are supportive, not fundamental: employee record-keeping, equal-opportunity compliance, compensation systems and records, and the like. Personnel may advise top management, but the responsibility for the development of people—the most critical of all management functions—lies with those running the business.

Motivating People

Midsize high-growth companies also work very hard at motivating people, using both financial and nonfinancial incentives to ensure that their managers' interests are the same as those of the company. Encouraging—indeed, ensuring—extensive employee stock ownership and tying bonuses to corporate performance are perhaps the two most conspicuous ways the winning companies achieve this goal.

One way to have employees behave like owners is for them to be owners. Based on our survey findings, employees own a large percentage of the winning companies' stock, and that stock is broadly distributed, often with a majority of all employees as shareholders. On average, they own 31 percent—in contrast with less than 4 percent in the case of the *Forbes* 100 giant corporations. Even excluding privately owned and closely held winning companies, more than 21 percent of the stock is employee-owned. And, while the CEO is almost always a substantial shareholder, in 93 percent of the companies other members of top management are also significant shareholders, owning, on average, nearly 9 percent of all shares. In 85 percent of the surveyed companies, employees below the senior management level owned nearly 7 percent of stock, on average (see Exhibit IV-2).

In addition, substantial performance-linked bonuses are common among the winning companies. Our ABC survey showed that the average CEO received 40 percent of his total compensation in incentive pay—and in more than a third of the cases, half of CEO compensation came in the form of bonuses. Among other senior managers, incentive pay amounted to 36 percent of total compensation; among middle managers, incentives averaged 25 percent.

In many cases, incentives are clearly linked to profits. Both Marketing Corporation of America and (as noted earlier) Kollmorgen have formulas that give employees one third to one half of the pretax profits from their profit centers, with half the remainder going to the government in taxes, the other half to the shareholders (to be reinvested in the company or paid out in dividends). Such systems leave little confusion as to which side of the bread the butter is on.

While not measured statistically, our interviews and work with midsize companies suggest that incentives are increasingly becoming tied to longer-term rather than short-term objectives. When Xidex set up its computer disk business, it set out to create entrepreneurial drive among those responsible for that new business by making them owners. It set up Xidex Magnetics as a separate corporation ultimately to be owned 77 percent by Xidex, 13 percent by division management, and 10 percent by the public. It initially sold those last shares to division managers for 4¼ cents each, and it told them that the company would go public if they succeeded. Two and a half years later, after a highly successful floppy-disk launch, they took Xidex Magnetics public, selling those 4¼-cent shares for $12.50 each—an impressive payoff for an extraordinary achievement.

Despite the potential financial gain represented by stock ownership and bonus programs, many of the CEOs we interviewed view nonfinancial incentives as even more important. Repeatedly, we heard a consistent theme in a variety of forms: "Monetary compensation is important, but it is not enough." As one CEO put it: "I think my team is terrific. Any of them could have made more money working somewhere else. The reason they stay here and stay motivated is that they like being a part of a winning team, and my most important job is seeing that we continue to win." The very success of the midsize growth company is a powerful nonfinancial motivator, but so is the fact that these companies

Exhibit IV-2
EMPLOYEE STOCK OWNERSHIP IN ABC COMPANIES
Percentage of total outstanding stock

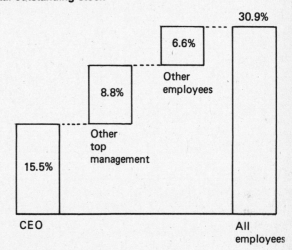

Sources: Survey of ABC membership; McKinsey analysis

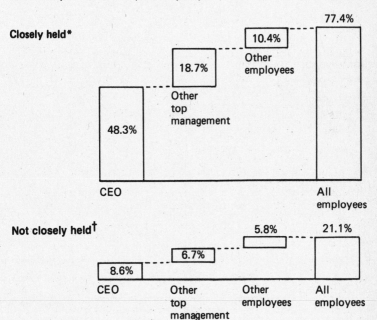

* Employee ownership exceeds 50%; seven companies represented
† Employee ownership is under 50%; 33 companies represented

Sources: Survey of ABC membership; McKinsey analysis

work so hard at keeping people involved and feeling that their work makes a difference. These companies also work hard at maintaining a sense of excitement, progress, and opportunity.

John Cullinane, the founder and now chairman of Cullinet, perhaps the nation's fastest-growing software company, likes to tell the story of why he went into business for himself. As Cullinane tells it, he was selected as "employee of the year" by one of his previous employers. He was told that the company president would personally pay him a visit and confer a cash reward. The suspense mounted as Cullinane and his family began to speculate what it might be worth to be an employee of the year—$10,000? $15,000? More realistically, maybe $5,000? The award ceremony finally took place, and the employee of the year found out that the cash stipend was $500 paid over three years.

It was at that moment, Cullinane recalls, that he decided to launch a company that would "really reward" employees for performance. And Cullinet does. For example, its key employee stock option plan defines *every* employee as "key." The "sales awareness plan" makes everyone equally aware of growth and progress. Every quarter, a proportion of new sales dollars is put into a pool from which funds are distributed equally among all employees. As Cullinane describes it: "We believe in dealing everybody in—and money is one way to say 'You're important!' "

They also consider motivation by example to be an important incentive; as one expressed it: "If the boss doesn't work hard and insist on high quality, why should anyone else?" At least every eighteen months, Harte-Hanks, the successful Texas media company that has recently gone private through a leveraged buyout, surveys every worker in the company—seeking suggestions for corporate improvements and ways to enrich the career experiences among the employee group. Both the specific ideas generated and the fact that people are asked for their views are visible elements of the company's concern for its people and thus are powerful motivators.

Job security is, also an important motivator. That's the point of Materials Research's no-layoff-even-in-tough-times policy. At another ABC company (which asked not to be named), employees earn the business world equivalent of academic tenure after a decade: They can be dismissed only with the specific okay of the president and only for grave cause.

The winning companies put extraordinary effort into thinking about organizational effectiveness. The best know they cannot afford to stop searching for improvements in the face of the internal trauma caused by growth in complexity and the external tumult arising from constant change. The distinction between the companies that succeed and the also-rans is that the high performers don't merely *recognize* the need to balance discipline and freedom, numbers and intuition, continuity and change; they don't simply agree on the need for overriding values that underpin commitment among their people. *They do something about it.*

The best of them exhibit all the qualities we have observed in our winning companies sample, and they continue to do so by making sure their ways of conducting business evolve as the company and the environment continue to change. They know that—when all the smoke blows away—organization consists only of people and that those people are the only enduring source of their companies' long-term success.

CHAPTER V
The CEO: Mainspring of a Winning Team

Dermot Dunphy has a vivid memory of his first taste of leadership—and he liked it. Just thirteen years of age, Dunphy was "hooker" for his Belvedere School rugby football team in Ireland, charged with hooking the ball with his feet as the mayhem called the "scrum" surged around him. He was also the team's captain, in charge of shouting out the plays over the noise of the game—there are no huddles in rugby. He remembers feeling a joy of command even at that early age that was to stay with him throughout his life.

Today, as a naturalized American citizen and CEO of Sealed Air Corporation, one of the nation's most successful packaging companies during the past decade, Dunphy is still very much in command and has built Sealed Air into a $166-million business (1984). The same competitive instinct and leadership drive that marked the boy are still evident in the man.

Sandra Kurtzig remembers how intensely her father worked at three jobs and she talks of how he built the family home with his own hands. His example clearly spawned the commitment to independence and performance that has motivated Sandy throughout her adult life. She had her master's degree at the age of twenty-one and paid her father back the $20,000 he lent her for college within a few years.

When she left General Electric in 1974 to start a family, she began developing computer software at home, which (perhaps inevitably) evolved from a part-time, spare-bedroom pastime into ASK Computer Systems, one of the most dramatically expanding computer software companies in the United States. Now the talk in California is about when Kurtzig—still only thirty-eight years old—will run for the U.S. Congress.

Jim Macaleer might never have started Shared Medical Systems except for the Korean War. Like his father, Jim was a chemical engineer who went to work for a large corporation shortly after graduation. When he was called up for service as a navy pilot, he looked on it as a four-year interruption in his career. But upon his return, two events caused him to conclude that life in a big corporation wasn't for him.

Soon after he got back to his civilian job, tremendous excitement swept his department one day over the promotion of one of their colleagues. But the promotion was minor, and the guy had been at his old post for fifteen years. That wasn't the fast track for advancement Jim had in mind. Not long afterward, the personnel department told Jim to take a two-week vacation. Jim pointed out that he had been back at his job only briefly, but personnel said that because he had credit for work back before his navy experience, he fell under a policy that required employees with more than four years' tenure to take a vacation every year. Jim used his two mandatory vacation weeks to look for a new job.

Jim and two partners took advantage of a hot venture-capital market in 1968, got a contract for computer information services from one of New Jersey's more forward-thinking hospitals, and launched SMS. Still led by Macaleer, SMS has grown at a compound annual rate of 25 percent and is one of only nineteen American Business Conference companies that hasn't had an earnings decline in the past fifteen years.

George Hatsopoulos departed from family tradition when he started Thermo Electron back in 1956. Born in Greece to a prominent family of professors, politicians, and lawyers, Hatsopoulos committed himself while he was in high school to a life plan that included moving to the United States, becoming an engineer and a professor, then starting a company. He turned the plan into reality after surviving World War II in a suburb of Athens, earning his doctorate in thermodynamics at MIT, becoming an assistant professor at that institution, and subsequently launching Thermo Electron on the basis of his doctoral thesis.

Jim McManus grew up on a Wisconsin farm with his grandparents, where he learned a great deal about planting seeds and making things grow. He earned his M.B.A. at Northwestern, spent seven years at Procter & Gamble (becoming one of P&G's youngest brand managers ever), and after seven more years at a marketing consulting and service firm, founded Marketing Corporation of America in 1971. He is still planting seeds: He spends 15 percent of gross profit on research and development every year, and he has presided over the founding of twenty new businesses.

He also still likes to see things grow: Marketing Corporation of America revenues topped $200 million in 1984, with a five-year compound growth rate in excess of 50 percent.

CEOs of high-performance companies come from all sorts of backgrounds, and early indications of future achievement aren't always evident. Each is distinctive—the stories of Dermot Dunphy, Sandy Kurtzig, Jim Macaleer, George Hatsopoulos, and Jim McManus certainly don't illustrate conventional thinking about specific "career paths." Their styles and personalities are equally diverse. But what these stories, and many others like them, do illustrate about the winning CEOs, we think, is their consistent eagerness to take charge, their relentless determination to succeed, and their extraordinary energy in putting that resolve into practical use. They need all these qualities to guide their companies successfully through their transition years.

How Hard They Work

The winning CEOs must love their job, because what it demands of them is unreasonable. They face extraordinary difficulty in taking a company from its entrepreneurial, informal stage, when it can be managed as a one-man or one-woman show, and turning it into a large, complex, often international corporation. Succeeding requires nothing less than the CEO's personal evolution from doer to manager to leader. And as the company grows and the distance between the CEO and the field of actual operations increases, the urge to take it easier, to enjoy the fruits of wealth, coupled with the lure of believing "Hey! I finally have it made!" can be a subtle temptress. Consider the contrast between two companies that were highly successful at the threshold: one that has sustained its performance, the other whose luster has tarnished.

As the oldest of seven brothers and one sister, SMS's Jim Macaleer knows what it's like to be the senior member of a close-knit group. As the founder and chief executive of a fledgling company, he knew that he had to have his finger on every detail of the business or he could easily go broke. Two incidents illustrate the depth of Macaleer's involvement in the business and the extent to which his determination to succeed sustained the company in its difficult early years.

One of SMS's earliest contracts for hospital information services was with American Medicorp, a private chain that operated three hospitals in the Philadelphia area. Within a few months, American Medicorp acquired hospitals in Florida, California, and Texas, and subsequently in other states. Jim and his partner Harvey Wilson had to take the company national almost overnight just to keep up with them. "There was no question," Jim says. "We had to follow our most important customers and meet all their needs."

Financing such rapid growth meant walking a financial tightrope. SMS's 1968 foray into the venture-capital market had brought in $2 million—four times the amount the founders had sought. But before the end of 1969, SMS had to return to the venture-capital market, where the company raised $3 million more. Largely because of its breathtakingly rapid expansion across the nation, it wasn't until two years later that SMS had its first profitable quarter—and by then the company had pumped more than 90 percent of its available capital into the business. "If we had gone just a few more weeks without becoming profitable, we would have been forced to go back for money in 1972—one of the worst venture-capital markets in history—and we would virtually have had to give up control of the company. We knew we had to get profitable, and so we squeezed down on the costs while we drove for productivity. And we made it." What seemed to be a cliff-hanger is, in fact, typical of the cool, disciplined, and highly rational management exhibited by Macaleer and Wilson.

In June 1970, SMS inaugurated new programming that enabled it to run data regionally rather than hospital-by-hospital. But the new program turned out to have a glitch in it, and instead of reducing the required amount of computer time as SMS had anticipated, the new program took *six times* as long. SMS was out of computer capacity instantly. Since the company's hospital clients were dependent on the information flowing through SMS's systems to carry out day-to-day operations, SMS found itself in a potentially mortal crisis.

SMS's response? The entire top management team moved into the computer center and spent the next seventy-two hours, around the clock, solving the problem—with Jim Macaleer leading the charge. Throughout SMS's history, whenever there has been a problem to be solved, its people simply did whatever it took to solve it—fast. Jim Macaleer doesn't look on that corporate and personal commitment as heroic: "If we don't serve our customer to the very best of our ability, someone else will. If the solution calls for twenty-four-hour days, then we put in twenty-four-hour days."

Jim's colleagues on that intensely committed top-management team shed some additional light on the discipline and determination of this leader:

- "Jim is tough and expects a lot of his people, but he's *always* fair. He is absolutely results-oriented and will not accept no for an answer. He assumes that a goal can always be achieved if you work hard enough."
- "From the outset, we were made to feel like entrepreneurs—and we were. We worked hard because we were owners. Jim and Harvey gave stock to literally hundreds of employees, and probably twenty-five of us are now millionaires as a result."
- "We give Jim Macaleer a monthly report a few days after the end of each month. He usually comes back at us with a list of questions the very same day. He still understands this business better than anyone, and he wants us to know that he cares about the details."
- "For a man as budget-conscious and disciplined as Jim, it's remarkable how much money we have poured into product improvement and development. We have three hundred people working on the enhancement of our product line."
- "Even though Jim has become a wealthy man, his lifestyle has not changed appreciably. He drives a Chevrolet for five or six years before trading it in, and he has lived in the same house in a suburban subdivision for the past ten years."

Discipline, a willingness to take risk, and commitment both to a vision and to the people you've selected to help you get there—without those traits in abundance, it usually doesn't work. Consider the head of another midsize company, a participant in a nationwide service industry, though not one of the companies we studied for this book. We'll call him Tom Walters and the company XYZ, Inc.

When it was founded in the late 1960s, XYZ was the leader in its field. Its distinctive niche allowed it to price at a premium over competition and to earn substantial profits. By 1981, XYZ had logged an enviable ten-year record of impressive growth in sales (which surpassed $200 million in that year), earnings, and return on investment. As Tom Walters saw it, such continued growth was inevitable, and so he turned his (and XYZ, Inc.'s) attention to what he believed to be its central challenge: how to structure XYZ to function as a half-billion-dollar corporation.

But Tom's obsession was misdirected. In reality, XYZ's real problem was dramatically different. XYZ was still pricing its core services at a premium, yet two major competitors had emerged in the late 1970s that were, in fact, providing better service. More critically still, one competitor had introduced a clearly superior service in markets that accounted for half of XYZ's business, and while its impact had not yet been felt, it was clear to others—though not to Tom—that the company's long-term survival was at stake.

And so, though the momentum of a growth economy was generating sales growth for XYZ, it was losing share rapidly. At the same time, service quality continued to deteriorate as operating people cut expenses in order to sustain—if only for a while—the profit growth of which Tom Walters was so proud.

The fundamental problem was Tom Walters. Tom was an energetic, attractive, bright young man who had succeeded the owner. He believed fundamentally in the power of positive thinking and in the power of sales and advertising. He didn't like hearing bad news. Those who pointed out the potential competitive problems—there are people in nearly every organization who notice such things early, and there were such people at XYZ—didn't find a receptive ear with Tom. In fact, "negative thinkers" either got nowhere or got fired, creating fear or plain resignation down the line.

Furthermore, having grown up professionally in a very small company, Tom hadn't developed an appreciation for the basic business disciplines needed to evaluate market forces, XYZ's performance against competition, competitive product and technological developments that could render XYZ's current services obsolete, or even the planning, budgeting, and cost control mechanisms that would allow a rational evaluation of expenditures versus benefits. His attitude was that he'd succeeded till now in running the company strictly by intuition, and his intuition told him that what was needed was to "get out and sell" and not listen to the naysayers.

And—not least—Tom was a strong believer in what he took to be "the balanced life." Tom was convinced that in a successful and well-positioned company such as XYZ, it was enough for a strong leader to work nine to five, sometimes ten-thirty to three-thirty. At the very time when XYZ's survival demanded nothing short of Herculean effort to change the product line and restore productivity at least to competitive levels, Tom was extolling the virtues of golf, sailing, and other extracurricular executive pastimes, and he was practicing what he preached. His board of directors consisted of old friends who were reluctant to raise tough questions with Tom, and so he continued to believe he was doing the right thing.

By 1981, the company was headed into big trouble. Only the nerve of a band of senior managers, willing to stick out their necks, rescued XYZ from the abyss. The combination of dedication to XYZ and alarm over Tom's neglect finally gave them the courage to confront him with the urgency of the situation and the need for major change. As a result, XYZ, Inc., has begun to pull itself up by its bootstraps, though it's still too early to tell whether the company can or will regain its earlier leadership position or reputation.

Tom Walters' plight illustrates poignantly the downright unreasonableness of the threshold company CEO's task. It demands that he have an early-warning system—the wisdom and the organizational support to identify and understand forces of change in the marketplace. It demands the wit and creativity to come up with timely, strategically sound responses to those forces, and the insight and the courage to make dramatic, sometimes risky changes in products or services. All the while he's got to keep on developing and nurturing an organization to carry out all these challenges—an organization that is innovative, adaptive, motivated, and responsive, and at the same time capable of re-creating itself over time to meet the demands imposed by a changing world.

Internally, the threshold company CEO needs to be a disciplined operator; a builder of systems; a wise parent, priest, and head of the clan. Externally, he must be a seer and prophet; a respected individual of boundless ability and integrity; a brilliant institutional marketer.

Overriding both these sets of impossible demands, he needs to be able to change his own role and know when it's time to do it; he has to give up the things he likes to do most, professionally and personally; he has to be a philosopher-king, creating values and meanings for his people.

The demands *are* unreasonable. But there *are* men and women who somehow manage to find ways of meeting most of them—and of knowing which ones they can let other people meet. The very difficulty of the job highlights the achievement and the great personal satisfactions of the few who succeed—the winning CEOs.

HOW THEY COPE

The styles, working habits, and quirks of winning CEOs vary across the entire human spectrum. In part, this stupendous diversity reflects the breadth of businesses and working backgrounds they represent.

People from at least three distinct and very different backgrounds become high-performance CEOs. The first identifiable group consists of successful founders: people like Sandy Kurtzig, whose energy, ingenuity, and spare room resulted in ASK Computer Systems; John Cullinane, creator of Cullinet Software, one of the largest and most successful companies in the burgeoning software field; Ray Stata of Analog Devices; and Jim McManus of Marketing Corporation of America, a remarkable combination of marketing service firms—to name just a few.

Then there are the successor CEOs who grew up in their companies and moved into the CEOship after years of experience in the company culture and disciplines. Some of these are the children or descendants of founders, such as Lee Brown of Brown-Forman, whose top-of-the-line potables make life agreeable for more people than those of any other American distiller; Bob Chilton of Chilton Corporation, the aggressively growing consumer credit-reporting company based in Dallas; Brad Boss of A. T. Cross Co., official purveyors of pens to the nation's Yuppies; and David Dibner of Burndy Corporation, maker of electrical and electronic connectors. Other successor CEOs joined when the companies were still small, when product lines and cultures were still in their earliest formative years—people like Abe Krasnoff of Pall Corporation, the leading filter company; and David Parkinson of Thomas & Betts, who produce connectors, terminals, fittings, fasteners, and other electrical and electronic accessories for the construction, maintenance, and office wiring markets.

And there are those who came into their companies at the very top—typically from much larger, more highly structured companies. Levitz Furniture brought Bob Elliot in as chief executive from Montgomery Ward to build the fundamental disciplines and controls needed to regain the company's momentum after it ran into rough water in the early 1970s. Roger Wellington joined Augat, Inc., in 1972, having previously run the Sylvania International Operations of General Telephone and Electronics International, Inc. (GTE), and promptly put a wealth of organization-building experience to work, bringing Augat from $14 million in 1972 sales to $257 million in 1984. Lester Colbert was hired as CEO of Xidex in the early 1970s and started that company on a dramatic growth surge that has continued ever since.

Among the winning CEOs, the range in management styles is as broad as their range of backgrounds. There are successful CEOs who believe in very tight control, and those who believe people perform better on a long leash; some who make all the decisions themselves, and others who delegate extensively; some who spend their time praising success and complimenting their people, and those who point out mistakes quickly and call for explanations and correction; those who operate mainly face-to-face, and those who rely more on written (even electronic) communication. There are, in style, product designers, salesmen, manufacturing engineers, accountants, generals, and philosophers—and just about every combination of all of these styles. But each, in proper balance, has been made to work.

On the other hand, there is much these successful leaders have in common. They all understand their businesses in depth; if not, they would lose the respect of their people or make other fatal mistakes. Most important, they all care deeply about the company—about its success, its reputation, its long-term well-being. But beyond these bedrock quali-

ties, there are four distinctive and perhaps uncommon traits that the
winning CEOs generally share. While the intensity and balance vary,
these individuals all tend to be:

- committed and persevering to the point of obsession
- builders, not bankers
- team players as well as individualists
- calculating risk-takers.

COMMITMENT AND PERSEVERANCE

The CEOs of winning-performance companies are a study in total
commitment. Whether they admit it or not, for the majority their company and its luster are the most important things in their lives. Their
commitment and perseverance were dramatically confirmed by our work
with the American Business Conference members as well as with other winning companies. These people are not only deeply involved; they love it.

Bob Elliot of Levitz Furniture is a good example. When we talked
with him, Levitz had close to a hundred retail warehouses in about half
of the states, and Bob knew the inventory, financial, and payroll situation, even the layout and the merchandising practices of every one of
them. It's no wonder: "I installed the systems to be sure I could keep on
top of these critical factors."

Don Brinckman of Safety-Kleen spends long hours maintaining his
familiarity with customer buying and turnover trends and with the performance of regions, districts, and individual salespeople. His involvement in the details is both pragmatic and symbolic. His sense of the
overall flow of the business—its strengths and weaknesses, its ups and
downs—is the basis for decisions on special incentive programs, sales
campaigns, and personnel evaluation. Symbolically, the power of his
involvement shows up in the organizationwide consensus not only that
Don cares but also that his high performance standards deserve to be
met. His penchant for keeping his finger on the corporate pulse has a
great deal to do with the motivation of his service, sales, and marketing
teams—which in turn underlie Safety-Kleen's continuing success.

Until recently, Josh Weston of Automatic Data Processing, Inc.,
designed the incentive plans himself that have been so effective in
motivating performance in that extraordinarily high-performing company.
ADP's people know that Weston will call them with well-informed questions when things anywhere in the company are not going well, and also
know that he'll take long-term employees out for dinner to celebrate a
special personal event or an unusual achievement. The knowledge that

"you know you're going to hear from Josh" and that he will be in possession of the facts is a major force in keeping the now-very-large ADP team pulling hard in the same direction.

At our first meeting with Dee d'Arbeloff, CEO of Millipore, he spent four hours describing the company—market by market, product by product, strategy by strategy. He demonstrated a level of familiarity with the organization, a thorough understanding of the business, and a grasp of the options that the company might pursue in the future that are unusual in a midsize company and impossible in a giant one.

At Donaldson, Lufkin & Jenrette, CEO John Castle spends weekends poring over detailed corporate reports. And at the recent Los Angeles Summer Olympics, visitors who didn't know him were amazed to find Tom Wathen, president and owner of California Plant Protection, carrying out routine security checks along with the other guards at key security checkpoints. They're typical winning CEOs—deeply involved in the details and enjoying it thoroughly.

Such intensive involvement was clearly reflected in the results of our survey of ABC chief executives. Despite the success of their companies and their own financial independence, the CEOs continue to work and travel extensively to keep in close touch with employees, customers, and the business environment. Until he shifted the responsibility to his group presidents not long ago, Robert Burnett, president and CEO of Meredith Corporation, the diversified media company that publishes *Better Homes and Gardens,* met with groups of employees in each of Meredith's widespread locations during annual all-employee meetings. His visits traditionally included stops at the company's plants at all hours of the day and night to ensure that he saw everyone—including second- and third-shift employees. The value of what he learned and the impact on his organization of having the boss show up to visit with them are incalculable.

Even CEOs who spend less time at work than the ABC's average sixty-four hours a week are deeply involved and well informed. Sealed Air's Dermot Dunphy claims to spend fewer than fifty hours a week actually on the job, yet he devotes most of that time to reviewing the critical performance indicators and to building the commitment of his top management group. He also does not count the hours he spends as a member of the boards of other businesses and philanthropic organizations, although fellow board members have frequently given him ideas useful to Sealed Air. In recent years, Bob Chilton of Chilton Corporation has shifted much of the burden for round-the-clock management to the tier of executives he developed immediately below him with exactly this purpose in mind. But all of them know that Bob stays closely in touch with the details through his frequent meetings and through travel; they know, too, that they have inherited an expectation—the mantle and the spirit of total commitment to the business that led to Chilton's success over the past two decades.

We speculated as to where the enormous drive and dedication of these people might come from. Perhaps their sheer energy is partially genetic—although their physical characteristics and backgrounds run the full spectrum of humanity. We found that they're all highly educated—99 percent are college graduates, and close to half have graduate degrees—but that didn't explain it. But then we made another discovery that may: These CEOs for the most part are "poor kids" who made it on their own.

Among our survey participants, 40 percent told us that when they were children, their family income was below average (16 percent said that they were downright poor). Only 17 percent classed their early lives as above average economically, and 43 percent estimated that they were middle income—findings that are especially revealing because when Americans in general are surveyed on socioeconomic background, roughly 70 percent rate themselves as middle class or above.

Almost two thirds of our survey participants had a paying job for at least ten hours a week after school when they were sixteen or younger, and three quarters of them worked during college. A third of them reported that they had been "broke" or "close to broke" at least once in their lives.

These data and our own experience in working with CEOs satisfy us that the combination of native intelligence and energy, strong family support, belief in the value of education, and just plain old ambition and competitive drive are among the major building blocks and forces that compel the winning CEOs—many of them almost to the point of obsession—to become superachievers. As one American Business Conference member said: "I think most of us knew what it was like to be poor, and we were motivated early on to escape it."

BUILDERS, NOT BANKERS

But once they have made it, money becomes almost incidental to the winning CEOs. It is the rare American Business Conference leader who could not retire tomorrow with a personal fortune in the millions; more than a few could sell their corporate holdings for tens or even hundreds of millions. These leaders do not need more money. What they're after, what they do need, is the satisfaction of leaving a legacy—a great institution with a reputation for leadership in its field.

Pursuing the Vision

The vast majority of CEOs we interviewed during our ABC work and for this book shared this sentiment expressed by one of them: "I met my financial goals long ago. I watch the increase in my personal net worth as a measure of how well I'm playing the game, but it's the inherent strength of my company and the way the business community perceives it that are of greatest importance to me." There are, of course, a few exceptions. One CEO, already worth well in excess of $10 million, told us that his personal goal is a net worth of $100 million.

The overwhelming majority of American Business Conference CEOs have set clear-cut and demanding financial performance objectives for their companies. But in talking with them it becomes clear that the winning CEO's greatest personal interest is to achieve competitive leadership and to build organizational strength, generating profits almost as a by-product.

Bob Swiggett of Kollmorgen has long held the company to two demanding financial objectives: doubling earnings every four years and achieving a 20 percent return on equity to shareholders. But those goals derive from Kollmorgen's tripartite vision: to be the leader in every market segment in which it operates; to be the pioneer in introducing new technology and new products; and to have a collaborative organization and culture in which capable people work together as though part of a family. Senior management spends much more time working with the company's fifteen divisions (and with each division's internal board of directors) on new ideas than it spends worrying about whether earnings and ROE targets will be met. Bob Swiggett's view is that the financial results will happen by themselves if organization and business decisions are made skillfully.

Their commitment to building institutions that will survive them leads these chief executives to take the long view and plan for the long haul. Says George Hatsopoulos of Thermo Electron: "When we had sales of three million dollars, I was already figuring out how to run the company when it reached a hundred million dollars. When we hit thirty million dollars, I remember starting to think consciously about what we'd have to do at a billion!" Bob Burnett of Meredith Corporation: "In the last analysis, it's only by encouraging an entrepreneurial attitude within the framework of formal corporate planning and decision-making that important things happen. The only excuse for formal planning is the generation of good ideas. And sometimes this requires a willingness to sacrifice current profits for future gain."

Dee d'Arbeloff, Millipore's chairman, had a vision of a company that would be the leader in sophisticated separation systems, not only in Millipore's traditional microporous membrane field, but in other related fields such as liquid chromatography and sophisticated water purification as well. Achieving that vision meant expansion by acquisition: As early as 1970, Millipore bought 20 percent of Waters Associates, the leader in high-pressure liquid chromatography. Then, in 1980, Millipore acquired Waters outright, and despite the two companies' earlier association, everybody knew that a period of adjustment was inevitable, since Waters represented a new culture, new technologies, and some new market niches. D'Arbeloff undertook the arduous task of combining the two companies. It took several years (as we'll discuss in Chapter VI), but the investment in innovation and in performance for customers is now paying off, with record sales and earnings in 1984.

We are convinced that the highly innovative, adaptive behavior of the winning companies is the product of eternal dissatisfaction with the status quo. It also reflects a strong market and customer orientation on the part of the CEO, who keeps asking not "How can we make more money?" but rather "How can we serve our customers better?" The people who grow up in or choose to join midsize companies are typically strategists by nature. They enjoy dreaming up new ideas and starting new businesses.

Building an Institution

The successful CEOs pay extensive attention to developing their staffs, skills, and management systems. Sandy Kurtzig, who could now retire in luxury and spend more time with her nine- and twelve-year-old children, has chosen instead to travel 80 percent of her time, promoting ASK Computer Systems. Bob Rosenberg at Dunkin' Donuts says: "My number-one job is to create an environment in which good people can work."

Still others told us about specific techniques they use for organization-building and the development and motivation of people—including communication programs to reinforce corporate values; management systems to monitor the external environment, new technology, and competitors; and awards and hoopla to emphasize successes, large and small. Millipore's d'Arbeloff uses monthly videotaped discussions to answer employee questions and to recognize notable contributions. Bob Rosenberg of Dunkin' Donuts drinks coffee and eats doughnuts at scores of his restaurants in order to meet the people on the firing line and keep in touch with whatever might be on their minds. To underscore California Plant Protection's motto, "We Take Pride," and the conviction that being a security officer is the most important job in the world, CEO and owner Tom Wathen regularly puts on a guard uniform and works the job. The firsthand knowledge these CEOs gain and the clear signals they send to their organizations are well worth the time that they take.

TEAM PLAYERS AND INDIVIDUALISTS

One of the toughest qualities of winning CEOs to generalize about—closely related to the emphasis on building the organization—is their combination of strong individualism, on the one hand, and propensity to have one or a few partners and their strong belief in team playing, on the other. They seem to sense—intuitively or analytically—that the complexity of their growing companies demands a multiplicity of skills at the top that they alone cannot fully provide. Typically, a CEO whose greatest strength is external, in the marketplace, will team up with someone or a couple of people who are strong in internal operations. If a CEO is a particularly strong "people person," he is likely to gravitate toward a partner who is more structured, more of a disciplinarian, who can provide the balance to himself. Thus, while there may be a few Renaissance leaders among the winning CEOs, most find a way to provide an important element of balance between freedom and discipline through the partnerships they form at the very top.

One of those who first mentioned the value of a strong team was the senior person we interviewed in the course of our work—Nestor MacDonald, born in 1896, past CEO of Thomas & Betts, whose counsel his successors, David Parkinson and Kevin Dunnigan, continue to value. Mac MacDonald told us in his office at T&B that each of his successor chief executives had had a strong, complementary number-two partner and that these relationships had been characterized by an extraordinary degree of cooperation and support between two very different personalities.

The company's founder and first chief executive, R. M. Thomas, relied on his Princeton classmate Hobart Betts from the time the company was established in 1898. Thomas was "Mr. Inside," the technical and production man—while Betts was "Mr. Outside," the sales manager. From the time G. C. Thomas, nephew of the founder, took over as CEO in 1929 until his retirement in 1960, Mac MacDonald was his chief lieutenant. G.C. was austere, a disciplinarian, a man who projected a clear-cut set of values that included absolute integrity and high product quality; Mac was the charismatic salesman, marketer, and ambassador to the industry who built T&B's strong relationships with its electrical wholesale distributors. After G. C. Thomas retired, MacDonald was paired with Bob Thomas, son of the founder and another relatively quiet but effective internally oriented operator. Since becoming CEO in 1974, Dave Parkinson, who came up through the externally focused world of sales and marketing, has worked hand-in-hand with President Kevin

Dunnigan, whose background is the internal world of manufacturing and operations.

Mac MacDonald put it nicely: "The history of our company—which has only had six chief executives in a hundred years—is the continuing saga of two imperfect men whose personal qualities are such that the ideal leader lies halfway between the two."

Another impressive team that has worked well for more than thirty years is that of Abraham Krasnoff, CEO, and Dr. David Pall, founder, at Pall Corporation. Krasnoff was its outside accountant, but in 1951 Dr. Pall persuaded him to join the still-fledgling company. Over the years, Dr. Pall has continued to be the product innovator, the inventor, and Krasnoff the organization builder.

A major share of the credit for Pall's unusual success in the tough field of filters is the respect and support these two men show for each other. Unlike many founders, Dr. Pall has consistently allowed Krasnoff to "run the company"—which has meant some strategic and organizational mistakes as well as notable successes. And Krasnoff has consistently shown his own high regard for the ingenious devices Pall developed to solve customer filtration problems. *Financial World* reported: "As far as president Abraham Krasnoff is concerned, Pall himself is the company's secret weapon: 'He's been the world's major contributor to the theory, science and art of filtration.' "*

Through our work with the ABC members, we were increasingly impressed at the number of winning companies that exhibit a similar pattern of effective teamwork:

- At *Millipore,* founder Jack Bush and Chairman Dee d'Arbeloff teamed effectively for many years during the company's early growth. More recently, d'Arbeloff and President Jack Mulvany have been the central partners with d'Arbeloff the prime strategist and external spokesman, Mulvany the tough-minded internal operator—but both involved in all the company's key decisions.
- At *Donaldson, Lufkin & Jenrette,* founder Dick Jenrette has provided the public presence, President (and recently appointed CEO) John Castle the driving operating force.
- At *Automatic Data Processing,* Henry Taub and Frank Lautenberg were the leaders in the early days, evolving into Lautenberg and Josh Weston prior to Lautenberg's election to the U.S. Senate in 1982.

*"Pall Corp.—The Secret Weapon Behind Its Growth," *Financial World* (August 15, 1979), p. 45.

- At *MCI*, CEO Bill McGowan and President Orville Wright share the load—McGowan the flamboyant entrepreneurial externalist, Wright the disciplined organization-builder and operating executive.
- At *SMS*, where the inside-outside roles are reversed, Chairman and founder Jim Macaleer is the operating disciplinarian, Vice Chairman Harvey Wilson the creative marketer and charismatic presence.
- At *Cray Research*, the technical skills of founder Seymour Cray have teamed up with the managerial and organization-building capabilities of Chairman and CEO John Rollwagen to create the world leader in supercomputers.
- At *Dunkin' Donuts*, the marketing and strategic skills of Bob Rosenberg go together with the finance and administrative wizardry of Tom Schwarz like . . . coffee and doughnuts.

As we reflected on the notion of team leadership, we were struck that only a few of the companies in our study have formal management teams—offices of the president or chairman, for instance. Yet in many of the best companies, the team at the top is clearly in evidence, both at work and publicly. (It's both interesting and instructive that many ABC members show pictures of groups, not individuals, in their annual reports.)

There are variations on the theme. Xidex Corporation does have a formal office of the president, consisting of CEO Lester Colbert and Executive Vice Presidents Gary Filler and Bert Zaccaria. Any one of them has full authority to make any corporate decision. As Colbert expresses it in characteristically colorful language: "If any two of us got splashed on the freeway to San Francisco, Xidex would still have an effective chief executive officer." At Kollmorgen, with its fifteen divisions and fifteen divisional boards, four men made up the core leadership group through 1984: CEO Bob Swiggett, Vice Chairman Alan Doyle, Vice Chairman (and brother) Jim Swiggett, and Executive Vice President George Stephan.

While several outstanding ABC members do not have as clearly identifiable a team at the top as these examples, a sufficiently large number of mediocre and shooting-star companies are anti-team for us to draw a connection. These nonwinners are typically led by chief executives who keep themselves isolated by geography or by personal style from their people. They lead by divine right; to them, the essence of leadership is financial ownership or appointive power rather than teamwork and mutual respect.

Perhaps it's *trust* that truly differentiates the winning CEO—an attitude that often manifests itself in teamwork but sometimes in other, less visible ways, a sense of collaboration and mutual understanding, formally or subtly, embracing just one or two confidants or an entire top-management group. As in team sports or on Broadway, a superstar sometimes makes the difference between success and failure but never can do it entirely alone. It's the whole team and the whole cast that scores on the field, at the box office—and in the winning company.

CALCULATING RISK-TAKERS

Winning chief executives agree on the importance of boldness—knowing when to take calculated risks. Among our survey respondents, more than 90 percent said they view risk-taking as a necessary characteristic in any high-growth company, and 74 percent said it had been "very important" in the success of their own businesses.

Taking Risk . . .

Winning company CEOs are frequently the initiators of courageous changes and investments that may come close to betting the company. Some of these high-risk moves come early, when a company is attempting to establish itself firmly. Such was Don Brinckman's decision to take Safety-Kleen national, opening more than a hundred routes across the country within eighteen months in order to preempt the U.S. market. Similarly, Jim Macaleer was willing to invest heavily in computer systems and use up 90 percent of SMS's capital in the first two years of its corporate life so as to cement its most important customer relationship and establish the capability to serve others uniquely well.

Other companies take risks in support of a determined effort to change direction at a crossroads in their evolution. Dee d'Arbeloff's acquisition of Waters Associates to establish Millipore as the premier company in materials separation is one example. And both Meredith Corporation and Unifi have invested surprising sums in high-cost, high-efficiency production capacity when their competitors were unwilling to make that commitment.

Another dramatic example that has had a high payoff in the long term was Bob Chilton's decision—described earlier—to invest $8.5 million between 1965 and 1969 to computerize Chilton Corporation's credit files—when its annual sales volume was only a fraction of that amount. Bob took the risk because he knew the investment would give Chilton a capability no competitor could match. The gamble paid off; customers valued the company's unparalleled storage and retrieval capability, and by 1974 revenues had soared to $20 million. In the early 1980s, Chilton invested massively again in its systems, this time spending $4.5 million on reprogramming so as to give customers better access to information and the ability to manipulate it. Now Chilton maintains up-to-date credit files on a third of all the consumers in the United States, and its 1984 revenues exceeded $85 million.

People decisions have been among the most important "bets" cited by the ABC membership during our study as well as among high-performing companies we have known well over the years. The outstanding CEOs seem to have the judgment and the confidence to put people into demanding jobs before they can be absolutely sure of success, and then make it work. Jim McManus of Marketing Corporation of America had ten losers after he took the risk of allowing his people to start new businesses, but far more important are the ten new winning businesses that have resulted from the same willingness to take chances on people. And Bob Swiggett of Kollmorgen created an organization to support sixty profit-center managers—sixty critical bets that have led to Kollmorgen's outstanding reputation and superior results.

Knowing the Odds . . .

To the winning CEO, calculating the risk is as important as the willingness to take it. Our survey showed that whenever they took a chance, most of these chief executives had assessed the odds of loss in advance, basing their judgment on in-depth knowledge both of the marketplace and of likely competitive responses, and on a thorough grasp of other external environmental influences. More important still, these CEOs had developed a clear idea—a contingency plan—for dealing with the possibility of failure and even turning it to advantage.

Pall Corporation again provides a good example. At least three times during Pall's early growth years, Abe Krasnoff, its president and chief executive, had to wind down major acquisitions or new businesses. In each case he did so without cost—selling an unprofitable heat-exchanger business "in bits and pieces" so as to "come out whole," for instance. Sometimes he was even able to make a profit, as when he sold a glass fiber plant that never achieved Pall's operating targets, and a pump manufacturer Pall had acquired but couldn't turn around.

. . . And a Little Bit of Luck

The willingness of winning CEOs to accept risk may be based in part on their sense that luck is on their side. While only 21 percent of the CEOs responding to our survey surmise that they are generally "luckier" than their competition, 68 percent acknowledge that luck or "good breaks" played some role or, even, was very important to their success.

We are persuaded that all companies in fact are equally lucky. The difference is in whether they have the intuitive smarts to recognize a break when one comes their way and the fortitude to take advantage of it. It's their ability to capitalize on lucky opportunities, not a disproportionate share of the luck, that really characterizes these leaders.

THE CHANGING ROLE OF THE CEO

However hard it may be for the proverbial leopard to change his spots, many midsize company leaders find it just about that difficult to change their roles and behavior patterns as the needs of their company and their position evolve. We referred earlier to the critical need for CEOs in the high-growth midsize companies to change; it's fair to ask why change is so important and just what changes are demanded in the managerial and psychological makeup of these leaders. Are there common elements in the kinds of change required? And what are the patterns of change—the devices used—to bring it about?

The fundamental driving force behind the need to change the role of the chief executive officer is *the need to manage the explosive growth in complexity* every midsize company faces. This complexity shows itself in product diversity, volume, technology, and systems relationships; in numbers, types and geography of distribution channels, and end consumers; and in growing pressures in the external environment—government, labor, competition, world economy, and society in general.

The character of complexity in any company and the ways it grows determine the skills required to manage the company, which in turn help define the roles the CEO can (and should) play. A company made up of highly independent business units—a Kollmorgen—depends on general managers in each division who can think as strategists and act as hands-on operations chiefs in their own businesses while wearing a corporate hat as well. To be successful, the CEO of such a company cannot be a highly directive, hands-on operating executive; if he is, the demotivating impact of his behavior will drive the best division presidents out of the company.

On the other hand, in a more centrally focused organization—an ASK Computer Systems—one dealing with a more closely related product line, yet one in which there is also a very high degree of professional and technological pride among its people, the CEO needs to provide overall strategic direction while maintaining a climate of freedom and innovation in which professional people will flourish. The open-collar, individualistic culture of Silicon Valley in California—noted for its phe-nomenal work intensity and its urgent day-to-day drive for innovation—is a good model of such an organizational frame of mind. It's no coinci-dence that ASK is located there and exemplifies that cultural trait.

In either case, and in every other type of organization and cultural climate, CEOs need the wisdom either to create structures and systems that will support the appropriate management needs, or to hire others who more comfortably can and to delegate the right measure of author-ity to them. The winning CEOs seem to have been sensitive to these varying determinants of success, primarily because they have been so intensely involved in the business that they have a deep understanding of what makes it tick and how that ticker is changing.

STAGES OF LEADERSHIP

In Chapter II, we touched briefly on the four stages of change in the typical CEO's role—stages that seem to apply regardless of the specific pattern of evolution in any single company. The typical characteristics and styles of CEOs tend to be quite different stage to stage, as do their roles in the company.

First, in the company's earliest days, the CEO is inevitably the true hands-on entrepreneur—the *founder/start-up CEO*. Almost by definition, this individual demands independence and total control. In an era of general concern over employment security, the founder/entrepreneur doesn't care to be an employee. Sometimes he is unemployable—a misfit in any organization—because he chooses to create and live by his own rules. He sets his own standards. Some founders have worked inside a structured organization before, and the shortcomings they saw there often were important reasons that drove them to start their own companies. Still others have no concept of organization; they simply get an idea and set out to give it life personally.

If the founder/start-up CEO is part of a founding team, he may focus more heavily on one or a couple of functions—research or product development, perhaps; maybe marketing; perhaps manufacturing or operations.

The fact remains, however, that the entrepreneur has his finger on the pulse of the business every minute of the day. He knows all the details intimately, frequently makes every decision, hires and fires, signs every check—in short, makes it all work by his personal energy.

It's generally at this stage that CEOs decide whether they personally want to make their companies grow. If not, they face a black-and-white choice between presiding over a company that will always be small, or relinquishing control to someone who does have the ambition to grow.

Next, as the business becomes more complex, a much higher proportion of the CEO's time has to be spent in managing through other people, and he becomes what we call the *hands-on operator.* His role is to conceive and launch new products and new markets, and to hire people to execute his vision of rapid growth. In essence, these CEOs are do-it-yourselfers. They frequently are creative and intuitive, and often generate ideas faster than they or their teams can act on them. They are unlikely to be obsessed with consistency, often moving from one focus or idea to another with lightning speed, frequently changing their minds and issuing conflicting directions. Those who choose to work with the hands-on operator need a high tolerance for change, ambiguity, and frustration, as well as the ability to interpret the boss's changing moods and directions. Subordinates also need to recognize that the boss is an exerciser of ego; it is rare that another strong will can survive under him. Furthermore, because of his disposition toward personal control and reliance on intuitive sense, the hands-on operator may well be a poor communicator, and disorder is frequently the result. CEOs at this stage are frequently not the founder.

The need for an *organization-builder* CEO emerges as complexity reaches the point where structured organization is essential. In a multibusiness, multimarket company, this phase may arrive when the company has only a few million dollars in sales, while in the larger one-product company it may not occur until the company has exceeded $100 million in sales. The point remains, however, that inevitably there comes a time when someone must bring order out of chaos by creating structures, controls, organizational systems, and lines of communication and decision-making that will ensure reasonable control and consistency of corporate direction if the company is simply to survive.

In many respects, this is the most critical phase. Increasingly, the CEO must let go of the operating reins but at the same time remain deeply involved in shaping the business and its culture. He must instill discipline, yet at the same time sustain within his growing organization the entrepreneurial spark that inspired its founder. This is the stage at which he truly creates an institutional climate that inspires his people to do their very best.

With high complexity, an *organization leader* must emerge. In contrast to the builder, the leader's primary task is to attract, motivate, and guide people with capacity to be builders and leaders themselves. While still in touch with the most critical activities of the company, the organization leader operates mainly at the level of broad directions, values, and philosophy, allowing others to devise and operate the organizational mechanisms needed to ensure success in their component businesses. Increasingly, external activities also consume more time—the need to deal with money managers and Wall Street, federal and state governments, outside boards, community interests, industry associations, and public forums that may be too attractive or too important to the overall image and well-being of the growing company to turn down.

These four stages are reflected conceptually in Exhibit V-1. Even in this simplistic form, the extensive change imposed by growing complexity on the time allocation, skills, and attitudes of the CEO is clearly dramatic.

Exhibit V-1
The changing role of the chief executive

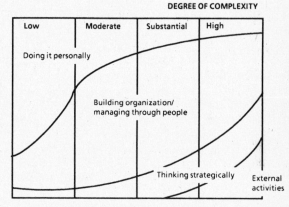

* Time allocation is generally representative but varies widely with industry mix, economic conditions, and CEO style

Typical of threshold companies in the transition phase, we found American Business Conference member companies in each of the last three stages of CEO transition—and every one of them highly conscious of the need for the role to evolve. In a good number, the founder or near-founder is still in place and still deeply involved in its day-to-day affairs—CEOs like Don Brinckman of Safety-Kleen, Lester Colbert at Xidex, and Jim Macaleer at SMS.

Other high-growth companies, as we have also noted, are at the other extreme—their corporations have become sufficiently large and complex that these individuals have truly become leaders of leaders. Among others, we include in this group Bill McGowan of MCI, Bob Swiggett of Kollmorgen, and Jim McManus of Marketing Corporation of America.

But at whatever stages they find themselves, each has had to face or is in the process of facing some very demanding alterations in his personal approach to management and leadership.

THE TOUGHEST ELEMENTS OF CHANGE

While the extent and nature of change are as varied as the businesses that make up the winning-performance group and the personalities and skills that characterize their leaders, there are three we single out as both the most important and the toughest:

1. *A heightened emphasis on team building.* Throughout the threshold transition, the CEO of the winning company has no more important job than to build a confident, turned-on team and simultaneously relinquish to that team many of the things that he still loves doing himself.

   For old-timers growing up in the business with him, he increasingly needs to provide the best development opportunity of all: giving them enough room to try and fail and try again. Instead of making decisions himself, he needs to set standards for others to meet, avoid asking the impossible, and provide adequate support while asking a great deal.

   For those he must bring in from outside the company, it's equally important to provide growing room—a chance to be assimilated into the company, to get to know its people, and to feel the satisfaction of a personal contribution.

   For both insiders and outsiders, the CEO needs to spend more time thinking through the balance, focus, and priorities of his management team, making selective changes in assignments that will lead to their continued growth and to new thinking about new and old problems alike.

   A final obligation that becomes more important and more difficult with growth is to face up to people problems. Nonperformance in the small company is readily manageable and the problem less intense because the CEO is in fact making all the decisions. Not so in the team-managed company: Many leaders have told us that the increasing need to bite the bullet on people is one of the most difficult challenges they have had to learn to meet.

2. *Greater skill in communication.* Communication in the small company is simple, passing directly between the founder/start-up CEO and those around him. The CEO can be emotional, contradictory, and even outrageous because the group is small enough and knows him well enough to deal with those inconsistencies.

By contrast, in the midsize high-growth company, inconsistent signals are frequently misunderstood, and conflicting priorities can lead to organizational paralysis. The CEO is literally the chief messenger, and his signals must clearly and consistently point the way to a complex organization. In contrast, in one troubled midsize company, a top executive told us just after leaving the company: "The confusion being caused by the CEO's conflicting statements was unbelievable. People on my level were spending about twice as much time figuring out what was really expected of them and how to protect their jobs as actually doing them."

The CEO in the winning company must be sure that formal controls and information are sufficient to identify major problems and opportunities, but not so "sophisticated" and complex as to become ends in themselves or require excessive time to generate or to use. He needs to ensure sound feedback to his team and be certain that two-way communication is taking place down within the organization. It's a tough, demanding, time-consuming job to hit the right balance of two-way communication. Perhaps most important, the winning CEO needs to be certain that the signals he sends are unequivocal, consistent, and clear—he can no longer afford the trial balloons or casual wild ideas of his earlier years.

3. *A higher level of personal discipline.* Delegation does not mean the CEO can work less hard. He has to find new ways to keep in touch that often call for extensive travel and spending time with customers and with his own people in widespread places—things that used to happen naturally in the course of carrying out the day-to-day business and now have to be executed by careful design.

For many CEOs, not meddling with operations and decisions they have delegated is one of the toughest disciplines. The winning CEOs have found that if they allow themselves the luxury of making a decision or carrying out a task that has been given to someone else in the organization, not only are other executives demotivated, but they now no longer know what their job is—they were told one thing, and something else has happened.

The winning CEOs know they have an obligation to be fair, to be consistent, and to avoid emotional outbreaks—denying luxuries that may have once been permissible and still are human but that undermine the workings of a high-performance organization.

If the CEO must change, and if the character of change is as difficult as we have described, what are the devices that the winning companies have used to succeed in carrying out this difficult process? Essentially there are only two avenues open to the CEO: to change his individual role and behavior, taking on new responsibilities himself and transferring others to his team, or to install a new CEO. Many companies have had to do both over the course of their successful histories; let's look at what they have done.

PATTERNS OF PERSONAL CHANGE

In simplest terms, there are only four ways that individuals successfully bring about a change in their own role and behavior within a company, and winning CEOs have used any one or all of them.

1. *Structural change.* Create a new division, delegate additional responsibility, appoint a chief operating officer, tell the chief financial officer to take over relations with the banks, install a payroll service that will relieve the CEO of signing all the checks—all these sorts of structural change allow other members of the management team to take charge.
2. *Changing people.* Very few high-growth companies succeed in passing through the threshold transition without bringing in experienced managers from the outside at high levels in the organization; none make it without major changes in the key players in key positions. For example, it is a rare bookkeeper from a $1 million company who can become the sophisticated chief financial officer needed by a $100 million company. Even a relatively stable growth company such as Thomas & Betts has found it necessary to go outside for key posts, such as the head of its financial function, from time to time—and this despite a ferocious dedication to internal promotion and development of people within the T&B culture. Beyond simply bringing in qualified individuals, the winning CEOs carefully lay out a program of personal objectives with their newly acquired executive, and hold frequent reviews to be sure that each is upholding his or her own end of the "contract." Such emphasis on communication, mutual review, positive feedback, and support can sharply improve the odds that new people will be effective and that the CEO will succeed in his ongoing effort to alter his own role within the company.

3. *Reeducation.* A surprisingly large number of winning CEOs have gone back to school to take management courses, or have joined groups such as the Young Presidents Organization to further their knowledge of what other successful business leaders are doing. One former winning company leader, Frank Carney of Pizza Hut, who subsequently sold his company to PepsiCo for more than $300 million, used to reeducate himself by volunteering to lead courses on such subjects as strategic planning. Having committed himself, Frank would then set out on a program of personal education to avoid embarrassing himself six months later when he had to stand up in front of a classroom full of his peers, who were all there to get the latest word on the subject.

4. *Reprogramming.* Parker Montgomery, chairman of CooperVision, the eye-care products company in Menlo Park, California, at one point set up offices for himself at opposite ends of the country. While there were practical business reasons for doing this, it also meant that each group of executives within that company would have to operate essentially on its own half the time, since Montgomery would be focusing for two weeks a month on the other group three thousand miles away. In addition to taking himself out of day-to-day operations, Montgomery found this a useful reinforcing device to encourage his associates to act like owners when he wasn't around.

Reprogramming can also mean turning over the chairmanship of key committees to other executives, not attending certain levels of operating reviews that the CEO used to sit in on, or encouraging off-site meetings at department and functional levels that the CEO does not attend. And it can mean taking on increasing external responsibilities that remove the CEO from day-to-day operations more frequently but still have great value to the company—a major reallocation of chief executive time.

Let's look at some illustrations of personal role change within the high-performance companies.

Bob Swiggett became a member of the Kollmorgen group in 1970 when it acquired his company, Photocircuits—the last and largest of eleven acquisitions that transformed the old periscope and bombsight manufacturer into an industrial holding company. Bob says Kollmorgen was "a conglomerate trying to manage itself as an operating company." Corporate objectives were vague, and the directives that issued from headquarters—"management by memoranda"—had little consistency and seemed not to make very much sense. With the recession of the early '70s, the underlying problem of unclear strategy and confused management came to the surface, and some businesses were sold or closed while others were consolidated. As a result of those traumas, Bob was appointed president in 1973, and in 1975 he became chief executive.

His initial challenge was to create a clear vision, culture, and structure that made sense for a midsize technology company with a broad range of products in separately managed divisions. He started by writing Kollmorgen's statement of management philosophy and asking his division presidents to assent to it. And he used all the tools of change available—structure, people, personal education, and a reallocation of his own time.

Once the newly defined culture and structure began to take hold, Bob's own role shifted from strong central advocate and builder of organization to team player who delegated operating responsibility to people down the line—supporting independent division managers with a small corporate staff, monitoring their performance, coaching them, nurturing the basic Kollmorgen principles. The change took Bob from deep personal involvement to much more hands-off, value-centered, symbolic leadership. It wasn't easy; it flew in the face of Bob's career-long focus on active involvement in the day-to-day operation of a single business. But he recognized the corporate imperative and succeeded in changing himself.

Sandy Kurtzig, founder of ASK Computer Systems, underwent what may be an even more dramatic example of a shift from hands-on doer to corporate leader. She says that when she founded ASK in 1972, she "wrote computer programs, sold them to a few customers, and swept the floor." At that time, she had little idea that her role would ever change; writing a little software was simply an adjunct to raising her two boys and being a housewife.

But the enthusiasm and support of one customer after another pushed the fledgling company to develop more and better manufacturing computer software systems, and Kurtzig's role gradually expanded to include hiring people who not only could continue to create software but also build the disciplines and systems needed to keep a small company solvent and under control. Still, in those early years she continued to do nearly all the important things, certainly all the decision-making, herself in her own way.

She still has a firm grasp on the overall strategic thrust of the company and spends time with her own people to encourage and motivate them, and with customers to maintain a feel for the market. But in almost every other respect, her role has gone through a complete metamorphosis since the successful initial public offering in 1979. The company employs 450 people. Kurtzig travels four days out of five, devoting most of her time to promoting the company's interests and image in the outside world.

Inevitably, she recognized the need to bring in people with specific management and decision-making skills to help meet the extraordinary demands of growing at a 50- to 100-percent annual rate. The shift in her role reached its culmination early in 1984 when she persuaded Ron Braniff, a longtime ASK director who knows the business well and also has big-company management experience at Tymshare, to be president and chief operating officer.* But the example she sets in good old hard work has not changed.

There are some who believe that the requirements for personal change by a CEO during the threshold company transition are so great that they can only be met by a *new* CEO. One said: "You haven't really proven that you have a winner until you have had three successful chief executive officers." That may be right. In the meanwhile, however, the CEO has no alternative but to make enormous changes in personal involvements and priorities in order to sustain the momentum of the company.

MANAGING SUCCESSION

Now let's look at the other approach. Sometimes the only way for a company to continue to succeed is for the CEO to replace himself or to be replaced. This may come at the normal end of his career through retirement, but equally often, if not more frequently, it occurs because the CEO is either unable or unwilling to undergo the dramatic personal changes needed to continue the forward thrust of his company.

The events and conditions that trigger a CEO change are numerous. A number of ABC company founders—Seymour Cray, David Pall, and Al Fielding of Sealed Air, to name just three—discovered that they genuinely preferred the scientific, technology-development side of the business to general management. In other cases, the trigger may be personal fatigue and stress on the part of a CEO who finds it difficult to stay on top of burgeoning complexity, or who genuinely loves hands-on operating management and gets bored or frustrated in the role of organization-builder. In some cases, a member of the board of directors may point out that problems are beginning to appear in the business or in the organization that perhaps can be better solved by another leader. And occasionally, the CEO simply realizes that he has created an effective team and groomed one or more individuals who are ready and eager to have their own shot at running the company. (In our experience, however, sensing that the time has come to turn over the reins to a new generation before reaching

*In June 1985 he was named CEO as well. Kurtzig remains chairman.

retirement age is both rare in general among all corporations and an impressive testament to the dedication of the CEOs stepping aside in the interest of the long-term building of organizational strength in the company. Both Dee d'Arbeloff of Millipore and Dave Parkinson of Thomas & Betts impressed us when they took this step during the course of our work.) At still other times, organizational rumblings of discontent send a loud signal to a CEO that a change is called for.

The personality and drive of the builder CEO are so pervasive and important that the loss of this individual and the insertion of a new CEO with different qualities can be traumatic. Although some of our partners disagree, we believe succession is far more sensitive in the midsize growth company, where the CEO's influence is so intense and immediate, than it is in large corporations, where a greater range of experienced general managers, staff support, and systems are typically in place to buffer the transition. Many of our survey respondents reported that managing the CEO succession process—in one way or another—was among the three biggest decisions they ever made.

The key to successful succession may in part be found in the words of several winning CEOs, which go something like this: "To build an organization, you've got to have the guts and wisdom to bring in people who are better than you are, and you've got to know when to give them the top responsibility." Whether successor CEOs are better, or simply different, is not an important distinction. What is important is keeping a clear view of the requirements of the chief executive office and to be sure that those requirements are met over a long span of time.

One way or the other, effective succession planning usually comes down to the will and objectivity of the CEO himself. But for the driving, obsessed, hands-on CEO to force himself to plan and execute his own succession is often a major psychological hurdle. There appears to be a pattern among the winning CEOs who have met the succession challenge. They:

1. Recognize that they are not immortal and therefore consciously plan for their own replacement. They may also recognize the need for new skills. Their thinking includes not only the requirements for normal retirement, but also a "hit by a truck" scenario that suggests what the board of directors should do in the event of catastrophe.
2. Determine how—in degree and direction—future skills needs and role requirements for the CEO job will differ from the past, and spell out these differences to guide the development and selection process.

3. Identify candidates, assess their strengths and weaknesses, and give them assignments in the organization that will prepare them for the top position as well as test their full range of capabilities. In the most thoughtful companies, a similar planning process takes place for candidates to replace those who may later become CEO that will prepare them for the next position as well as test the full range of their capabilities.
4. Carefully develop a relationship and understanding with the successor CEO, to ease the transition. The experience of the successful companies shows that extensive communication between predecessor and successor CEOs greatly improves the odds of success.
5. Draw on trusted advisers—frequently one or more key board members —to test and refine their own thinking and to strengthen their resolve. Letting go can be difficult, and a number of CEOs have told us that it is consequently important for them to have "someone to talk with."

When succession plans work, each new leader brings a new wave of strength and growth. As we described earlier, Automatic Data Processing evolved from a small local payroll processing firm in 1949 to become by 1984 a $1-billion company doing business throughout the United States as well as in other major world markets. The role of the chief executive has gone through three dramatically different phases, each under a different CEO:

- Founder Henry Taub led the hands-on start-up stage that extended through the 1950s, creating the fundamental values and operating disciplines under which the firm established itself as a reliable supplier of payroll services.
- Even prior to becoming CEO in the early 1970s, Frank Lautenberg had emerged as the driving spirit behind ADP's rapid growth through acquisition in the 1960s and 1970s. ADP acquired nearly one hundred local data processing firms and specialized computer information companies as it extended its business coast to coast and internationally.
- Josh Weston, the present CEO, is the organization builder—the architect of a highly disciplined systems management stage at ADP, one in which a broader team of operating managers is responsible for managing the many divisions and groups of businesses that make up ADP, within a very clearly defined set of objectives, policies, and philosophies.

Each transition was smooth and natural, as Taub and Lautenberg in turn reached the point when they saw the value of fresh leadership to ADP and wanted to take on new areas of leadership for themselves—

Taub in the philanthropic world, Lautenberg as U.S. senator from New Jersey.

Perhaps the wisdom and the skill to carry out effective transition are among the ultimate tests as to whether the winning company has truly achieved a lastingly effective organization.

In brief, the chief executive of the midsize growth company plays a unique role. He is the architect and builder who creates and sustains the strategic and organizational qualities that underlie the success of his company. His ability to sustain the traits described in this chapter, while undergoing necessary personal changes and adaptation, is a critical characteristic that distinguishes the leaders of the high-performance companies.

CHAPTER VI

When Bad Things Happen to Good Companies

Even the best companies can get in trouble. The problems may result from forces in the outside world—new technology; the luck, skill, or creativity of competitors; a downturn in the economy; even the strength of the U.S. dollar that undermines export markets and diminishes the value of international profits. More frequently, corporate problems are self-inflicted—a lapse of discipline, strategic errors, organizational hardening of the arteries. For everyone, it's a demanding and rapidly changing world, but it's especially vexing for companies attempting the transition from small to big, and sooner or later it almost always catches up with them. Like most adolescents, at some time they get in trouble.

One test of a winning company, then, is how it deals with adversity—the skill and agility it shows in dealing with environmental trauma and with its own mistakes, and in how well it learns its lesson. This chapter takes a look at the kinds of problems some of the winning companies have encountered—what went wrong and how they coped.

First, it is important to recognize that bad things *do* happen to the best companies; no one is immune. Even among the eighty-one publicly listed American Business Conference members, no company other than ADP has had an unblemished two-decade record of sales and earnings growth. Eleven of those eighty-one have unbroken growth records through 1983 but were founded or went public much more recently, most of them in the mid-1970s. Among the seventy longer-established, publicly owned ABC members, the facts reveal more than an occasional blip of trouble. In the two decades between 1964 and 1983:

- Fifty-one have suffered at least two years of profit downturn.
- Thirty-two have seen their profits decline in at least two *consecutive* years *and* at least one other time as well.
- Eighteen had earnings declines in at least *five* of the twenty years.
- Twenty-eight companies showed an actual *loss* in at least one year (seven during the 1981–82 recession).

Extending our analysis to a broader high-growth midsize sample—to the one hundred fastest-growing midsize companies in the country during the period 1966–71 that were still in existence in 1981—confirms the pattern. All the companies increased their sales by at least 35 percent a year in the earlier period. But in the comparable five-year period a decade later, one of the strongest periods of economic expansion in recent history (and one of high inflation as well), 40 percent of that group showed sales growth rates below 10 percent, and several were actually in decline. Only one in nine continued to grow at 35 percent or more.

The message is crystal clear. With exceptions so rare as to be statistically insignificant, even the best companies can look back on—or forward to—difficult times. The winners, however, can look back with satisfaction, because they have learned from adversity and sharpened their corporate characters as a result.

RESPONDING TO TROUBLE

The best responses to adversity are reminiscent of the response of a golfer whose game is off: single-minded commitment, a tremendous sense of urgency, and a redoubling of time and attention to the basics.* The underlying attitude of each is the same: I am a winner. I not only will solve this problem, but I'll be even stronger and better as a result.

As the examples we will examine in this chapter illustrate, the actions these companies take to recover from a stumble are as varied as the niches they compete in and the people who make up the companies. Sometimes they sell divisions that no longer show promise or meet financial standards. Sometimes they invest in new product lines or tech-

---

*A true championship golfer does not, for example, blame his caddie, or claim that the rules are unfair.

nology. Sometimes they reorganize to recapture their former simplicity by combining divisions with related products or markets—but if it makes sense, they also split up divisions to create smaller, more entrepreneurial, faster-response businesses. Some have doubled their research-and-development spending to regain a product advantage; others have put top priority on trimming the inefficiencies that crept into their cost structure during periods of high growth, severing unproductive people, but also adding new skills that may be key to coping with the new problems.

How the winners *don't* behave in times of trouble is as illuminating as how they do. They steer clear of unsound business practices, such as shipping poor-quality products in order to generate short-term cash. They avoid unsound financial practices, such as overvaluing their inventories, booking sales to customers with poor credit, or using up important reserves. They don't indulge in shortsighted organizational steps, such as terminating people who will be needed in the future, or consolidating unlike businesses for ephemeral economies. They don't drop development programs that are creating tomorrow's products and businesses; they don't assume, at least not without compelling evidence, that the problems will solve themselves if the company simply "stays the course." They follow common sense.

Let's take a good look at the experiences of a handful of American Business Conference members.

Donaldson, Lufkin & Jenrette

In twenty-five years, Donaldson, Lufkin & Jenrette went from darling to dog to star performer.

Since its founding in 1959 by three Harvard Business School graduates still in their twenties, DLJ has been applauded as one of Wall Street's star pioneers. As DLJ president John Castle told us: "Success in the investment banking business is a function of being in the right niches—and DLJ started out in the perfect niche." An innovator in venture capital and other investment-banking and investment-management services, it was the first to draw a bead on institutional investors, then just beginning to emerge as a powerful—and lucrative—segment. Institutional portfolio managers were willing to pay well for sophisticated research, and DLJ became famous for the caliber of its reports. In 1970, DLJ innovated in a different way: It became Wall Street's first financial house to go public.

But in the mid-1970s, DLJ ran into rough sledding. Earnings were down in three of the five years between 1973 and 1977; DLJ even suffered a substantial loss in 1974.

In Castle's opinion, the sharp downturn in DLJ's fortunes that started in 1973 was only partly a function of weak market conditions on Wall Street. "Our overwhelming success during the first fifteen years led to overconfidence—a sense of invincibility—that proved part of our undoing in the mid-seventies. We had too much success and thought that we could take on all comers in a financial services supermarket. This led us to make a major mistake. We decided to try to go head-to-head against well-established competition in mature segments of the investment-banking, fixed-income, and retail-brokerage businesses. The result was an unintelligent allocation of scarce resources. In short, we lost our focus on what we were good at and strayed onto dangerous competitive ground.

"To compound the problem, at a time when our business was becoming far more complex and potentially volatile, we had not established the necessary controls to manage constructively the creativity, personal freedom, and originality of our large professional staff. These latter qualities are good in our business, but we lacked the basic disciplines to monitor how well we were doing and to maintain profitability when times got tough."

DLJ's response to these problems was a combination of strategic refocusing on a few niches and of building a better balance of discipline with entrepreneurial energy. It took several years to complete the fix, but the result has been a series of dramatic record years since 1978.

DLJ began by reassessing its strengths and taking a searching look at emerging investment trends to see where the firm might best focus its efforts to remain distinctive. Building on its leadership in investment research, DLJ identified investment management as the niche in which it could become preeminent. And it did. At one point DLJ was managing almost half the non-trust company employee benefit and similar funds under management on Wall Street. DLJ also restored its former heavy emphasis on brokerage, commodities transactions, and investment banking in a relatively small number of distinctive market niches where it could maintain or establish its position as a leading participant.

In tandem with that sharpening of DLJ's strategic focus, Castle and Chairman Dick Jenrette (the only one of the three founding partners still active in the firm after 1973) set out with their colleagues to strengthen the firm's basic management disciplines. They developed and installed a structure of profit responsibility and controls that would supplement but not replace DLJ's traditional freedom and spirit of entrepreneurship. Among the most important steps was their adoption of one of the most demanding monthly operating reviews in the industry. The process involves meticulous preparation of detailed information on each division and performance-review meetings each month.

At these meetings, which managers must attend no matter how inconvenient, DLJ analyzes progress in each of its component businesses and on action to be taken toward achieving the plan agreed upon at the previous month's gathering. Managers also go over a series of exhaustive profit-and-loss statements.

"We must have two inches of P&L statements to go through each month," Castle says. "This sounds like a hell of a lot of detail, and it is. But it gives us the basis for really knowing what's going on in each of our businesses." He goes on to explain, "It's particularly helpful since we continue to put high emphasis on creativity and the entrepreneurial spirit within DLJ by maintaining a series of small, free-standing business units. So these monthly reviews ensure that the people running every unit know the extent to which top management is staying on top of the business. As a result they're far more disciplined in controlling expenditures and in meeting their volume and earnings targets than they otherwise might be."

In addition, the firm adopted a set of incentives under which an executive can earn a substantial bonus for developing his business and controlling the costs. Castle uses this incentive plan partly as a surrogate for stock ownership.

"We also have regular cost-control targets to be sure we're eliminating nonproductive expenses. At any one time, we must have a score of projects under way, each consisting of a searching review of one or more of our businesses and divisions—particularly divisions that may have been behind plan or in trouble recently. This is a process that we began in 1979, and it has paid off handsomely."

DLJ also carries out an intense strategic planning process each year, including development of multiscenario contingency plans indicating how managers will deal with possible downturns in their businesses. These plans get particular attention in difficult times (as they did, for instance, in early 1982, when market activity was down sharply). Castle credits the process with helping DLJ maintain its focus on its core businesses and avoid a repetition of the problems that resulted earlier when the firm strayed from its areas of strength.

The payoff from this refocusing on its core strengths has been dramatic. Between 1978 and 1984, DLJ earnings increased more than 1,000 percent.

Thermo Electron

Among the success stories that abound among Boston's Route 128 high-tech community is Thermo Electron, the brainchild of MIT professor George Hatsopoulos in 1956. Thermo Electron is a leader in specialized products and services built on the laws of thermodynamics. From 1976 to 1981, Thermo Electron's net income grew eightfold on a fourfold increase in sales, then for two years spiraled downward close to breakeven before recovering sharply in 1984.

Founder and CEO Hatsopoulos says, "Most security analysts don't understand Thermo Electron. They see us as a conglomerate producing cogeneration equipment, measurement instruments, and artificial hearts, and don't realize that we are simply a group of engineers whose mission is to provide products at the leading edge of technology that build on the laws of thermodynamics: putting energy to work more efficiently and more economically."

By 1981, pursuing this mission had resulted in a $231 million company with earnings of nearly $9 million. It had also resulted in substantial complexity (TE had thirty separate business units) and volatility (most of those businesses were in fields highly susceptible to recession).

Thermo Electron had simply spread itself too thin. The company was in too many niches, it had too broad a product line, and it wasn't monitoring and evaluating the performance of its people properly. TE's zealousness to produce innovative products had simply taken the company beyond manageability.

By the end of 1983, revenues had declined to $182 million, and earnings had all but disappeared. Just a year later, though, Thermo Electron was sitting on the largest order backlog in its history and expected record profits. Its common stock is approaching an all-time high.

How did Thermo Electron climb from the trough of 1983 to the triumph of 1984?

Sheer recognition of its problems was the first major step. Seeing volume and profits slipping, CEO Hatsopoulos and his senior team came together in 1982 and developed a program consisting of three major elements:

1. "We determined the limits of our ability to manage." Recognizing a need to cut the number of business units in half, the management team examined each of TE's thirty business units and decided whether to leave it alone, sell it, close it down, or consolidate it with another unit. The process was painful, but necessary to restore growth. TE now believes that its current number of business units will remain practical until the company reaches approximately $500 million in volume.

2. "We reviewed and reduced our staff. Several hundred people had to go." This was the most difficult step of all and required making tough decisions. TE's senior management believes the smaller but stronger organization that remains is far better equipped to build on the corporation's strengths over the next few years.
3. "We increased our research and development." As an overall goal, TE fixed on greatly accelerating its record for innovation, and it almost doubled its research-and-development budget in 1984 in order to accomplish it. Drawing on analysis and on interaction among technical and marketing people, the company zeroed in on a few fields they believed deserved top priority, such as electroplating, a small-scale cogeneration module, and biomedical businesses, including the artificial heart.

At about the same time, Thermo Electron spun off a small group working in its R&D center—a new company called Thermedics, which develops biomedical products. According to Hatsopoulos, Thermedics now has a market value of about $100 million.

In brief, TE's response to adversity was to attack—to simplify and strengthen the company's structure; to upgrade the average capability of their people while reducing current costs; and to improve products and technologies. At this writing, Thermo Electron's aggressive program appears to be succeeding. In 1984, sales increased 29 percent to $235 million, and net income rose to $6 million.

Sanders Associates

Just over the border of Massachusetts into New Hampshire, amidst scenic hills, sits the corporate headquarters of Sanders Associates. The largest industrial employer in New Hampshire, Sanders is today a leader in the research, development, and production of sophisticated electronic warfare equipment for defense and computer graphics for the commercial market.

Jack Bowers, chairman of Sanders Associates, is a man given to understatement, who describes his job as chief executive as "encouraging technical inventiveness and preventing debacles." And in the six years from 1979 to 1984, Bowers and his management team have succeeded impressively. Sanders' sales of high-technology products and services have increased from $164 million to $746 million during the period, more than tripling annual profits, to $70 million.

Technical inventiveness is the hallmark of success in electronic warfare and surveillance, and Sanders encourages the technical work force through, for instance, a program of major awards for excellence that recognize technical achievements and through the appointment of engineering fellows (who make technical contributions and serve as mentors to others). In addition to many classified technical innovations in defense, Sanders' scientists invented and patented the technology for popular television games (which has brought more than $20 million in royalties to the company over the years); and the company's pen plotters (which can produce thirty inches a second of drawings accurate to one one-thousandth of an inch) were cited by *Electronics Products* magazine as one of the most technologically significant new products introduced in 1983.

Sanders not only learns from its successes, but from its misfortunes— including an unsuccessful venture into commercial business terminals in the early '70s.

The commercial computer terminal debacle was one of those business ventures that sound appealing and do not fail for lack of resources or commitment. During the late 1960s, Sanders decided to produce business terminals that would ultimately be used in applications such as the Avis Wizard reservation and billing system. This new business was quite different from Sanders' earlier successes in designing and developing radars, electronic components, and antisubmarine warfare systems. The new business pitted the then comparatively tiny enterprise in head-to-head competition with giants like IBM and catered to a customer group that valued ease of use more than state-of-the-art precision—though that was Sanders' strength among its sophisticated defense customers. As one veteran of the episode explained to us: "We had a damn good terminal, but it didn't bring success. We just didn't have the marketing and service know-how. Our design was terrific but got copied, and wasn't really appreciated by lay users."

After years of trying (and years of losses), Sanders sold the business to Harris Corporation and settled its differences with IBM—for which it now develops and produces computer-aided design and computer-aided manufacturing (CAD/CAM) terminals. Not only did the doomed commercial business take its toll in losses; it also consumed top-management attention that might have been focused on Sanders' core business. As Bowers explained to us, "We realized we had been in the wrong commercial business—but were still interested in finding new growth areas."

Sanders refocused its efforts on its military business, building its electronic warfare capabilities into related areas such as command and control systems, ocean surveillance, and computerized test equipment. And it also undertook a two-year strategic study that identified a new commercial product line—interactive graphics. Unlike the earlier failed business terminal venture, interactive graphics built on current Sanders technical strengths. The company had, for example, developed and built displays for the NASA Saturn program, and at the time computer graphics represented some 14 percent of Sanders' business. More important, Sanders positioned itself this time in the most sophisticated segment of the business—the high-technology end rather than the consumer-oriented segment—where technically oriented customers could appreciate technical value. To augment its skills, Sanders acquired two companies: Cal Comp, already a leader in digital plotting (albeit a cash-short one at the time of its acquisition), and Talos Systems, a participant in the digitizer field.

By 1984, the revised strategy had paid off. Graphic Products and Systems accounted for $255 million in sales and $25 million in profits. And Sanders' sales of defense electronics systems and products had risen to nearly $500 million.

Millipore

For twenty years, from 1960 through 1979, Millipore, the materials-separation company, was one of the hottest high-tech stars. The financial community came to rely on Millipore's highly predictable, 20-percent-plus earnings growth. From scarcely more than $1 million in sales, it increased its sales to $195 million and operating profits to $19.6 million (restated) by 1979. The company took justifiable pride in this outstanding performance, and that pride was evident in the intensive work pace of the Millipore environment.

Then came a modest decline in operating profits in 1980, followed by a steep drop of 43 percent in 1981. The following year, 1982, operating profits recovered substantially but still lagged 17 percent below the 1979 peak. Not until 1983 was the company able to resume its practice of breaking its own growth records and in 1984 profits soared, up 48 percent on sales growth of 14 percent.

The story of how Millipore confronted its problem and managed to emerge stronger as a result can be instructive to other companies.

In part, Millipore's difficulties were a result of deep recession in its key markets, and of the strengthening dollar, which came at a time when its international business was expanding rapidly. But in hindsight, it seems clear that four internal forces were more to blame.

1. *Strategic expansion through acquisition of new businesses and different cultures.* In its early days, Millipore had a single product line—microporous membranes used to filter contaminants from such fluids as missile fuel, wine, and blood. During the mid- and late 1970s,

Millipore began to acquire other companies in a move toward broadening its base in materials separation—bringing the company into a far wider range of both technologies and markets. In 1975, Millipore acquired Worthington Biomedical Corporation as a step toward coupling its early membrane technology with organically active materials, an approach designed to improve certain kinds of applications. In the words of Chairman d'Arbeloff, "the acquisition proved to be a story of synergy that never happened."

Most significantly, in early 1980, Millipore acquired Waters Associates, the leading company in liquid chromatography, a wholly different technology for analyzing and separating materials. The acquisition of Waters, even more than the others, imposed on Millipore the burden of understanding new technology—Waters was not only in chromatography but was also in electronic instrumentation, where Millipore had no experience. Furthermore, Millipore had to assimilate a new and foreign corporate culture. Waters had a different management philosophy, oriented toward the long-term development of a relatively small number of potential customers based on extensive scientific discussion and trials. This comparatively low-key, technology-based focus stood in bold contrast to Millipore's hands-on direct marketing approach and aggressive sales follow-up among a much larger base of many smaller customers. So different was Waters' culture and so difficult the assimilation of its organization into the Millipore way of life that Waters went through three presidents within three years of its acquisition by Millipore—changes that required time and attention by top Millipore management, and inevitably affected Waters' growth and profitability during the transitions.

2. *Business and organization complexity.* Millipore exemplified the patterns of high-growth transitional companies we've described in this book—evolving, over the twenty years to 1980, from a company with one relatively narrow product line into a complex organization that marketed diverse technologies through multiple sales forces to customers in more than a hundred niches around the world. The ability of top management to focus on all these markets and on the people responsible for developing their profitability was clearly diluted.

In 1967, Millipore's organization consisted of half a dozen key executives who would meet around the conference table in Bedford, Massachusetts. All the company's activity took place at a single site, and communication was clear and virtually instantaneous.

By the mid-1970s, Millipore decided it had to divide itself up into divisions—creating, as CEO d'Arbeloff put it, "a number of small business units that would each have the vitality and focus that the total corporation had when it was small in the late 1960s and early 1970s." Millipore experimented with a matrix structure, delineating multiple formal reporting responsibilities for every employee—a structure that is complex and difficult even in a stable environment and virtually impossible in a rapidly evolving organization such as Millipore. The company even subdivided its core Millipore Products Division, the microporous membrane business, into several separate profit centers, leading to duplication of staff functions and thus to increased costs. Decentralization and divisionalization also weakened the company's historically strong marketing force because several sales forces were approaching the same customers, none large enough to service all the needs of each customer all the time.

The company having thus fragmented itself, objectives were no longer as clear as they had been. Business units were left to make their own decisions about such matters as how much emphasis to place on technical and product development versus marketing. Not least, the uncertainties introduced by the new organizational complexity led to bureaucracy and the weaknesses that always accompany it: avoidance of experimentation and risk, spending too much money to avoid mistakes, and the sluggishness that comes when major decisions have to be cleared through multiple channels.

3. *Values: the quarterly obsession.* From its founding, Millipore had put heavy emphasis on the quality of its products and on sustaining a high level of innovation that would improve its customers' performance. Yet a second value began increasingly to capture the attention of down-the-line management—the company's extraordinary record of increasing sales and earnings by more than 20 percent from quarter to quarter. After twenty years of consistently higher earnings, maintaining the pattern became an objective in itself. Management at the division and plant level began to perceive making the budget each quarter as a more important goal than investing in development of innovative, high-quality products that might pay off several years in the future.

As a result, says d'Arbeloff, "we started putting our problems on the balance sheet. As new products came on line, we somehow overlooked old inventory that was becoming obsolete, and failed to write it off as quickly as we should have."

In brief, with top management's attention diverted by the complexity of assimilating new cultures, a gap developed between Millipore's long-term values and the short-term pressures perceived by operating managers.

4. *Inadequate controls and financial information.* While Millipore's budgeting system was strong, its external monitoring systems did not keep up with the burgeoning complexity of the business. For example, the company didn't generate data on sales and profits either by product line or by end-user market. Thus it was difficult, at best, to identify market turns or competitive inroads in a severely competitive, quickly changing business. Furthermore, lack of adequate financial information led to surprises; problems such as rising expense and staffing levels didn't get noticed until they were acute. As d'Arbeloff put it, "We weren't watching our balance sheet—we simply didn't keep up with our tremendous growth and were not sufficiently sensitive to growing competition."

The problem of inadequate data extended as well to long-range planning. Sheer complexity began eventually to result in confusion about priorities among the array of business opportunities facing the company.

At a company of lesser skill and resolve than Millipore, this litany of converging forces could have led to disaster: years of deteriorating performance, the loss of key people, takeover by a larger corporation. In our view, Millipore seems to be passing this test of its adaptiveness and strength with flying colors.

In 1980, even before the problems had begun to turn up on the P&L or balance sheet or had become evident outside the company, Millipore began to address them aggressively. In early summer, Millipore's top management team—the dozen or so key people responsible for major divisions and functions—met in Lenox, Massachusetts, for a searching review of the company's values, objectives, and general direction. Some participants in that session faced the potential for substantial personal criticism. But in that and many subsequent meetings, Millipore set up a program to pull up its corporate socks. Says Jack Mulvany, then president and chief operating officer: "We decided to bite the bullet."

The first step was perhaps the most important. Millipore declared its intention to confront the adversity and overcome it. Once it had made that commitment, management was in a position to take the steps that led to the beginning of 1983's turnaround and 1984's record performance.

• Senior management pledged itself to reduce expenses and staffing levels under the direction of a task force consisting of members of each major division charged with evaluating every significant cost category.

- Millipore sold Worthington Biomedical in 1982. The sale generated a $17-million profit that allowed Millipore to reduce sharply its long-term debt.
- The company reintegrated its Millipore Products Division, enabling it once again to give more complete service to all customers through a larger sales and service force.
- A core team of managers from all parts of the company was assigned to review Millipore's basic strategy, and to reaffirm or modify it to reflect the fundamental values and priorities the management group believed should drive the company over the next several years. The core team broadcast the message throughout the company that top priority would go to quality, innovation, and customer service, in combination with compassion for and a focus on developing Millipore's people. This effort was vital to putting short-term financial goals back into perspective, reasserting their importance as a commitment to be met, but never at the expense of the values of the company.
- Millipore resolved to establish a set of profit standards for every product and market segment it served, and to monitor business performance against those standards carefully. Toward this objective, Millipore brought in John Gilmartin, a seasoned financial executive from Pfizer, the large pharmaceutical company, to devise a suitable control system.
- Millipore cleaned up its balance sheet—taking write-offs and making adjustments as realism dictated—and adopted policies to ensure conservatism in its accounting practices in the future.

The results of the massive effort were a management team more sharply focused on and committed to the company's basic strategic goals and operating strengths, a far stronger organization, and a return to record performance levels. In a business as competitive and rapidly changing as Millipore's, the company has to expect to confront new problems and stresses almost continually. The ability it demonstrated to conquer the array of forces that assaulted it in the early 1980s, though, suggests that Millipore has the corporate confidence and ability to win.

Even at this writing, two of the high-performance companies we have chronicled are coping with profit pressures—Augat and MCI.

Although Augat's growth in sales and profits has been impressive, it has not always been steady. In 1975, for example, the worldwide electronics industry suffered a downturn, and Augat suffered with it. But during that tough period, Augat consolidated its position—acquiring control of a Swiss subcontractor that had supplied precision machine contacts to its integrated circuit socket business and staying in the

integrated circuit packaging panel business while four other competitors—
TRW, Texas Instruments, Litton, and AMP—exited.

The past three years have been difficult ones as well. The cable
television industry—a prime customer group for Augat's products—has
been less aggressive than expected in its growth, and the recent hysteria
caused by some 150 companies seeking to market personal computers
has led to major expansions and contractions in demand for interconnection parts. But the most serious blow—and one that Augat has learned
from—concerns an earlier environmental problem: chemical spillage on
the property of Augat's plating subsidiary. In addition to taking a $3.5-
million extraordinary charge to earnings in 1983 for cleanup, Augat's
plating plant was shut down for three months during 1984, disrupting
production of those components that needed to be plated and requiring
the company to have plating done by others—at a premium cost.

The good news about the bad news of the environmental spill is
how Augat has learned from it. To avoid future problems of this sort,
Augat created an internal environmental audit (parallel to its financial
audit activities).

It produced training films—that are now used by other companies
in Massachusétts—to teach employees how to prevent environmental
problems. Always an innovator, Augat has retained an outside independent "environmental auditor"—the research and consulting firm Arthur D.
Little—to audit its environmental affairs just as Deloitte Haskins &
Sells audits its finances.

Despite this one-time environmental problem and some softness in
its major markets, Augat plowed some $16.7 million into research, devel-
opment, and engineering in 1984—up from $12.5 million in 1983.

MCI—perhaps the fastest-growing billion-dollar company in America—
was for five years one of the fastest growing in profit as well. But
recently, profits have dipped markedly—reflecting in large measure the
post-AT&T divestiture increases in access charges by the regional operating companies. Thus payments for MCI access to local lines increased
from 21 percent of revenues to 44 percent in fifteen months—and the
effect was lower profits and a drop in MCI's stock price. MCI's response
has been to invest—increasing investment levels in its network from
$623 million (1983) to $1 billion annually (1985) and aggressively (and
expensively) expanding its coverage to all phones in the United States to
prepare for what the company sees as an era of equality in quality and
convenience among long-distance providers. Although the jury is still
very much out on who will profit from—indeed, survive—the telecommunications shake-up of this decade, many analysts, as well as MCI
President Orville Wright, are optimistic about a return to higher prof-

itability levels. "We have survived many problems in our short history. The setback in profitability is just another that time and careful management will correct," he predicts. More important, most MCI employees believe it—70 percent of them continue to purchase common stock in the company voluntarily and regularly.

WHAT HAPPENED?

These winning performers encountered rough sailing that traced to combinations of external and internal forces:

1. *Trouble in the economy.* Most businesses suffer when there is a business downturn; some sectors, such as capital equipment for heavy industry, can be hit exceedingly hard. Other economic twists can also hurt, depending on the industry. For example, the strength of the U.S. dollar against most other currencies has made it increasingly difficult to export profitably, has invited substantially greater imports in competition with domestic manufacturers, and has diminished the value in U.S. dollars of profits earned abroad. Dee d'Arbeloff of Millipore notes that "currency exchange rates were the difference between our achieving margins of ten percent in 1982 as we planned, and the six percent we actually realized."

   The 1984 decline in oil price is another example of an economic shift that can have a strong impact. While a boon to oil users, the price decline severely hurt the profits of oil producers, refiners, and marketers as well as companies in oil-field equipment and oil-drilling syndication.

   Changes in the role of government can affect companies, too. As this book was being written, the impact of the new prospective payment plan for the nation's health-care system, essentially scrapping years of cost-plus pricing in the hospital and medical products markets, was causing major dislocations for some of these companies.

2. *New competitive tactics.* New technologies, new and superior competitive products, and new ways of doing business can catch even an innovative and resourceful company off guard from time to time. The shift of many industrial products from electromechanical to electronic operation came with remarkable speed and left some companies with obsolete products and a daunting challenge to catch up. NCR— formerly National Cash Register—is a well-known example. In the

early 1970s, electronic cash registers took over the market NCR had led for decades, and when it was slow to develop its own new product line, NCR lost share rapidly.

3. *Strategic errors.* Many winning companies have experienced a time in their corporate adolescence when they diversified beyond their strengths and into fields they either did not understand or in which far stronger competitors stood ready to give them more than their share of trouble. Still others failed to adapt to changing market conditions even after they had recognized the advent of a new technology or competitive conditions. And companies will sometimes launch a product line for which it turns out there is simply a very limited market willing to pay prices that will yield an acceptable return.

4. *Organizational weaknesses.* As size and complexity demand formalized structure and management systems, and introduce new people and new ideas into the company, the opportunities for breakdowns and malfunction multiply. Layers of organization can add drastically to response time. Functional specialization can lead to major problems of coordination and control: Is manufacturing really providing what sales is selling at the time it was promised? Systems may fail to monitor costs that get out of line. Leaders may lose their in-depth understanding of business dynamics or even their fundamental zeal for the business at all. People throughout the company may lose motivation and morale, adopting a nine-to-five mentality.

There is, of course, no pat formula companies can follow either to recognize the nature of problems or mistakes, nor a formula that tells them what to do to recover. By definition, if a company wins by doing things differently from the competition, then when it stumbles, it will stumble for distinctive reasons, and when it recovers, its road to recovery will also be distinctive.

But there are some broad patterns that seem to characterize the way the high-performance companies we have discussed in this chapter came to grips with their problems and resolved them.

- They were alert enough to recognize the existence of a problem at an early enough point to do something about it before it became cataclysmic.
- Once they identified the problem, they didn't hesitate to bite the bullet.
- Once they sensed things were awry, they conducted a complete inventory, making sure that in the sweep, they caught *all* the things that were contributing to the dysfunction.

- Once they bit the bullet, they mustered all their organizational resolve and resources to addressing it. As in any life-and-death situation, there was no higher priority than the rescue.
- And—not least—this sense of urgency translated into speed and agility.

In short, they moved quickly to address their problems in a substantive way.

In most of the examples we looked at, for instance, the companies let down their guard, just a bit, when times were flush. Some of them allowed staff to grow a little too large. Some of them moved into new product or service areas that they should have recognized were not good strategic fits. Some of them softened the relentlessness with which they monitored a few key variables.

But as soon as each of them had its moment of recognition, it moved swiftly to cut loaded staff, to spin off the strategic misfits, to restore the organizationwide 20/20 focus on the critical performance indicators.

Virtually every midsize high-growth company has experienced strategic and organizational problems. The winning performers are the minority that moved to correct them quickly and creatively, typically returning to even stronger positions than before. They understand that success itself breeds problems. They know they have to anticipate change and adversity, and that they must therefore build in the discipline of an early-warning system to detect internal missteps and external disruption soon enough to turn them into opportunities.

More important still, since no system can be perfect, they build into the cultural bedrock the conviction that when trouble arrives at the door, dealing with it is everybody's top priority. In brief, they have been tested and found not wanting.

CHAPTER VII
Putting It All Together

Some of our colleagues have trouble believing all this. The questions they have been asking us during the course of our research into the qualities of winning performers sound something like this: "Come on, now. Are there really companies that have *all* these qualities? And, if so, do any keep it together for long? In the long run, aren't all companies doomed to stagnation—even decline and deterioration? Won't success ultimately lead to complacency, and size to bureaucracy, finally causing even the best of companies to trip over its own feet? And even if these things don't happen, won't changes in the prevailing economic winds, changes in the competitive ground rules, technologies, and market forces ultimately shift against a company and drag it down? Just look at the railroads, the big steel companies, the automakers—is anyone exempt?"

Their questions are valid. Of the top hundred companies on the original *Fortune* 500 list thirty years ago (1955), only forty-six remain in the top hundred today. Furthermore, at the extremes, the numbers catch up with the fastest-growing companies eventually. (It would only take forty years for a $100-million company to become a $1-*trillion* company if it found some way to sustain a sales growth rate of 25 percent.) And even for the best companies, some loss of youthful vitality, clear vision, innovativeness, and adaptiveness becomes the ironic price of success. But while corporate immortality may be neither a feasible nor an attractive goal, in our view, companies that have sustained for at least a decade or two the traits we describe in this book have proved something important— they have institutionalized a corporate way of life that is not only right for its time, but contains within it the ability to adapt to inescapable changes. By so doing, they have greatly improved the odds of continuing to survive as quality companies.

This chapter looks at three very different companies that have impressive records of sustaining high performance coupled with adaptation over more than ten years.* These companies—Cray Research, Automatic Data Processing, and Sealed Air Corporation—represent very different industries, competitive and environmental settings, strategies, organizations, and leadership styles. The first is a very high-technology manufacturer of the most advanced large-scale computers; the second, an information services company; the third, a medium- or low-tech make-and-sell company, predominantly in the packaging business. They are not unique in their accomplishments; 119 publicly owned companies have, like them, sustained sales and profit growth rates of 20 percent or more over the past decade;† a few private companies have done so as well, and others that have grown less rapidly have equally resourceful management capabilities. We chose these three not to elevate them above the others but simply to represent all those who have sustained over time the qualities described in this book.

THE GENIUS OF CRAY RESEARCH

Cray Research—one of America's youngest but arguably most successful companies—puts it all together as the world's leading designer, producer, and servicer of supercomputers for leading-edge customers in the scientific community. Founded April 6, 1972, Cray is one of only two companies to make *Inc.* magazine's list of the hundred fastest-growing publicly held companies for five consecutive years (in the sixth year Cray had grown too big to qualify).

Cray's sales and profit growth since 1977 are impressive in their own right—from $11 million in sales to $229 million in 1984 and $1 million in profit to $45 million—but overshadowed by the importance of its innovations to the nation's scientific, technological, and defense posture. As *Forbes* magazine reported in September 1983, "No question about it: Seymour Cray [the company's founder] isn't just another scien-

---

*Cray was founded in 1972 and turned its first profit in 1976, but it has averaged more than 20 percent growth since by a wide margin.
†See Appendix B for a complete list of these companies.

tist; he is a national resource."* Cray computers, its largest models capable of making one billion calculations in a second, have become indispensable to those who push the "state of the art" in nuclear physics, oil exploration, weather prediction, aircraft design, and weapons research.

Cray Research stands out as an example of an enterprise that exemplifies almost all the lessons of our research and experience. Its strategy is *innovation*—continuously creating new generations of supercomputers that at times threaten to put Cray out of its "old" business by making obsolete the pioneer machines of the previous year. Cray leads in a *niche market*—perhaps as few as four hundred customers in the world—whose requirements are so sophisticated and need for having the fastest supercomputer so great that only the best, fastest, and most powerful will do. Cray *builds on strength*—broadening its product line by finding new applications for its machines but sticking to what it does best—go-fast computers. Cray competes on the *value* of its product. It produces and markets among the most expensive computers in the world—selling them to price-conscious government agencies, research institutions, and universities—because they get the work done cheaper and faster, and make possible research that could not be done before.

Cray has an *organizational culture* that transcends wealth creation and business administration. Founded by five men who sought to escape the administrative bureaucracy of a larger company and specialize as technical purists, the company's *shared values* and commitment to a small company spirit require few rules as Cray celebrates autonomy, common sense, and fun. Cray engineers are *close to their customers*—be it at seminars for current and potential customers in the woods near Chippewa Falls, Wisconsin, or via its monthly user magazine, *Cray Channels*, which laymen find difficult to understand but users find provocative. But more important, Cray shares the common interests and needs of leading-edge scientists—the best for the brightest. Quite naturally, *people skills and rewards* figure prominently in a company in which the most valuable resources are people who succeeded, but weren't happy, at other leading companies. *Top-management leadership*—the obsession of Seymour Cray to build the most powerful scientific computer, and the institution-building skills of John Rollwagen (now chairman and CEO)—has been harmonized through an unusual but successful top-management transition.

Let's look at how Cray Research combines the qualities described

*"War Games," *Forbes* (September 12, 1983), pp. 108–10.

in the preceding chapters, and what lessons it holds for those who dream about business success and impact that go beyond the bottom line.

STRATEGIC POSITIONING

To most Americans, supercomputers have an aura of excitement and high fashion—because of their high-technology basis and the sophisticated uses to which they are put. The supersecret National Security Agency has a picture of a Cray computer on its recruiting brochure, for example, aimed at appealing to recent college science majors NSA hopes to attract. Several of the popular science-fiction movies have featured a supercomputer as an inanimate force that either held the key to the future or played some sinister role in a nuclear holocaust or near-miss. But despite this current notoriety and fashionability, the supercomputer market was not one that the biggest and most established giants have pursued with success.

IBM, the undisputed worldwide leader in computers, made two brief forays into supercomputers—in the 1950s with its "super stretch" effort and in the mid-'60s with its Model 90—and each time abandoned the project.* Control Data Corporation, founded by the iconoclastic and socially conscious Bill Norris and others, including Seymour Cray, was for a time the leading producer of supercomputers. But CDC also saw the supercomputer market as a tiny one with modest growth and profit potential—and turned its forces to the bigger business of commercial mainframes and business applications, as well as less-related areas such as innovative finance through its acquisition of Commercial Credit Company. In fact, recently another supercomputer entry, ETA Systems, has spun off from CDC. This lack of corporate excitement about supercomputers—founded on market research that predicted only handfuls of customers sophisticated enough to demand these one-of-a-kind machines—left Seymour Cray and his four colleagues free to seek an unpopular but demanding goal—as Cray told his hometown paper, the *Chippewa Herald Telegram*, in May 1972, "to design and build a larger, more powerful computer than anyone now has." In essence the fledgling supercomputer company ignored the conventional wisdom and set up shop to serve an undefended—indeed, unpopular—market. How they went about serving, expanding, and leading in this neglected segment holds the lessons of success of the company's rapid rise from twelve

---

*"Supercomputers: Only A Few Success Stories," *Computerworld* (Nov. 9, 1981), p. 18.

technical apostles who lost a half million dollars in 1973 to a $229 million company in 1984 and a stock market success story.

Innovation as a Way of Life

The foundation of Cray Research's strategy is, has been, and will be innovation. Technological innovation is what most distinguishes the company, but it has also been creative and practical in finance and marketing.

In 1983, for example, Cray Research was first in investment per employee on the *Business Week* research-and-development scoreboard of some 776 major U.S. companies that spend at least $1 million a year or 1 percent of their sales on R&D.* In that year Cray Research invested nearly $21,000 per employee in research, nearly four times the average of the thirty-one leading U.S. computer companies (ranging from established giants like IBM, Honeywell, Sperry, and Control Data to newer companies like Apple, Tandem, and Amdahl). On another accepted measure—percent of sales devoted to research and development—Cray ranked fourth out of the 776 research leaders, investing more than 20 percent of its sales revenues—about seven times the National Science Foundation's estimate for all U.S. industry and almost three times the average level for the major computer makers.

This double tithe of corporate resources to research was not accidental. From the very beginning, Cray Research decided to invest every year a minimum of 15 percent of its revenues in research—believing that continued technological superiority was central to its mission and that its leading-edge customers—for the most part sophisticated scientists in their own right—would pay the premium for continuing innovation.

Even before founding Cray Research, Seymour Cray had earned his reputation as a technical innovator. The first machine he worked on at Sperry Rand was the Univac 1103. After helping found Control Data, Cray was the principal architect of the CDC 1604 mainframe, where he pioneered using transistors as a substitute for vacuum tubes. He subsequently led the design of the 6600 (the then vanguard scientific computer and first one to use germanium transistors), the 7600 (the first "supercomputer"), and the 8600 (never marketed).

Cray's technological genius—which has fathered at least three generations of supercomputers—has not been as a fundamental scientific inventor, but, in his self-effacing description, as a packager of things that already exist. As one of Cray's early collaborators told the *Twin Cities*

---

*June 20, 1983, p. 122. A year later, Cray was still in the top fifteen in the nation as measured by dollar of research-and-development spending per employee—but no longer first of all.

Reader in 1983, "Seymour said it before. 'We're packaging engineers. We take a product that's existed for quite some time and just package it differently. That's all.' "*

John Rollwagen, a man who appreciates irony and describes perversity and contrariant thinking as among the most important Cray cultural norms, told us that the Cray-1 Computer—at the time the leading edge of technology—was "a collection of trailing-edge components." As he explained, the company "couldn't afford anything other than old, on-the-shelf parts!" And with few exceptions Cray Research has continued to follow Seymour's advice to his colleagues—to take the "low technology" approach. "You know my rule: Keep a decade behind."†

The creativity and innovation of Cray's leading-edge technology is the achievement of simplicity and conceptual "block-busting."

In a field where calculations per second are measured in the hundreds of millions and operating cycles measured in nanoseconds, keeping it simple works. For example, in the Cray-1 model (which Cray and Rollwagen jokingly refer to as the "world's most expensive love seat" because it looks like one), some of the wires are four feet long. But in the newer models, maximum wire length has been reduced to sixteen inches. Short wires mean less distance for electricity to travel, and less distance means more speed.

A major challenge in computer technology, especially the supercomputer variety, is how to control and contain the heat that can make microprocessing components fail. Teams of talented scientists devote their lives to building refrigeration systems. The Cray-2 computer is a triumph of common sense—the computer is submerged in a fish tank filled with an inert fluorocarbon coolant—leading Cray and Rollwagen to refer to this major advance in computational power as the "world's most expensive aquarium." Thus it is not surprising that when Cray, questioned about special tools he uses to design these machines, explained, in *Datamation Magazine,* "I don't use special tools when I design except paper and pencil."‡

Cray's innovation isn't limited to technology. The company prides itself on its imaginative financing for customers—creating leases for nonprofit institutions, finding financing for computers sold to the intelligence community where the customer and the machine's location are state secrets, or creating convertible notes early in the company's history.

*"Meet Seymour Cray," *Twin Cities Reader* (August 31, 1983), pp. 14–16.
†"Cray's Mark Remains Speed with Simplicity," *Update*, University of Minnesota alumni magazine (Spring 1983), pp, 8–10.
‡"Four Expert Opinions," *Datamation Magazine* (December 1982), pp. 143–50.

In the marketing realm, Cray has become expert in federal procurement practices that baffle even its customers, who are government agencies. In a market where the practice is to demand competitive price bidding—a method that would seem to be a barrier to a company like Cray—Cray Research only and always quotes list price and nearly always wins the "competition."

Leading in Niche Markets

At last count, excluding those installed in the Warsaw Pact nations, some 144 supercomputers were in use in the world. Ninety-seven of them are products of Cray Research.

By way of comparison, more than 122,000 general-purpose, American-made computers, 17,000 mainframes, and 2 million medium- and small-scale computers are in use in the world today—supplemented by more than 1 million minicomputers and untold personal computers.*

But Cray Research has never taken its eye off the original handful—now one hundred—of customers: the government agencies, academic and research institutions, and sophisticated corporations that need to make trillions of calculations on a regular basis. As Cray Research's one-page mission statement makes clear, "Cray Research is a company whose primary business is the design, construction, marketing, and support of large-scale scientific computers which provide superior computational power within existing systems."

As society's aspirations to figure out the impossible through simulation and quantitative analysis have grown, this once-tiny market niche has expanded. Some of the original handful of customers now have more than one supercomputer. For example, the Lawrence Livermore National Laboratory has six and the Los Alamos National Laboratory has five. NASA and the National Center for Atmospheric Research each have two.

At times the idea of expanding Cray's customer base by offering a machine a little less sophisticated has been discussed at Cray—and rejected vehemently. Rather, Cray Research has allowed some of the world to catch up to it—to enter its niche. While Cray Research still focuses on the tiny technically purist segment, it sells models with Cray-1 level of performance (at reduced prices that reflect advances in the components it uses and manufacturing economies) to the newcomers for what are their state-of-the-art needs.

Building on Strength

Cray Research's first objective is to stay and lead in its niche—in

EDP Industry Report estimates.

the words of its mission statement, "to lead in the development and marketing of high performance systems which make a unique contribution to the market they serve." And its second objective is to build on strength—again in its words: "To foster and support entrepreneurial developments of products which are natural extensions of our current capability."

For Cray, this edging out on the sturdy limb of current capability has taken the form of finding new applications for nontraditional customers who are very sophisticated customers. For example, during the past two years Cray has installed supercomputers for eight of the ten largest oil companies—to help them better focus their exploration activities—and has installed machines for General Motors (to help in car design and simulate crashes); for Boeing and NASA (to simulate tests previously done in even more expensive wind tunnels); and for a movie company (because the supercomputer—believe it or not—can create scenery more economically than the studios).

In edging out, Cray has not changed its hardware concept, even though each supercomputer is still specially tailored to meet customer needs. But it has embarked on a program to create software for its newer "nontraditional" customers. Previously, Cray had relied on its state-of-the-art customers—research institutions and the like—to create their own software for their one-of-a-kind applications. Today, some two hundred of Cray's more than two thousand employees are engaged in software development. About one third of its research budget is devoted to software, and Cray has worked to help make its machines more compatible with other computers its newer customers might already have.

Edging out has paid substantial dividends for Cray without compromising its philosophy of developing even more powerful computers. Each year the company has increased the number of new computers installed—reaching twenty-three new machines in 1984 alone, eleven of them for new customers who almost all ordered the "low end" of Cray's line. The other twelve installations were with repeat customers—in the traditional state-of-the-art category—who quite naturally ordered the latest top-of-the-line models.

Competing on Value, Not Price

"The Cray Style," an operating philosophy of the company that we will visit later in this chapter, explicitly addresses the basis of competition:

Economy comes from high value, not from low cost.

True to this declaration, Cray supercomputers—the most expensive in the world—owe their value to delivering economy to customers. Cray supercomputers cost anywhere between $5 million and $20 million for the equipment, plus a monthly service fee that ranges from $25,000 to $50,000. By comparison, a top-of-the-line mainframe goes for about $4 million.

This high initial and operating cost, however, pays for itself in lower computing cost. For example, a Cray-1 costs about 1 percent of what an IBM 360-50 would to perform a standard simulation, according to the NASA Ames Research Center analysis reported in *The Economist*.* And a Cray-2 costs even less—approaching one tenth of 1 percent per simulation. For scientists who conduct masses of simulations, the Cray machine quickly pays for itself.

In the commercial world, the high cost of a Cray computer can be dwarfed by the economic and strategic benefits it permits. For example, *Business Week* reported that "Because of its Cray system, Boeing was able to increase by 12 percent the aerodynamic efficiency of the area of its new 767 jetliner where the windshield joins the body. . . . Those kinds of problems weren't being solved before because of economic problems."†

That is not to say that Cray isn't cost-sensitive—or that it doesn't pass along savings to its customers. In 1982, for example, Cray was able to cut the cost of its Cray-1 by using new components. It cut the price in half—from $8 to $4 million each—creating a new price performance curve for supercomputing and closing the price gap between a supercomputer and the top-of-the-line mainframe. For about six months, the market was confused—it couldn't believe Cray was offering comparable performance at half the price. When they discovered it was true, a number of new customers bought the machine—Cray had expanded the total market as well as its share.

FOCUSED ORGANIZATION

As Seymour Cray was realizing his dream of building winning supercomputers, his partner, John Rollwagen, focused his attention on building a winning organization. During the past ten years Cray Research has progressed through the stages of corporate development that most companies take much longer to accomplish. From a standing start with no product, customer, or business, Cray took four years and considerable financing to produce its first product. In short order thereafter,

*"Supercomputers Come Out Into the World," *The Economist* (Aug. 11, 1984), p. 78.
†"The Hot Market for Supercomputers," *Business Week* (December 20, 1982), p. 70.

the company's success brought growth and business complexity—working out of three major production and management locations; operating four domestic marketing and service regions and an equal number of overseas subsidiaries; adding two generations of supercomputers, software development, and numerous modifications to its original product line; and expanding from twelve employees to more than two thousand.

In managing this decade of change to become a world-class force that nations and consortia of giant competitors would like to equal, Cray has overcome the challenges that the trade press and industry observers predicted might bring it to its knees. First, the company has transformed itself from one almost entirely dependent upon the skills, leadership, and technical genius of one man—Seymour Cray—to an institution well respected in its own right and that in a unique way continues to draw upon the founder's talents. Second, it has performed its encore— successfully developing and succeeding commercially with a second generation of supercomputers—the Cray X-MP—applying a new approach, parallel processing, to the original Cray-1. This is the achievement of a team led by a second Cray Research computer designer, Steve Chen.

The design challenges of an organization to meet these requirements—complexity, growth, augmenting the talent of a genius, and performing a state-of-the-art technical and business encore—has in our view been as difficult as the design challenges of a new generation of supercomputers. And Cray Research's experience in meeting these organizational challenges holds important lessons for other threshold companies. Cray's blueprint for success included a conscious and well-executed effort to define and institutionalize Seymour Cray's mission and shared values; careful attention to and mastery of the business fundamentals most critical to the enterprise; a successful campaign to vaccinate the company against latent bureaucracy; an ongoing effort to understand customers well enough to have their interests at heart; and high priority on developing and motivating people. Here's how Cray did it.

Institutionalizing Mission and Shared Values

As is the case in many entrepreneurial ventures, Seymour Cray and his early compatriots had a strong and well-understood set of shared values that provided the philosophical underpinning for their new venture. These shared values included a mission of technical superiority, a distaste for the bureaucratic impediments of larger organizations, a respect for individual contributions, and a belief that people get better results when they have fun.

As the company succeeded and grew, Rollwagen sensed a need to reinforce those aspects of the culture that had contributed so much to

Cray Research's position—and convened a philosophy committee, of which he served as secretary. After months of deliberation and widespread contribution from people throughout the company—old-timers, technical folks, administrative staff, new employees—the committee published a creed: "The Cray Style." We reprint it in full because it is a model, in our view, of a corporate philosophy.

"The Cray Style" speaks to five corporate values that those we interviewed (and our observations of the company confirm) are very much at work.

First, *quality*—in products, working environment, people, tools, components. Cray's strategy is clearly a quality- (versus cost- or price-) driven one, and the company has decided to emphasize quality in every aspect of its work.

Second, *informality*—Cray, Rollwagen, and the others at Cray are convinced (and their record is convincing) that the most important breakthroughs and innovations come from small groups working together. Although the company is getting larger fast, great effort is made to make the place manageable. As an exemplar, Seymour Cray usually works with small teams of five or six people—usually picking the most junior, least experienced new engineers because "they don't know what's impossible." Cray Research organized its four regions into profit centers—to encourage a small-company spirit. The Cray X-MP—its second generation of supercomputers—is a big hit that was designed by a team separate from that which designed the Cray-2.

This appetite for small-company spirit manifests itself in the systems the company uses to manage itself. First of all, there are no policy or procedures manuals. As Margaret Loftus, the head of Cray's burgeoning software operation, explained: "I have only one corporate policy and that is the policy of no harassment. My belief is policy books inspire harassment."*

How does Cray get away with it? The shared values, mission, and philosophy of the company are so strong, so well understood, and so committed that rules and regulations just aren't necessary.

The next corporate value is *fun*. As the preamble to "The Cray Style" states, "At Cray Research, we take what we do very seriously, but don't take ourselves very seriously." And indeed they do—and don't. Seymour Cray again is a clear role model. For example, although hundreds of articles have appeared about Cray Research over the past decade, Seymour Cray is usually unavailable to the press. But when he does speak,

---

*"People," *Datamation Magazine* (April 1, 1984), pp. 167–68.

the Cray style

At Cray Research, we take what we do very seriously, but don't take ourselves very seriously.

We have a strong sense of quality — quality in our products and services, of course; but also quality in our working environment, in the people we work with, in the tools that we use to do our work, and in the components we choose to make what we make. Economy comes from high value, not from low cost. Aesthetics are part of quality. The effort to create quality extends to the communities in which we work and live as well.

The Cray approach is informal and non-bureaucratic. Verbal communication is key, not memos. "Call, don't write" is the watchword.

People are accessible at all levels.

People also have fun working at Cray Research. There is laughing in the halls, as well as serious discussion. More than anything else, the organization is personable and approachable, but still dedicated to getting the job done.

With informality, however, there is also a sense of confidence. Cray people feel like they are on the winning side. They feel successful, and they are. It is this sense of confidence that generates the attitude of "go ahead and try it, we'll make it work."

Also, there is a sense of pride at Cray. Professionalism is important. People are treated like and act like professionals. Cray people trust each other to do their jobs well and with the highest ethical standards. They take what they do very seriously.

But Cray people are professional without being stuffy. They take a straightforward, even simple, approach. They don't take themselves too seriously.

Because the individual is key at Cray, there is a real diversity in the view of what Cray Research really is. In fact, Cray Research is many things to many people. The consistency comes in providing those diverse people with the opportunity to fulfill themselves and experience achievement. The creativity, then, that emerges from the company comes from the many ideas of the individuals who are here. And that is the real strength of Cray Research.

it's clear he doesn't take himself too seriously, as the following interview with *Datamation Magazine* shows:

Datamation: "What problems do you find in working with gallium arsenide?"
Cray: "Well, it's hard to pronounce. Once you get over that . . ."

Datamation: "What technological developments in the past five to ten years have had the biggest impact on your niche in the computer industry?"
Cray: "I guess there haven't been any."

Datamation: "No developments in mathematics, architecture . . . ?"
Cray: ". . . I just do my own kind of work, so if there were something new in mathematics I wouldn't know about it."

Datamation: "What has surprised you most in how your products are used?"
Cray: "I don't know what all this supercomputer talk is about. They certainly aren't supercomputers; they are kind of simple dumb things."*

The fourth element of "The Cray Style" is *professionalism*—that "people are treated like and act like professionals [and] trust each other to do their jobs well and with the highest ethical standards." The simple approaches are seen as professional ones to get the job done. There are no time clocks; every employee—executive, designer, assembler, or secretary—is treated and expected to perform as a professional. As a Cray vice president told us, the company encourages the ultimate in flex-time. (Seymour Cray reportedly likes to arrive in the afternoon and leave in the dark hours of the night.) Small teams rather than massive groups tackle major technical and business problems. Cray achieves this measure of what Peters and Waterman term "productivity through people" by instilling pride and professionalism throughout the work force.

Finally, Cray celebrates individual *achievement* and the *creativity* of individuals. While this last element of the creed may strike the cynical among us as perhaps a platitude, mouthed by institutions good and bad, at Cray it is an important part of the culture—finding its legacy in the history of five men who celebrated their diversity and sought to create an environment that was conducive to the individual. No part of Cray's business system is taken more seriously nor is more central to its

---

*"Four Expert Opinions," *Datamation Magazine* (December 1982), pp. 143–50.

success than the design of computers, and yet two successive generations of supercomputers (the Cray X-MP and the Cray-2) were designed by different teams following different technical approaches (i.e., two approaches to parallel processing and two approaches to chip design). Both succeeded technically—and the diversity of approach was celebrated.

Mastering the Business Fundamentals

Quite obviously, the most fundamental business skill at Cray Research is designing, producing, and servicing supercomputers for leading-edge customers. And no subject so overwhelms the attention and effort of the company.

But strategic planning and finance also receive considerable attention—in part reflecting the skills and inclinations of Rollwagen, the current chief executive. And along with the early group of designers who joined Cray, Cray Research has built its other fundamental disciplines by attracting skilled specialists in marketing, finance, and human resources.

Fighting Bureaucracy, Encouraging Experimentation

Seymour Cray and his early colleagues in part began the company to escape the gnawing bureaucracy of their previous employment. And as earlier discussions of their shared values and "The Cray Style" disclosed, a dread of bureaucracy is one of those closely held shared values today.

But even more than rejecting bureaucratic structure and systems— the most tangible way to ensure small-company spirit and informality— Cray Research is also an experimenter by nature. Some experiments are highly successful—such as the X-MP project. Others—including a research project in Boulder, Colorado, and a subsidiary called Circuit Tools—have been tried and either abandoned or reconstituted. But the "go ahead and try it" mentality pervades the organization.

Understanding Their Customers

In one of Seymour Cray's rare published interviews, he had the following to say about his market:

. . . We keep selling computers to the same old people and they are getting old at the same rate I am. We don't even need introductions when we come out with a new computer because we already know the people. It's just the same market for us over and over again. . . .*

As it was explained to us at a meeting of the Cray Research top management team one afternoon, Cray is so close to its leading-edge customers that they become partners, as it were, in the search for greater computational power to unlock the future of science. Customers visit Cray's research, design, and manufacturing facilities—and jointly "benchmark" the machine so that each can be configured to the scientists' highly specific special needs. (Despite the closeness in determining needs, however, Cray retains control over the ultimate design of the machine, its technical "architecture"—although jokingly, Les Davis, an executive vice president of Cray, allows that "each machine can be any color the customer wants.") Furthermore, Cray—perhaps borrowing a page from the IBM success formula—stays with the customer, not only through the supercomputer's installation and shakedown, but on an ongoing basis to make sure it works right throughout its useful life.

Attention to People

Although much of the outside world may view Cray Research's technological knowledge and reputation as its prime asset, the management of Cray sees its people as still more valuable. Hence the high levels of attention to professionalism, individual achievement, and creativity in "The Cray Style" are not surprising. And in contrast to many Silicon Valley high-tech firms that seek to lock their people in with "golden handcuffs," Cray's profit-sharing vests as quickly as the law permits. The reason: Cray Research wants to keep its best talent because they *want* to stay, not because they are waiting for a vesting date. As a company founded by purist pilgrims who left other leading firms, Cray finds that providing continuous challenge, recognition, and fun is far more powerful than legally binding employment contracts or mere financial incentives.

EVOLVING CEO LEADERSHIP

We also found Cray Research a good example of the elements of leadership that we have come to see as widely associated with superior performing midsize growth companies. Not only were the traits of perseverance, institution-building, teamwork, and calculated risk-taking

---

*"Four Expert Opinions," *Datamation Magazine* (December 1982), p. 150.

prominently present, but most important, Cray Research has accomplished an effective—albeit unusual—transition of chief executives.

By all accounts of those who should know, Seymour Cray is a genius—a man who transforms Boolean algebra into practical computer hardware that can compute hundreds of mathematical transactions in a microsecond (one millionth of a second). And his dedication to doing this better than anyone else has marked, even determined, the course of his career.

Cray, the son of a city engineer, had an early interest in applied science, serving as the electrician at the Chippewa Falls High School junior prom and winning the high school science award in 1943. He studied electrical engineering at the Universities of Wisconsin and Minnesota. After early employment at what is now Sperry Corp. (a pioneer in the field of computers), Cray helped found the maverick and entrepreneurial Control Data Corporation (CDC), where he became a vice president and director at the age of thirty-one. At this rather tender age, he was recognized for his interdisciplinary skills in designing sophisticated scientific computers—and at the time CDC had cornered the market for "supercomputers."

To capitalize on Seymour Cray's eclectic interests (which ranged from circuit designs to logic architecture and software development), CDC set up a lab near Chippewa Falls where Cray could think, create, and produce. As CDC began to diversify its interests into the commercial applications of computers and into financial services, Cray began to question the company's seriousness about the mission he embraced with single-minded intensity—to produce the fastest and most powerful computer in the world. Although the market for sophisticated, state-of-the-art, high-speed machines was thought to be tiny (by some estimates only a dozen opportunities), Cray was obsessed by a vision of technological achievement, scientific purity, and quality.

In 1972, with a team of four other technological purists, Cray set out to design the best. As one of his early compatriots, Les Davis, told us, "We really didn't know exactly what, if anything, we would produce. We might have become an engineering think tank or we might have assembled the fastest computer—but we were in the business of advancing the state of the art!" This team spent four years and raised millions of dollars before selling a single computer. In fact, as a Harvard Business School case* (used to teach aspiring M.B.A.'s the art and science of business) on Cray Research reports, it takes at least two years of

*Francis J. Aguilar and Caroline Brainard, *Cray Research, Inc.,* Harvard Business School (1984), p. 8.

effort to design, market, manufacture, and install any supercomputer. And Cray Research's newer markets, such as automobile and petroleum companies, had, respectively, seven- and five-year gestation periods between initial contact and the first sale. This perseverance is not limited to the founder. As Robert Gaertner, the company's human-resources chief, told us, Cray's ultimate success in penetrating the petroleum industry was the result of the effort of one manager, George Stephenson—who kept at it for five years.

But more significant than the long lead times and financial risks associated with the business has been the obsession of Seymour Cray and his technical associates with creating ever more powerful and faster generations of supercomputers—and their single-minded goal not to let unrelated opportunities cloud their focus or barriers (whether technical or administrative) stop their progress. As one industry wag tells it: "The first supercomputer was like winning a Nobel Prize. But these guys are not satisfied unless they win the prize every year!"

Institution-building has been as significant an accomplishment at Cray as computer-building. Institution-building includes, but is far more than, Cray Research's practice of investing heavily in research and development for the future. And it is more than the early (and current) efforts to raise capital. It is all those actions taken to build an organization and corporate culture that can sustain the enterprise over many years.

John Rollwagen's role in building the institution ranges from decisions that are visible and tangible (e.g., installing financial control and strategic planning systems) to intangible (such as instituting the effort to articulate, codify, and reinforce Cray Research's operating philosophy).

Cray Research is a model of calculating risk-taking, too. For four long years, Cray and his associates raised and spent a lot of money—much of it their own—accumulating losses of some $4 million as they worked to design, refine, and perfect a computer second to none. Finally, in 1976, they had a computer that worked—even faster than the ones Cray had designed for Univac and Control Data—and they provided it to Los Alamos National Laboratory on approval. (As those of us who were once stamp collectors know, "on approval" is the process of sending goods in the hope that the customer will see the benefit and later pay for them.) The machine worked and the research laboratory bought it—the price finally covering the costs of the start-up research as well as the machine itself and justifying the tremendous risk in dollars, personal time, and reputation that the founding team had at stake. Today Los Alamos has five Cray computers that help this national research laboratory continue its pioneering role in nuclear physics and weapons research.

Any enterprise that seeks to advance technology beyond the state of the art, and to create and serve markets that previously were thought not to exist, is by any definition risky. And Cray Research, as a matter of day-to-day business, places these bets. What distinguishes Cray Research is its calculation in taking them.

First, Cray believes in internal competition. It is not unusual for small teams of Cray professionals to be at work on differing approaches to solving similar problems. As Seymour Cray told his college alumni magazine, "We're not going to participate in any national effort . . . we've got competition within the company. I've got a group here five miles away who I know are trying to outdo me."*

Andrew Scott, Cray's vice chairman and counsel and one of the founders of the company, explained to us that Cray has consistently passed up opportunities to join in government-sponsored and -funded research to advance the state of the art, preferring instead to stick to its fiercely independent internal competition—in at least one case selling a machine to an agency after that agency had financed considerable research by two would-be competitors to design a supercomputer.

As John Rollwagen explained the practice of risk-taking at Cray Research: "We have no alternative—no choice—but to make the bets. But we make several bets at once."

Cray Research provides a good example of effective teamwork and transition at the CEO level. John Rollwagen, an MIT engineer and Harvard Business School graduate, likes to tell the story that his linkup with Cray came from being in the right spot at the right time—in his case in a Mendota Heights, Minnesota, barber shop. Rollwagen is another Control Data Corporation alumnus who had gone on to become the marketing chief for a computer time-sharing business. Sitting by chance in a barber chair next to another former Control Data officer and Cray founder, in the building in which Cray had his business office, Rollwagen decided to stop by to chat. He was hired three years later as a vice president with undefined responsibilities and quickly became chief financial officer, later president, and finally chief executive. For the past decade Rollwagen and Cray have led a productive partnership—marrying Seymour Cray's scientific genius, his obsession with quality, and technical purity with John Rollwagen's financial creativity and marketing savvy to build Cray Research into a world-class institution.

In many ways a company's success has not been tested nor its future assured until it has successfully orchestrated a transition from founder chief executive to a successor. In the case of Cray Research, this inevitable transition was feared by customers and Wall Street alike—

*"Cray's Mark Remains Speed with Simplicity," *Update,* University of Minnesota alumni magazine (Spring 1983), pp. 8–10.

because of the oversized technical and philosophic contributions of its namesake, Seymour Cray.

Fortunately, as the company grew in size and complexity, Seymour Cray had the vision, self-confidence, and introspection to realize that the prospects and demands of running a multihundred-million-dollar enterprise was neither a burning passion for himself nor in the long-term interest of the institution. In 1980, after months of far-ranging, candid, and intense discussion among Seymour Cray, John Rollwagen, and Andrew Scott, an unusual—but thus far successful—role change for Seymour Cray and top management succession was announced as the company displayed to the public the prototype of the Cray-2 model.

In essence, Seymour Cray went into business for himself again—as the prime "independent contractor" for and consultant to the company. On a single sheet of paper, Cray, Rollwagen, and Scott devised a simple agreement under which Cray went about his research and development independently but supported by the company. Cray was to have none of the despised administrative duties of a chairman or company officer but was freed to do what he did best and most wanted to do— design supercomputers. Cray Research provided the staff, leased the laboratory facilities from Seymour Cray, and had the right of first crack at his research—which Seymour Cray would solely decide and direct.

At the time of the announcement, many Wall Street observers and industry experts questioned how and indeed if such an open-ended, unusual arrangement could work. Obviously, it requires extraordinary goodwill on the part of both parties. But apparently it has, as the agreement was extended through 1987. In our discussions with Rollwagen and Scott it was clear that Seymour Cray was—and is—a special resource who has to be given quiet and support to do his best work. The agreement is intentionally ambiguous—both Cray the man and Cray the company know it can work only so long as both want it to.

So now, John Rollwagen, at the time of his promotion thirty-nine years of age, faces the challenge of running the company in a way that keeps Seymour Cray and the legions of upcoming Seymour Crays productive and creative in the face of stiff competition.

The challenges for Cray Research today and in the future are greater than in the past. When it went into business in 1972, there was but one competitor—Control Data Corporation. But in the past two years, giant consortia of top computer companies have announced massive cooperative programs whose ambitions are to beat this relatively tiny company.

The heralded Japanese eight-year $100 million National Superspeed Computer Project (Fujitsu, Hitachi, Mitsubishi, NEC [Nisson], OKI Electric, and Toshiba); the Austin-based Microelectronic and Computer Technology Corporation (MCC)—combining the resources of fifteen giant American companies, including Control Data; and the European Esprit program, as well as others, are each seeking to catch up with and better the results of this small, highly entrepreneurial, fast-moving company. *The Economist* reports that some fifty teams in America's universities are also trying to build their own supercomputers.* In some measure, this incredible competition is Cray's own doing, as the little midwestern computer company has demonstrated beyond reasonable doubt that the tiny neglected market niche of supercomputers is an exciting one. And only time will tell how long "The Cray Style" will continue to prevail against the massive resources of nations, industries, and universities. So far, Cray has outwitted them all.

THE INTENSITY OF AUTOMATIC DATA PROCESSING

Because his immigrant family could not afford to prepare him for a career in medicine, law, or even teaching, Henry Taub aimed from his earliest years at a career in commerce. His first jobs were in selling newspapers and caddying, but by the time the United States had completed its first year in World War II, fifteen-year-old Henry Taub was working nights for Associated Transport. Six years later, at the age of twenty-one, he was to found Automatic Data Processing, one of the most dramatic success stories of the modern era among midsize growth companies—in fact, among all corporations.

But in 1943, young Taub had to get home from his job at Associated in time to do his high-school homework, and so he rapidly became a work expediter, with an eye for methods of improvement. He found new ways to sort out the stacks of bills that daily came across his desk and to structure the process for calculating the net amount to be entered in each invoice. He learned to type eighty words per minute, and he kept finding ways to improve productivity. "I guess we drove that organization, because I had to get back to my homework. My high-school record was important to me because I had to have a university education."

To earn his tuition during his undergraduate years at New York University, Taub continued working, this time with a small accounting firm. Little of his time went to traditional accounting and auditing activi-

---

*"Supercomputers Come Out Into the World," *The Economist* (August 11, 1984), p. 78.

ties. Working for small clients, Taub's primary job was to act as book-keeper, payroll clerk, and accountant for these clients. He did their billing; he posted their accounts receivable; he made out their payrolls. And so, by the time he was graduated from New York University at age nineteen, he had years of office experience and an unusually good understanding of the difference between efficiency and inefficiency in administrative management.

Taub still had no idea of founding a company. After graduation from college, he joined a larger accounting firm but soon found that the slow pace and bureaucratic climate of such a firm were not for him. He next joined a friend as office manager in a small lingerie firm. It was a historic event when the payroll didn't get out one week because one of the clerks was sick—and Taub learned quickly just how devastating to morale and productivity it can be when workers aren't paid. This prob-lem led one of his colleagues to conceive the idea of a company that would manage the payrolls of other businesses, guaranteeing that no matter what happened, they would never miss a payroll. With that col-league and $6,000 put up by a third partner, the entity that was to become ADP was launched, with Taub the back-office man.

Business developed slowly—"We only had two accounts"—when Fate again took a hand. Taub's working partner, Irving Levine, got mar-ried, and shortly thereafter was offered the security of a chief financial officer in a larger, established company. Taub then went to the money partner and offered to assume responsibility for the $6,000 investment if he could have all the equity in the fledgling company. And so it was that at age twenty-one Henry Taub became the sole proprietor of a new business. He had two small clients, a $6,000 debt commitment, and a pretty good sense of what clients needed and how to provide it. His aspirations were modest—never to let his clients down, and to make sure his small company survived.

Just another small company with modest beginnings. Yet a founder who works night and day from boyhood, and a business that demands 100-percent accuracy and on-time delivery can lead to unusual intensity—of purpose, of commitment, of day-to-day execution. In ADP's case this intensity generated a thirty-five-year record of sales and earnings perfor-mance that—to our knowledge—no other listed company on any United States stock exchange can match.* And it shows up clearly in ADP's strategic, organizational and management practices, which parallel closely the findings of this book.

---

*For another view of ADP's achievements, see "How to Manage an Evolution," *Forbes* (April 23, 1984), pp. 96–103.

ADP'S STRATEGY

ADP was born through an *innovation* that created a new business *niche*—a foolproof outside service to help small businesses meet their weekly payrolls—an area once the sole and secret province of the business owner. Its *high value* lay in the owner's peace of mind—he could be sick, he could travel or take a vacation and still know his people would get their pay envelopes on time.

Since the earliest days, ADP has *built on the strength* of its trusted relationships and intimate knowledge of payroll processing and reporting requirements. As succeeding waves of employment regulations were passed at state and federal levels, ADP was ready before the starting gun to provide the extensive analyses and reports that were called for. ADP was creative in understanding and meeting its clients' internal information needs in personnel management. And its operating, sales, and service skills—which have consistently allowed it to be low-cost producer as well as value leader in payroll systems—were the foundation for rolling its business out geographically across the United States. As its operations evolved from mechanical calculators and accounting machines through successive generations of increasingly powerful computers, ADP was able to maintain commanding cost and service advantages over its competitors—and an ROE averaging about 17 percent.

As its skills in managing and marketing computer services expanded, ADP began to apply them in a series of new market niches—and the pattern of service innovation, value to the customer, and continuing to build on strength were and continue to be the strategic thrust for the development of each. Its approach has been consistent and highly disciplined; rarely did ADP pioneer by starting a niche business from scratch, but rather its innovations lay in buying small and marginally successful companies and then reshaping their product line, operating methods, and sales approach to the ADP style. ADP has done this perhaps a dozen times. Let's look at three examples.

1. *Wall Street "back office" operations.* While the notion of a sound computer-based system for managing trading transactions, account records, and general brokerage accounting was not new in the early 1960s, ADP's "innovation" after buying a small pioneer firm already in the field was to develop the first system that really worked—and one that later proved it could meet the huge peak trading volumes that characterized the tumultuous days of the late 1960s and beyond. By doing this better than anyone else, ADP now serves about 20 percent

of the potential market for such services and is the leader in the "third party" market—those brokerage houses using outside computer services. In part, ADP has done well because many competitors have had systems that failed when confronted with massive trading days, and still others have been frightened off by the sight of well-known brokerage firms going out of business as they lost control over back-office operations. ADP's systems—and its clients—don't fail, and its customer list keeps growing.

2. *Collision estimating.* One of ADP's businesses that best illustrates how an innovative system can create a "sustainable competitive advantage" is its collision-estimating service, which combines a proprietary data base with cost-efficient data communications. The business, previously owned by Itel Corporation, was later acquired by ADP. The key to its subsequent success is the high value that ADP generates for both the individual consumer and for the insurance companies who pick up the tab for repairing cars damaged in accidents, by providing data available nowhere else. What the service does is simple: It describes clearly what it should cost to repair any kind of damage on any make or year of automobile, protecting both driver and insurance company against price gouging by upwardly mobile body shops.

In its computers, ADP has all the data it needs—based on actual experience around the country and the judgment of a panel of experts—on the time required to carry out every sort of repair. They also have prices on both new and used parts from all over the country, and wage scales for each labor trade within each geographic region. An insurance adjuster feeds detailed information on a damaged auto into ADP's computer communications network and within two minutes gets back a detailed printed estimate of the work involved to carry out the repair and what the cost should be. This becomes the basis for the insurance company to pay its policyholder and for the driver to obtain a reasonable price quotation for the work from his body shop.

ADP recently expanded its market by extending this service to isolated areas where computer terminals are not available to connect with the ADP network. ADP simply provides an 800 phone number to generate the same information by telephone—an innovation typical of the small incremental moves ADP makes continually to expand the scope of its markets and the strength of its position. Today, it would be very difficult for any competitor to recreate as extensive a data base and communications network as ADP has achieved in this high-value market niche.

3. *Automobile dealer services.* ADP's original entry into the automotive

market—one of the most complex information networks in the United States—started with the acquisition of a very small regional business in 1975. The problems it deals with relate to a number of the most fundamental needs confronting automobile dealers:

- keeping track of vehicle inventories
- vehicle leasing, servicing, and ordering
- for prospective buyers, locating cars throughout the country that have the precise characteristics and equipment they want
- locating critical parts that may be held by other dealers
- general dealership accounting, as well as other services.

ADP's system contains all the data, reports, and communications capabilities needed by the nation's car dealers to meet these demands—a function no individual dealer could perform on his own. In continuing to serve this niche, ADP has improved the service by selling or leasing a computer to the dealer, rather than handling all the data processing on ADP's own computers—a major shift from its traditional practice of centralized processing, and an example of ADP's adaptiveness in providing high-value service to customers.

Other new niches where ADP has built on its core strengths are banking services, "pay by phone" bill paying, funds transfer and other financial services, and massive data bases and data communications networks tailored to major industries. In each niche, ADP's goal—not always but usually achieved—has been to become an indispensable part of their customers' own way of doing business.

Not that ADP's efforts to enter new niches are universally successful— ADP too is only human. For example:

- At one point some years ago, ADP entered the business of preparing income taxes for certified public accountants. The field proved far too seasonal for ADP, with the work load peaking sharply in the weeks leading to April 15. And the cost and administrative headaches of tracking myriad changes in federal, state, and municipal tax codes left little room for profits. After two years of operation, ADP sold the business.
- With the acquisition of two small companies in the early 1970s, ADP entered what was to become a major growth market for computer services—the hospital-information market. As Josh Weston described ADP's experience to us, "It was the right market and the right timing, but we didn't give the business either the senior management attention or the operating talent needed in the formative years of an explo-

sively growing and changing field. That was a big mistake and after four years we were so far behind our expectations that we decided to sell the business."

Because of such experiences, ADP today is committed to intensive analysis and extensive senior management involvement in each niche it enters.

In summary, ADP was born through innovation; has grown through intensive commitment to a series of market niches; has built on its fundamental strengths in computer and communication-network design, operations, and marketing; has learned from its mistakes; and has staked its success on providing such high value to its clients that ADP can sustain its unusually successful profit growth rate and return on investment.

ORGANIZATION: DISCIPLINED FREEDOM

From its earliest days, ADP's need for organizational discipline has been overriding—but so has its need for individual freedom to promote rapid adaptation, innovation, and responsiveness in the rapidly changing world of computer-based information systems. When the company was small, both the discipline and the creativity came personally from Henry Taub; his brother, Joe; and Frank Lautenberg, later chairman of ADP and now U.S. senator from New Jersey. With growth, ADP has had to build both qualities into the organization—a challenge of the first order. Let's start with discipline.

To make the point one more time, payrolls are sacred. People must be paid at the right time, in the right amount. As a result, from the very beginning, ADP emphasized speed, accuracy, and reliability, and it supported these goals with very tight budgets, incentives, and controls. Computer operations had to be backed up in case there was a breakdown; if getting out the payroll meant working all night long, that's what was expected and done.

With growth and diversification, these disciplines had to be adapted and extended again and again. The company added new divisions as it moved out into new niches. To learn more about the disciplines and controls of large, successful companies, ADP brought in new talent from other corporate cultures at high levels (unlike many other winning-performance companies we've studied, several current division general managers came into ADP well up in the organization, with experience in other major companies). Structural and systems changes were frequent and necessary to stay on top of rapidly changing and increasingly complex businesses.

By the early 1970s there was a growing recognition that maintaining an adaptive, innovative organization in a climate of intensive controls and discipline needed more attention. Applying their own personal discipline and intense involvement to the problem, ADP senior management undertook a number of steps to achieve a better balance, including but not limited to the following:

- Increasingly, several levels of management came together frequently to talk about the business in all of its aspects. Line managers, corporate functional managers, and senior corporate management all attended, and the meetings were noted for their open and interactive quality. These sessions were no-holds-barred, direct, and sometimes combative—but they did provide a forum for all to participate in the most important aspects of the development of the company. Equally important, all managers knew they had a say in the corporation's future, and access to the ear of the chairman and president.
- ADP hired a senior human-resources manager to assist the chief executive officer as an "appointed renegade" in a tightly disciplined organization. His job was to give emphasis to the human side of the company and to remind people—particularly general managers—of ADP's strong desire for creativity, personal initiative, constructive criticism, and informality in its demanding, fast-moving environment.
- In 1977, top management appointed a task force—"Task Force '80"—and charged it with making recommendations to corporate management on major priorities for strategy and organization for 1980 and beyond. This task force included the general managers of each of the major service divisions as well as top corporate staff executives, and the reports and recommendations they produced led to significant changes in both structure and management systems at ADP.

As you may have guessed, ADP is not a restful place to work. The work pace is intense and an important part of ADP's success. CEO Josh Weston sets that pace, and when he's in town you can usually find him at his desk by seven-thirty after an early-morning jog of two miles or so. When traveling, Weston's normal schedule is to start over breakfast with one or more of ADP's field people, followed by a program of visits with both customers and ADP employees at several levels of the organization, wrapping up with a dinner and frequently postdinner conversation. These exposures keep Weston on top of his business, and the example is not lost on the rest of the organization, which operates with similar intensity.

To get a more complete picture of how these qualities of discipline, freedom, and intensity add up to winning, let's have a look at each high-performance organizational characteristic as it applies to ADP.

Mission and Values

ADP's management team shares a common view of the company's mission and values. These have been painstakingly spelled out in ADP's "Corporate Philosophy," which was first published in 1980 and updated in 1984. Significantly, ADP's philosophy simply does not allow for trade-offs among short-term performance, long-term performance, and the development of a strong organization—ADP wants it all. The notion of trade-offs has become all too popular in American business management, where the rational left-side brain leads managers to say: "If you want me to invest in developing products and markets for the long term, that will cost money in the short term and I can't deliver as high a near-term profit. And if you want me to develop people, we can't spend as much time and money in the development of either long- or short-term profits."

ADP's attitude is that there can be no trade-off—its people are expected to do all three. This attitude generates adrenaline and creates tension, but it also results in a higher level of corporate achievement. Perhaps the lesson is that the dissatisfied organization, the one with high standards that can never be fully met, is the one that will create constructive tensions that lead to long-term success.

ADP's outstanding long-term profit record reflects this point of view. Profit goals are crystal clear, and incentive programs are tied to their achievement.

Among its primary objectives, the client comes first, as its philosophy makes clear: "Client service is number one at ADP. Our growth objectives leave little room for losing clients. Each of our clients is precious. They need us only if we provide them with accurate, efficient, and responsive service. The client is preeminent and should be treated accordingly."

ADP's philosophy then goes on to spell out its high standards for quality service, continuing product improvement, and high-value innovation, its dedication to market leadership and outstanding financial performance, and its commitments to its people and culture: "Let us end where we began, with the people of ADP, who are the backbone of our success."

Empty words? Far from it, as we have learned from discussions with people from all parts of ADP. But perhaps most impressive, and a measure of the dedication of the organization to these values, is the widespread view that ADP is far from meeting its own high standards. Here is one of the most outstanding records of any company under $1 billion in sales today (although ADP will cross the $1 billion mark by the time this book goes to press), and yet its people—rather than rejoicing in their success—are more likely to say:

- "We don't begin to spend the time developing and motivating people that we should."
- "We still put too much emphasis on making our short-term financial goals, and not enough on thinking through how we can serve our clients better in the future and continue earning the right to still higher levels of profit."
- "We aren't nearly as innovative as we should be, or as aggressive in moving into new areas of high potential as we should be."

A clear mission, high standards, an unresolvable tension among three unshakable values, and an eternal sense of dissatisfaction—quite a recipe for success!

Attention to the Fundamentals

The single most vivid characteristic of ADP's management system and organization is its intensive discipline. Born of the need for error-less accounting services delivered on time to clients, the company's fundamental controls and disciplines are comprehensive and very strong.

At the first level of the organization, this discipline is institutionalized in the Tuesday night sales meetings referred to as "roll call." At some fifty separate meetings around the country, each salesman in turn gets up to report the sales that he has made during the prior week and any other major developments. This practice has two effects. First, no salesman wants to get up two, let alone three weeks in a row without having some good news to report in the form of new business, so the pressure for performance is intense. As Josh Weston puts it, "Each salesman sees his peers fifty times per year, so there is nowhere to hide." Second, these meetings give immediate feedback on competitive and market developments. Most companies are on a monthly sales cycle; if one of their customers, markets, or salesmen is having trouble, it will not show up for two or three months. At ADP, it takes only two or three weeks.

ADP's incentive systems are yet another discipline. Bonus incentives are tied directly to the achievement of sales, service, and profit goals, and the fact that both success and the lack of it are widely communicated is another major motivator.

The disciplined management of ADP's operations begins at the very top of the company with its rigorous annual operating plans for each profit center, and three- to five-year strategic plans for each business. But the real significance of these plans is not in their existence, since such plans can be found in most companies. The secret is in the clear expectation that managers will achieve their plans or find a way to correct shortfalls and get back on plan—a highly disciplined and intensive focus on success.

Fight Bureaucracy, Encourage Experimentation

Given its strong disciplines, ADP has developed an equally strong set of practices to keep it from becoming too rigid or bureaucratized. Some of these were outlined at the start of this section; here are several more:

- *An emphasis on decentralization.* ADP has more than a dozen individual businesses that are run with a high degree of independence, and within them ADP maintains offices in more than a hundred cities, with each local manager responsible for his own client development and service, as well as financial performance. ADP has consistently stayed with its philosophy of maintaining small business units with a high level of delegated authority and responsibility.
- *Small staff.* "As in a Japanese company, if you look for staff around here, you will have trouble finding it." Overwhelmingly, line business managers at ADP take responsibility for doing all those things necessary to the success of their business, rather than delegating them to staff.
- *Intensive effort to improve communication across organizational lines.* ADP has a Human Resources Council, made up of the division presidents. Its mission is to draw on the experience of all the council members in devising new ways to accelerate and improve the development of ADP's executive group. ADP also has a Strategic Council, which provides high-level interaction beyond day-to-day operating issues, and an Executive Committee consisting of ADP's three line group presidents, the president of the company, and the chief financial officer. To get even broader interaction, ADP's senior management group, made up of the top forty to fifty executives in the company, meets two or three times a year to address the fundamental issues facing the company.

Think Like the Customers

Every twelve months, and every six months when a business is changing rapidly or new approaches are being tested, ADP sends out a customer survey to each of its clients asking for a performance evaluation on ADP itself. In one instance, this important means for measuring broad customer reaction brought to the surface the fact that client service response time and response quality had been deteriorating in a major Northern city. Normally, ADP's customer service is performed by small teams of five or six customer service representatives with responsibility for a relatively small number of clients and with a good deal of continuity in their relationship with those clients. When the client survey pointed out that things were not going well, further investigation found that client service teams in that city had grown far too large—up to fifteen people—and were handling far too many clients to give the personalized attention to each client that ADP's business—and its policies— call for.

The solution was to go from two client-team clusters to four, and service once again improved markedly. Another significant fact: It was ADP's president who called the local customer service manager, four levels below him, to bring attention to this problem and initiate action— both a symbol of ADP's dedication to cutting across lines to get things done quickly, and a reminder to all managers to monitor results.

Calling directly on customers gets heavy emphasis, and Josh Weston's practice of calling on customers periodically is as much designed to set an example for others as it is to keep his own finger on the pulse of the marketplace. Once again, a mark of ADP management's eternal dissatisfaction is the conviction that most managers still should be spending more time with customers, identifying little ways to improve service and relationships.

An Emphasis on People

Bob Miller, ADP's vice president of human resources, initially turned down a job at ADP because he was not sure the company put enough emphasis on the development of its executive manpower. According to Miller, the reason he later accepted was the "dirty dozen."

In the late 1970s, when ADP was expanding rapidly and needed a large influx of skilled managers and functional specialists to support the growing company, the company thought the appeal of its dramatic growth story would be irresistible. Not the case. Twelve times between 1977 and 1979, people whom ADP sought to bring into the company in key positions turned them down. To find out why ADP had been a rejected suitor, Josh Weston had follow-up interviews conducted with each of these twelve people in an exercise that became known as the "dirty-dozen study."

The results of the study indicated that ADP had not been sensitive to the need to spell out in detail what the role of an executive introduced into ADP management at higher levels would in fact be. Those being recruited from far larger corporations were accustomed to very clear job descriptions and future career tracks, as well as to a much clearer picture of what the compensation and promotion prospects might be. ADP's entrepreneurial mode was to say, "Come on aboard—there's so much going on that your talents can contribute to, we will figure out your assignments as we go along." This and other aspects of ADP's unsuccessful recruiting approach all surfaced during the dirty-dozen study and led to major improvements in ADP's practices. It also led to Bob Miller's belief that ADP really did care about its people, and shortly afterward he joined the company.

CEO Josh Weston sees his own most important role as the development and encouragement of people. The week prior to one of our discussions with Weston, he had visited Chicago, San Francisco, and Los Angeles, spoken individually with thirty-five members of ADP's field organizations, and had talked with more than two hundred people in groups—as well as making a number of customer calls. Weston tries to maintain human contact and has been known to call field managers and treat them and their spouses to a night on the town when they have made an unusual accomplishment. He sees his central role as one of creating and maintaining a culture that turns on the energy and creates interaction among ADP's people, and on the other hand that minimizes politics.

Yet Weston confronts his organization with a dilemma. He is seen as someone who is so organized and rational that it is difficult to deal with him on easy human terms. Some years ago, Josh was presented by his managers with a parking meter—the significance being that when you saw Josh you had a finite and limited time to state your case before the time was up. Characteristically, Weston has tried to deal with this dilemma by setting up a counterforce: "I encourage pushback—debate—from all levels of management to give me a check and balance on my own eccentricities. I know they will come back at me, and so with people like that around I can afford to be myself." Weston understands ADP's constant need for a balance of tensions, even at the very top.

CEO Leadership: A Man for Each Season

Perhaps in the most important sense, the story of Automatic Data Processing is a tale of three leaders—each a very different personality who fulfilled or is fulfilling a different role. As much as any company, ADP highlights both the critical role of the CEO and the vital importance of having that role change as corporate conditions change. In our view, ADP's history could not have been written without each of the three chief executives who have led the company, nor would it have done nearly as well had there been a change in the order of their coming.

Henry Taub was the entrepreneur with the vision to create a payroll business and the relentless commitment to make it work—the man with the patience to spend twelve years bringing his company to $420,000 in sales while frequently working into the wee hours of the morning, then returning to his desk at the crack of dawn. Taub told *Forbes:* "We were young, none of us was married, time didn't have the value it has when you get older."* Yet he was a man with the breadth and leadership quality to continue as CEO of that company as it grew from $420,000 in 1961 to $188 million in 1976. And he had both sufficient charisma and judgment to attract a Frank Lautenberg in the early 1950s and enough ego control to turn over the CEO title to him in 1976.

Today, Taub continues to lend his full support to Josh Weston, serving as chairman while Weston is president and CEO. Now, most of Taub's time is devoted to philanthropy, which he pursues with the same joyful obsessiveness that he showed in his early round-the-clock years at ADP.

Taub's major contributions at ADP go well beyond the establishment of the business itself. He established ADP's dedication to reliable, high-quality service that remains the underpinning of the firm to this day. In summary, Taub matches our model of the winning-company CEO: innovator, obsessed leader, corporate builder who put the success of his enterprise above personal ego, a risk-taker who took not only the entrepreneurial risk at the outset, but the management risk on successive generations to whom he gave over control. He modified his role sufficiently to give Lautenberg and Weston extensive management control at ADP even before he stepped down as CEO, and he planned not only his own but a second successful CEO transition as well.

Frank Lautenberg met Henry Taub in the early days of Automatic Payrolls (as ADP was known at the outset) and formally joined the company full time in 1954, devoting himself primarily to sales. Well before becoming chief executive in 1976, he had embarked upon the course that set his stamp forever on ADP's future shape: the dramatic acquisition program that rolled out ADP's core employee services/payroll business across the nation, gave it the scale advantage of massive computer power, and took the company into a broad array of new related niches. Lautenberg is widely credited as the architect and chief negotia-

*"How to Manage an Evolution," *Forbes* (April 23, 1984), p. 100.

tor of ADP's acquisition program, a master of the art of edging out who completed about a hundred acquisitions before his departure to the Senate in 1982.

Lautenberg's determination to build ADP into the preeminent computer services company in the country also made him an aggressive hirer of outside talent. From the likes of IBM, Digital Equipment, Burroughs, and many more top companies, he brought in a host of key early players in ADP's growth. As Lautenberg told us, "I knew that I had to professionalize management, that ADP was rapidly growing well beyond my control. So I brought in people with the skills to run a giant company."

Fate seems to have played a vital card in 1970, when Lautenberg hired a man away from Popular Services, Inc., whose general manager was Josh S. Weston. "When Josh argued with me and tried to keep me from taking his man, I quickly learned just how good Josh was," Lautenberg said. "I also probed a bit and found out that Josh was running the whole company, but that he had no equity in the business. Before long, I hired Josh, and—with Henry Taub as chairman—we ran the company as a team for the next decade."

In brief, Lautenberg was a team and corporate builder, a risk-taker who brought the company into many new fields, and, together with Taub, engineer of the succession of Josh Weston to the CEO position at the time of his own departure for the Senate.

Lautenberg later told Josh Weston: "Your problem is that you don't yet have your own Josh Weston." At this writing, there is for the first time since ADP's earliest days no clear number-two man at ADP, although one may emerge in the next year or so. For now, Weston looks to the Executive Committee as a forum in which each member can continue to develop and contribute to running the day-to-day business. ADP is a far larger, more diverse and dispersed company than most of the winning performers we've looked at, and given today's rapid change in both technology and market structure, it probably makes great sense to let ADP's next leader emerge from a core group of sector managers and functional heads.

In a real sense, Josh Weston's obsession with the business may be the most intense of the three. But perhaps most important, while he is seen as a hands-on operating man to this day, Weston has truly begun to "professionalize" the management of ADP. Time and again, he has brought in talented outside executives and given them extensive high-level responsibility.

In business decisions and new product introductions, Weston is cautious. He insists on extensive analysis, experimentation, and planning. The risks he takes appear to be on people—in the introduction of key new blood into high positions in the company.

In brief, the strength of Automatic Data Processing derives from its leaders, who have championed its intensive, niche-oriented strategy and its self-critical organization. For longer than any other company we know, ADP has been able to balance the demands of a rapid-growth company, a fast-changing industry, and the retention of its own historic operating performance.

The lesson from ADP is one of balance and commitment. ADP's moves have not been abrupt—they have been calculated, they have been incremental. But they have been so many and so skillful—despite its failures and businesses that have yet to show a profit—that the company's performance stands out as one of the most dramatic the country has seen in the past thirty-five years.

THE WINNING TEAM AT SEALED AIR CORPORATION

"You have to admire a company that consistently doubles its sales and earnings every three years by selling air!" This remark was directed at Sealed Air Corporation, the creator and developer of the market for trapped-air "bubble packaging" used to protect fragile things.

Sealed Air doesn't really "sell air"—it markets protection against shock, vibration, abrasion, corrosion, and electrostatic discharge. It also markets more than packaging materials—it sells systems that protect customers' products while they are in storage, manufacturing, or distribution, and that lower customers' packaging costs by improving their productivity (output per worker in some cases has increased more than 100 percent).* Sealed Air's motto is: "Our products protect your products"—corny perhaps, but an apt description of Sealed Air's mission.

In contrast to the high-tech genius of Cray Research and the business intensity of ADP, Sealed Air's story is a lot less sexy. Packaging is generally low-tech, mundane stuff—a product whose destiny is to be

*"Air Bubbles Pay Off in Five Ways for a Packager," *Canadian Packaging* (May 1981), p. 20.

thrown away after serving a fleeting purpose. But Sealed Air has made it an exciting business for both shareholders and employees by creating or acquiring a series of high-growth niches, and, through technical and marketing agility, building a leading position in each. Sealed Air exemplifies the full range of qualities—strategy, organization, and leadership—described in this book. But in our judgment, the premier secret of its success is organization. It has built a culture not of scientific geniuses or around-the-clock computer-systems whizzes, but of solid make-and-sell businessmen who feel part of a winning team.

Under this team, Sealed Air's performance has been extraordinary. From 1971 to 1984, sales grew at a compound rate of 27 percent and earnings at 29 percent. The company's one downturn during the period came in 1982, and it was quickly reversed through cost-cutting, product development, and increased marketing effort, bringing Sealed Air out of the recession with substantially improved market shares.

SEALED AIR'S STRATEGY

Sealed Air has consistently displayed the characteristics of innovation, niche orientation, building on strength, and high value that typify the winning companies. In markets characterized by relatively modest growth and gradual technological change, it has also made continuous improvements and entered new niches that provided the basis for sustaining its market position and rapid growth rate, and got itself back on track quickly when faced with business downturns.

A film clip of the Sealed Air strategy and business position would reveal a company whose foundation lay in *innovation*—the creation of a wholly new cushioning material that guaranteed a far higher level of protection to sensitive and valuable products than the traditional excelsior, sawdust, or crushed newspaper. That product is "air cellular laminate" —layers of plastic film with thousands of air bubbles trapped in between—the kind your kids (and maybe you) like to pop after unwrapping it from your new videotape recorder. Building on this original idea, Sealed Air continued to innovate, adding eighteen patents for product and process improvements.

Sealed Air has been innovative in developing new applications as well as new products. As founder Al Fielding put it, "At the beginning, we probably had two hundred ideas on how to use our air cellular material—packaging simply proved to be the best of these. But we have always sought new and high-value uses for AirCap [Sealed Air's registered trademark for its best bubble wrap]." Sealed Air's innovativeness has also been applied to the systems that are used on its customers' packaging production lines and in its own manufacturing and distribution processes. For example:

- In 1976, Sealed Air purchased Instapak, a foam-in-place system that squirts a blend of plastics through a special applicator "gun" into the carton that holds a personal computer or some other bulky, fragile product. Within fifteen seconds, the plastic expands to 140 times its liquid state, forming a foam cushion that holds the product in place and protects it from impact. Not only has Sealed Air's continuing research led to major innovative improvements in the appearance and performance of this material, but it has repeatedly improved application speed through, for example, automatic cleaning attachments to keep the "guns" free of gummy plastic, and the development of semi-automated and automated production equipment for applying the material at higher speeds. The trade journal *Modern Materials Handling* cites one example in which production speeds were improved by a factor of four—a major cost reduction for Sealed Air's customer.*
- Building on its film-coating technology, Sealed Air created a new easy-peel masking film—Poly Mask—which adheres to the shiny metal surfaces of parts and products (such as stainless steel furniture or household appliances and fixtures) during manufacturing, handling, and shipping, protecting them from scratching until they are installed and the Poly Mask is peeled off.
- Sealed Air has created a variety of products that incorporate its bubble packaging material, such as cushioned mailing envelopes—its "Mail Lite" and "Bubble-Lite" products—which provide very lightweight and highly protective containers for small gift items, audiocassettes, and other small, fragile things. Over the years it has continued to add features (such as self-sealing) to these products.
- Sealed Air dramatically improved the economics of distributing rolls of its feather-light bubble packaging material to customers by utilizing huge trailer bodies of extremely light weight. Sealed Air no longer has to pay the high price of trucks capable of carrying forty thousand pounds or more to "ship air" around the country!
- Meanwhile, development goes on in other new forms of packaging and protection that offer value and economies to customers. One of the latest of these is Instafil, a substitute for the familiar polystyrene cushioning "peanuts."

*" 'Smart' Foam-in-Place System Shortens Molding Time by 75%," *Modern Materials Handling* (November 5, 1982), pp. 60–62.

Each of these innovations has been designed to create or meet the needs of a *market niche* and to *make money for customers* in that niche. For example, Sealed Air has recently entered a new niche market—for cushioning material requiring a high level of flame resistance—by offering a material that is the least flammable plastic on the market today. In yet another niche, Sealed Air caters to major electronics and computer firms that have special problems of moving very sensitive and high-cost products around the world. And Sealed Air also offers products and application systems designed for manufacturers of high-quality glassware, marketers of commemorative plates, wine retailers, and scores of others. It achieves its high growth by finding one tiny niche after another.

Sealed Air has consistently *built on strength* in entering new niches and growing its businesses. The Poly Mask product was based predominantly on the company's skills in plastic coating and its sales and distribution capabilities in a very broad range of product protection markets. Sealed Air has made seven acquisitions over the years, and every one of these has been an extension of Sealed Air's marketing or manufacturing capabilities. Each has also been integrated into Sealed Air to achieve low cost along with high value, and thus maximum benefit to Sealed Air's customers. For example, Instapak is managed as a separate product line (but not a separate business). Instapak is thus seen as one of a number of ways to provide protection to customers' products—through the same sales and marketing organization as bubble wrap, rather than as a freestanding division.

In the late 1970s, Sealed Air entered a market niche that builds on its unique position in plastic air bubble manufacturing: a swimming-pool products line that keeps the dirt out of pools and the heat in. In simplest terms, Sealed Air found that its Air Cap material could not only provide a lightweight cover for swimming pools, but also absorb the heat of the sun during the day, warming the pool, and provide insulation against the cold at night, retaining heat as well as preventing loss of water through evaporation. Sealed Air took the business a step further by adding a passive solar panel, which adds incremental heat to the pool and in some cases eliminates the need for a heater.

Virtually all of the Sealed Air products we've described, and others we haven't, make money for Sealed Air's customers. That's a key to its strategy. In terms of value to the customer, Sealed Air's philosophy and practices were well summarized by CEO Dermot Dunphy in his remark, "There is no such thing as a commodity." Dunphy's point is that there will always be innovative ways to improve a customer's packaging economics, not only through better materials but through faster application; by improving the availability of materials and supplies so that customers can reduce their inventories or eliminate downtime on their packaging lines; or simply through more consistent product quality than competitors.

One other major value that Sealed Air provides its customers is its packaging engineering service—twenty-four labs across the United States and abroad to which customers can bring their packaging problems and develop solutions with help from Sealed Air's people. In short, Sealed Air has made its customers' profits Sealed Air's own business, and by providing value to customers it has continued to enhance its own profit and returns.

Responding to Trouble

The packaging industry is cyclical, particularly those materials and systems sold to package recession-prone industrial products rather than more stable consumer goods. Sealed Air has shown itself highly adaptive strategically in tough times, and especially so in the 1981–82 downturn. It not only bounced back quickly, but it used the dislocation to take market share away from competitors.

The dip in Sealed Air's profits in 1982 was more than just a result of a general packaging industry downturn during the recession. During the late 1970s, somewhat lulled by rapid expansion and high profits, Sealed Air allowed marketing and staff expenses to build up excessively. Because its emphasis had shifted toward marketing, it had also gradually slipped in technological leadership, causing a slow response to some competitive product improvements.

Once Sealed Air management spotted the problem, it was quick to take action, even before the recession started. In 1980—two years before these problems showed up in financial results—feedback from customers caused Sealed Air to undertake a strategic reappraisal of its market position. This effort turned up the fact that one of the company's major competitors in the foam-in-place packaging business had developed both a more aesthetically attractive material and a more reliable application system. At that same time, Sealed Air also reached the conviction that the balance of management's attention had shifted too much toward marketing and that the time for reemphasis on product development was at hand.

Sealed Air's new commitment to technical development was accelerated by the sense that a recession was on the way, believing that most competitors would cut back on product development during this period. Sealed Air managers saw this as a major opportunity to take market share away from competition if they could come out with superior products at precisely the time that financial pressures were most affecting their competitors. With that in mind, Sealed Air tripled its research and development budget; increased the company's capital investment in research facilities; and made a major drive to hire people at the Ph.D. as well as technician levels to strengthen Sealed Air's research competence.

One of the outputs of this enhanced research-and-development effort was substantial improvement in the foam-in-place product and in the speed and reliability of its applicator systems. On the basis of these improvements, Sealed Air recovered its clear leadership position in this core market. In 1980, *Financial World* estimated Sealed Air's share of the foam-in-place market at 80 percent.* The company also made major improvements in its bubble wrap products, and extended the line into uncoated films to meet new competition for products with less demanding protection requirements.

Sealed Air also had the courage to lower its prices (at the temporary expense of some margin dollars) during the recession in order to take share from weaker competitors, leaving fewer dollars to the competition for both marketing and product development. With the return of market growth, Sealed Air allowed prices to rise, and competitors that had been experiencing far worse financial pressure than Sealed Air followed.

Simultaneously, during the recession, Sealed Air stepped up to the need for a more disciplined approach to staffing and expense levels. The company carried out an exhaustive review of all its executive manpower and made significant reductions, with each case handled individually and personally by the chief executive. The sensitive way this was perceived to have been handled has helped materially to retain the high morale that characterizes the organization.

ORGANIZATION: A CLASSLESS SOCIETY

Sealed Air's innovative, make-money-for-the-customer strategy and its success in emerging from an adverse period stronger than it had been exist only because of a committed team of people operating in a "classless society"—to use a phrase we heard often from Sealed Air people.

The team spirit that underlies Sealed Air's success over the past fourteen years was dramatized on one of our visits to corporate headquarters in the fall of 1984. Unlike most of our corporate meetings, we began not with a lengthy solo interview with the chief executive but in a

---

*"It's All in the Packaging," *Financial World* (March 1, 1980), p. 48.

joint meeting that included Dunphy; his senior management team; one outside director; and Dunphy's administrative assistant, Barbara Lewis. We later interviewed each of these key players individually, but Dunphy wanted them together at the outset—to symbolize Sealed Air's team approach to running the business.

The presence of an outside director at this initial meeting was also unusual in our experience, although not for Sealed Air, and confirmed what we had been told by others outside the company: namely, that board members are treated virtually as members of management. They are expected to be fully informed and to make contributions to corporate thinking. Robert L. San Soucie, the director, whom we interviewed later that day, told us that he typically spends five hours or more per week on the company, which is far above average.

The presence of Alfred Fielding, today executive vice president and in 1960 cofounder of Sealed Air, was another clue to the openness and supportiveness of this team organization. In the average midsize company, once a founder is no longer chief executive, he is rarely seen. At Sealed Air, Fielding is regarded as one of the most valuable members of senior management and continues to provide active leadership in his field of greatest interest and expertise—the development of new products and market niches. As Seymour Cray did more recently, Fielding decided in the late 1960s that technology, not management, was his primary interest, and gave up the CEO responsibilities. Time and again, in our discussions and in his speeches, Dunphy emphasizes the importance of Fielding's perspective and insights to the management of the company. Founder Fielding later confirmed our sense of Dunphy's ability to make people feel productive and part of a team: "Dermot has a way of bringing out the best in us and building on the best ideas. He creates consensus around the best thinking, and he ends up with everyone in the boat together on any major decision that we make. In part he achieves this because there are no recriminations for small mistakes—they are regarded as part of the learning process. The question is—what do we learn from our mistakes and how do we capitalize on what we have learned?"

In contrast to the major changes that have taken place in Sealed Air's strategy over the past decade and a half, there is remarkable stability and continuity in management. All but one of Sealed Air's senior management team were with the company a dozen years ago, when Sealed Air was a small company of $5 million in sales, and Dunphy was brought in by the board as CEO. Conventional wisdom says that a new CEO coming in from outside the company brings his own team with him—"a new broom sweeps clean." In Dunphy's case, he built on the team already in place, and as a result he has a strong management group with a continuity of perspective and a sense of identity with the company that has strengthened over the years.

Given its culture, it is not surprising that Sealed Air strongly exhibits the six qualities of effective organization described earlier in this book in its mission and values, attention to fundamentals, avoidance of bureaucracy, emphasis on trying new things, its commitment to its customers, and its focus on people.

Mission and Values

Closely related to the value Sealed Air places on maintaining a "classless society," one often hears another phrase that for some might sound either trite or obscure—"success and humanity." At Sealed Air, the phrase has real meaning. When we first read those words in Dermot Dunphy's handwritten response to our eighty-two-item ABC questionnaire, we had no idea how often we would hear them from multiple levels of Sealed Air management during our interviews. They summarize the spirit that drives the company—to be winners, but to do so by dealing people in and by helping people develop their full potential. In the words of George Shegog, senior vice president, finance, who joined Sealed Air in 1970: "When I came here from Price Waterhouse, I thought I'd probably stay from two to four years—I'm shocked that I'm still here fourteen years later! There's a strong sense of winning in this company that extends from the janitor to the president, and it's given me opportunities to grow far beyond my expectations. Just as vital, we are all part of the team, and we all treat each other as equally important." Success—winning—*and* humanity.

Sealed Air has expressed its mission in a set of strategic guidelines that are articulated and understood deep in the company:

1. Focus on differentiated, proprietary products that produce economically measurable benefits to our industrial and consumer purchasers.
2. Stimulate new product development to utilize our well-established distribution channels.
3. Seek market leadership because market leadership maximizes long-term profit.
4. Foster technological leadership because it is the only long-term guarantee of market leadership.
5. Exploit the greater market potential and develop the increased competitive effectiveness that result from multinational operations.

Part of the power of these guidelines is that they were announced publicly in Sealed Air's annual report for 1980. When management is on the record, the commitment to make good on its promises is substantially increased—and so far Sealed Air has run ahead of plan.

And Dunphy reinforces these objectives and values through periodic memoranda and speeches to employees—"Sealed Air Code of Conduct"; "The Conflicting Roles of a Controller in a Decentralized Financial Organization"; "No Such Thing as a Commodity"; "Role of the Plant Manager"; "The History and Significance of Technology at Sealed Air Corporation"; and many more designed to emphasize the dual role of all managers within Sealed Air both to carry out their functions fully and to support each other and the interests of the corporation consistently.

Underlying all these and the focus on accomplishment is a strong sense of fun. Dunphy's sense of humor is seldom far below the surface. At our kickoff, we rarely went five minutes without some good chuckles, and that was cited by the attendees as pretty much standard operating procedure. At Sealed Air they get a kick out of winning.

Attention to Fundamentals

There is a powerful discipline at Sealed Air that imposes on management the obligation to adapt as well as to operate effectively. Perhaps it was best summarized by Elmer N. "Pete" Funkhouser III, senior vice president, international: "Five minutes into any discussion, someone says, 'How does this fit into what we are trying to accomplish in the company?' " With all the pressures of day-to-day operations and with the hundreds of details that must be resolved daily, this discipline constantly reminds Sealed Air executives to focus on the fundamental value of every action to its customers and the company and to test whether it really fits with the corporation's long-term objectives, values, and interests.

Sealed Air also gives discipline to the common cause of its executives with clear quantitative financial objectives: an earnings growth rate of more than 20 percent, a 7 percent net margin on sales, a 20 percent return on investment, an equity-to-long-term-debt ratio of at least 2 to 1, a current ratio of at least 1.5 to 1, and the ability to remain substantially self-financing while simultaneously paying dividends of approximately 20 to 25 percent of earnings.

Sealed Air has strong current operating reports, budgeting systems, and competitive information. The company's emphasis on sustaining high profits and self-financing, as well as the fiercely competitive nature of its business, led to a very cost-conscious approach to running the business— managers do not want to waste a penny and are consistently finding new ways to squeeze costs out of the business. Their strong orientation to discovering new ways to improve their customers' economics through product and application improvements carries over into the discipline they apply to their own business in the constant search for improvement.

In brief, Sealed Air has outstanding internal and external information and puts it to use in a highly disciplined environment.

Fight Bureaucracy

Pete Funkhouser points out that he runs his $30-million international operation with a staff consisting of himself and one secretary. Because the company considers the development of its people a central task of line management, Sealed Air does not have a human-resources executive. The company does not use organization charts, nor does it have job grading or formal job evaluation procedures, since this—in Dunphy's words—could lead to "evaluating the job rather than the performance of the person in the job." By avoiding bureaucrats, Sealed Air helps avoid bureaucracy.

The company makes extensive use of small task-oriented teams. The company's development of Instafill, its answer to the polystyrene "peanuts" that you find on your floor the day after Christmas, was accomplished by a team consisting of a chemical engineer, a chemist, and a salesman, all spending less than full time. One salesman and two technical people teamed up to develop the automated Instapak machine, and Merle Brown, senior vice president, technology and manufacturing, reported that he had recently met with ten technical project teams at work on separate product and process improvement efforts.

Encourage Experimentation

One Sealed Air practice is to encourage experimental thinking through what it calls "vertical/horizontal" management. Under this concept (which is similar to Analog Devices' concept of dual career ladders), Sealed Air seeks to ensure that managing other people is not the only road to success in the company. It wants high-achieving individual performers who can contribute new ideas, and the leading and most visible example of success is Executive Vice President Al Fielding—who is well paid, highly respected, and has no one reporting to him. Sealed Air, more than most companies, emphasizes that there are two distinct roads to high position and esteem in the company as well as to high financial rewards: personal accomplishment and managerial leadership.

Dermot Dunphy reflects the creative, experimental attitude of Sealed Air in these comments on Richard Sperry, the inventor of Instapak: "I once asked Dick Sperry how someone with a degree in biology, which he has, became an inventor of mechanical objects. He replied that it was perfectly logical, that everything had already been invented in nature and that by analogy, he merely transferred some of the ideas into steel and plastic.

"Accordingly, we do not look always to the most formally trained engineers or chemists for our innovation but seek to identify and nurture the creative spirit wherever we find it."*

Sealed Air also expects and accepts mistakes, looking at them as an integral part of learning rather than as a reason for punishment. In the words of director Robert San Soucie, reflecting on our kickoff meeting with Sealed Air management: "Everyone at that table has made a serious mistake at some time in the past. We don't fire them—we say work your way out of it and learn from it. And we end up with better managers as well as good new ideas as a result."

Think Like the Customer

The most powerful incentive to understand a customer's business as well as the customer does is the will to beat competitors. But beyond this fundamental drive, Sealed Air has created a series of organizational devices to be sure it remains close to the people who pay all the bills.

- *Technical conferences* in which a large number of customers' technical people are brought in and asked to present their problems to the whole group. Not only do these provide direct help to customers, who get ideas from others that help them improve their own operations, but it leads to substantial ideas for product improvement at Sealed Air.
- *Buyer seminars* in which purchasing executives from customer and potential customer companies are brought in and informed of Sealed Air's packaging capabilities. These seminars often lead to new application ideas and directly to new customers.
- *Sealed Air's packaging service laboratories,* where new packaging applications and production techniques are tested out for customers.
- *Executive visits* in which members of the Sealed Air executive group visit frequently with customers to determine their needs and how well Sealed Air is meeting them.

The central thrust of Sealed Air's business is to understand its customers' protection requirements and find the most economic way of meeting them.

Sealed Air's account representatives not infrequently end up their days working on the packaging lines of their customers. This not only

*Speech by T. J. Dermot Dunphy before the Newcomen Society of North America, in New York City (May 13, 1982).

cements the relationship by helping the customer to improve his packaging performance, but it gives the Sealed Air representative an in-depth and detailed understanding of his customer's needs and problems. As Larry Chandler, senior vice president, North American operations, put it, the company succeeded because "we became a consultant to our customer, a partner to our distributors, and a participant in our industry."

Emphasis on People

In a 1984 talk to a Sealed Air technical meeting, Dermot Dunphy summarized some of the innovative technical improvements in the company that had created new products, improved old ones, and generated savings in Sealed Air's manufacturing costs. Most important, his comments reflect a view of people in organizations that is fundamental to the company's culture and continued success:

> My first lesson [in the management of technology] was to seek out and nurture the creativity that exists in all of the people within our organization. The human mind is our fundamental resource; and nature has concealed at the bottom of everyone's mind talents and abilities of which he or she is not aware. As Albert Einstein put it, "the important thing is not to stop questioning. Curiosity has its own reason for existing. One cannot help but be in awe when contemplating the mysteries of eternity, of life, of the marvelous structure of reality. It is enough if one tries merely to comprehend a little of this mystery every day. Never lose a holy curiosity!"

That attitude of mind—that everyone can be a creative contributor—is the backbone of Sealed Air's emphasis on people. It helps explain why there is a high continuity of leadership in the top positions of the company. And it also makes believable the comments of Barbara Lewis, Dunphy's administrative assistant for the past five years: "This is a very civilized group. Even when we have had to terminate people during a business downturn, it's amazing how frequently they left as friends and continued to stay in touch with us afterward. There is a sense that this company really cares and believes in the ability of its people to contribute." *Forbes* magazine in 1979 questioned whether Sealed Air's consensus management, supportiveness for its people, and slowness to terminate might undermine corporate discipline in a tough competitive environment.* We think its record turnaround in the past four years shows the Sealed Air culture to be its greatest asset.

---

*"What Turnaround?," *Forbes* (October 1, 1979), p. 89.

Sealed Air backs up its philosophy of attaching high value to peo-ple with strong incentive and equity ownership plans. Senior managers typically earn a third of their annual compensation in the form of incen-tives based on performance, and Sealed Air's performance-based stock ownership plan extends well down into the ranks of middle manage-ment. In a company whose share value has increased a dozen times since the early 1970s, this is a powerful way to keep the team motivated!

DERMOT DUNPHY: THE JOY OF LEADERSHIP

When Dunphy was at Harvard Business School in the mid-1950s, he vividly recalls a time when the desire to become a leader in business became a major goal in his life. Dunphy was taking a course called "Manufacturing" and was impressed when the professor, General Georges Doriot, read a quotation from Joseph Conrad's *Typhoon** that captured the loneliness of command:

> Jukes was uncritically glad to have his Captain at hand. It relieved him, as though that man had, by simply coming on deck, taken at once most of the gale's weight upon his shoulders. Such is the prestige, the privilege, and the burden of command. Captain MacWhirr could expect no comfort of that sort from anyone on earth. Such is the loneliness of command.

As Dunphy later put it, "at that moment, I decided I wanted that loneliness of command, of leadership, more than anything else. The romance of business suddenly opened up for me."

When Dunphy was graduated from Harvard Business School in 1956, he joined Westinghouse's air conditioning division, where he remained for several years, ending up in charge of sales for a major sector of the country. Then he succumbed to the lure of leadership and became president of Custom-Made Paper Bag Company, a small manufacturer of Popsicle wrappers and vacuum cleaner bags, purchasing more than half of the company's stock. Over the next eight years, through smart selling, cost-cutting, and plain hard work, he built up the company's sales and made it profitable. Selling out Custom-Made to Hammermill, the paper company, in 1967, Dunphy simultaneously established a capital base for himself and cleared the decks for his next career move.

At that time he was asked to go on the board of the then-tiny Sealed

*(Garden City, N.Y.: Doubleday & Company, 1919), p. 75.

Air Corporation by the company's investment bankers, who had purchased a large share of Sealed Air stock. Recognizing the opportunity for growth and the need for a builder CEO, the board made him president and chief executive of Sealed Air in March 1971.

In taking the company from $5 million in 1971 to $166 million in 1984 sales, Dunphy's earliest contributions were to solidify and encourage Sealed Air's small management team and to build the company's sales and marketing effectiveness. He led the development of strategy, personally taking the lead in the company's acquisition program, the most important being the acquisition of Instapak. He provided balance, shaping the team-oriented corporate culture while at the same time overseeing the design of Sealed Air's disciplined information systems. And finally, starting in 1980, he led the rebalancing of Sealed Air's priorities to give the company the research and technical strength it needed to match its marketing and sales strengths. Above all else, he brought a winning spirit.

Here is what his leadership team has to say about him:

- "The way this company is run gives each of us an exceptional opportunity to grow. Dermot constantly stimulates sound thinking and rarely gives orders. Each of his speeches, each of his meetings is designed to stretch our horizons—for example, his recent speech 'No Such Thing as a Commodity' in front of our salesmen. He pointed out that there are always ways to distinguish our product and service from our competition and create incremental value for our customers. This got our people thinking differently about our product line."
- "Dunphy is one of the rare CEOs who doesn't think you have to do it his way. He encourages us all to feel responsible, to think out our own best way of reaching a goal, and if it doesn't work, figure out how to change it. That attitude and that approach are great motivators."
- "The openness of this society keeps us working well together as a team, even after a tough debate. We went through a major deliberation in a series of meetings two years ago when we had to decide how we were going to distribute and sell our solar pool blankets. All of our key officers were involved in the discussion. A straw poll indicated a six-to-five split among the officers, after which Dermot made the decision in favor of the minority! But Dermot first spoke for over an hour, carefully weighing the pros and cons. Both his skill and fairness in weighing the issues and his obvious concern for the opinions of those with whom he ultimately disagreed made it easy for all of us finally to concur in the decision. In effect, we developed a consensus after the decision was made. In this type of decision-making there can be uninhibited debate with no losers!"

Dunphy is clearly an organization builder, a team player committed to the success of Sealed Air. The one dimension in which he claims he is not representative of our findings for the winning performers as a group is in hours spent on the job. Dunphy states that he works only fifty hours a week and that the reason he can do so is that the strong team spirit that exists at Sealed Air allows others to cover many of the bases that he would otherwise have to handle himself.

Dunphy does, however, display tremendous tenacity and is willing to take risk. He pursued the Instapak acquisition for nearly five years before completing it, and the year before it was done he was told by Instapak's board to forget it. Instapak cost Sealed Air $7 million (in cash and stock), compared with Sealed Air's net worth at the time of $13 million. A close friend and HBS classmate, Salomon Brothers partner Harold Tanner, said of Dunphy at the time: "He's a riverboat gambler—the Instapak acquisition was a bet-your-company move!" Since then, Instapak's foam-in-place line has become one of Sealed Air's most successful businesses.

Dunphy has given a good deal of thought to management succession and has identified at least two potential successors in Sealed Air today and others in the wings who may emerge. But at fifty-two, Dunphy sees a long time still ahead before he turns over the reins of leadership.

In brief, Dunphy appears to have combined a clear vision of the business of making money for his customers by "protecting their products with Sealed Air's products," to have built an enthusiastic team with the same energy and drive characteristic of Dunphy's rugby teams in the 1940s, and to have taken some "calculated risks" that have paid off mightily for his company.

SOME LESSONS FROM SUCCESS

Cray, ADP, and Sealed Air each illustrate the common elements of midsize success we examined earlier. They also graphically depict why general statements about the roots of success are so difficult to make—even at the broad level of the findings of this book—because only by "putting it all together" is the potential of winning performance realized. The particular combination of practices can—and does—vary as dramatically as those of our three example companies.

Many less successful companies have some—even all—of the elements. They compete in niches, innovate, provide value to customers, build on strength. Many also-rans have a sense of direction, good people, disciplines, and a commitment to fighting bureaucracy. And there are losers with brilliant, obsessed leaders. The elements may be right, but the combination is wrong.

Small companies succeed because of the individual qualities of one person. Having become complex, midsize companies succeed only if the entire institution takes on and sustains the winning qualities. Midsize companies are complex organisms, much like human beings, where all the parts must support and contribute to the whole, and do so at the right time and in the right way. To push the analogy, a strong heart is essential to a successful athlete, but no more so than clear vision, good lungs, a sound vascular system, or strong arms and legs. And that heart has to respond when and only when it's needed—one can no more run a record mile with a pulse of 70 than sleep with a pulse of 180. It all has to work, and work right, together, all the time. Isolated events may succeed on occasion, but only the consistent institutional strength of the entire organism can be a longtime winner.

It all fits together; the whole depends on the parts, and each part on the whole.

Winners are in niches—innovate, build on strength, and add value—as Cray, ADP, and Sealed Air do. Such companies also anticipate changes, respond to adversity, and adapt to a changing world. In turn, their strategies and their adaptiveness are products of their organizational strength—their clear sense of direction, their people, systems, values, and structures. They combine competence with motivation, the skill, and the will. And there are no such organizations except those created and sustained by committed, able leaders—who not only put it all together but keep it that way.

Style and external appearances may vary enormously, as our three diverse examples show—Cray's innovativeness, playfulness, and individuality; ADP's intensity and organizational discipline; Sealed Air's team spirit. Their pivotal institutional skills or focuses may vary just as much—from Sealed Air's product development and marketing, to ADP's low-cost operations and service reliability, to Cray's technological uniqueness.

The concepts of what leads to midsize success are common, but the execution is unique and suited to each company in its time. The elements of success are common, but the combination of ingredients is unique. And what finally counts is that unique combination—putting it all together.

CHAPTER VIII

The Entrepreneurial Corporation

Nearly two decades ago, the respected economist, influential social commentator, and public servant John Kenneth Galbraith delivered his eulogy for the "entrepreneurial corporation."

In his best-selling volume *The New Industrial State,* which intellectually conditioned a generation of college-educated Americans, Galbraith reported that "the entrepreneurial corporation has declined."* To emphasize his belief in a new economy characterized by planning, oligopoly, and scale, the distinguished professor almost always referred to the entrepreneurial corporation in the past tense. Although Galbraith's obituary for an entrepreneurial economy was indeed premature, the facts he marshaled at the time suggested that the death rattle of entrepreneurial management might have been in earshot.

At the time of his writing, Galbraith reported that the five hundred largest companies accounted for the lion's share of the nation's sales and assets. The rise of the modern conglomerate had begun to take form. Students at Harvard College, where Galbraith taught, had little interest in business and even less in entrepreneurial achievement at the time—they were more concerned with the Vietnam War, civil rights, and other political and moral issues of the day. In fact, in 1967 Harvard Business School—deeply concerned about the new generation's antipathy toward business—invited (and paid) fifty top-ranking college under-

---

*John Kenneth Galbraith, *The New Industrial State* (Boston: Houghton Mifflin Company, 1967), p. 388.

graduates to spend the summer with the school, in large measure to find out why the world of commerce was so unappealing to that generation's best and brightest and to introduce them to highly regarded businesses.

The world and America's economy have changed since then. Business is alive and well, especially among the young urban professionals who were the college students of the '60s and '70s. And energy devoted to and interest in the entrepreneurial economy has become the order of the day, with record levels of new businesses established and the advent of entrepreneurs as national heroes. For 1984 *Time* picked an entrepreneur, Peter Ueberroth, as its Man of the Year, the first business leader since Walter Chrysler was on the cover in 1928, and soon after, *Business Week* profiled a new corporate elite—half of whom were entrepreneurs.

While the large enterprises that Galbraith identified in *The New Industrial State* have grown in absolute terms, their impact upon the economy has remained stable. For example, in 1967 the largest five hundred companies accounted for more than a third of corporate sales; in 1982 their share was the same.* But in terms of providing jobs, exports, or exciting the public's imagination, small and medium-size businesses substantially outpace the growth rates of the largest, most solidly established multinational enterprises.

This profound change in the economic order has in large measure been articulated by the rebirth and renaissance of the entrepreneurial corporation—the midsize growth companies we have examined that are neither the tiny proprietorships nor the massive oligopolies that comprised Galbraith's economy.

As we shall argue, the innovations, management practices, and spirit of the entrepreneurial corporations have relevance not only for the fraction of 1 percent of the nation's businesses that are midsize (but which account for a quarter of national product and a fifth of employment) but indeed also for their larger and smaller business siblings.

The entrepreneurial corporation is alive and well, not only among our midsize growth companies but in smaller enterprises yet to cross the threshold of size and complexity, as well as among operating divisions and subsidiaries of larger companies. For example, the strategic and organizing concepts and practices of such high-performing giants as 3M (Minnesota Mining and Manufacturing), Citicorp, or Johnson &

1984 Update: Mergers and Aggregate Concentration (New York: McKinsey & Company), p. 25.

Johnson seem to have most of the winning-performance attributes at work in their many decentralized businesses.

Although managing a complex business well requires doing many things right (just as flying an airplane or conducting surgery do), there are three major challenges for creating and sustaining an entrepreneurial corporation—whatever its size or venue. These three elements are managing purposeful innovation, orchestrating spirit and discipline, and providing entrepreneurial leadership. Let us look at each of the three in turn.

MANAGING PURPOSEFUL INNOVATION

As far back as 1969, the management writer and expert Peter Drucker had advice for those who sought to become business leaders during the final quarter of this century. In his own contribution to an anthology he edited, Drucker presciently wrote: "Tomorrow's business leader, it is clear, will need to be able to organize for entrepreneurship . . . will have to know how to anticipate innovation and how to make innovation economically effective."*

From our observations and study, Drucker was indeed correct. His tomorrow has arrived: Innovation has become the basis of competitive advantage for the high-performance companies—and there are at least five important lessons they hold for those who see their future the same way.

The first lesson is that *innovation is technological but not necessarily technical.* To explain the distinction, the dictionary tells us that technology is "the systematic treatment of an art." Technical, on the other hand, has to do with the specialized knowledge of mechanical and scientific subjects. From a management point of view, technology is the systematic application of some body of knowledge—and that knowledge need not be scientific or technical—to create or improve a product or service.

Many of the nontechnical innovations of our winning performers are technological because they changed the system of the business, but they were not technical. Lenox China's bridal registry is hardly scientific, unless one includes the anthropology of weddings as a science. Similarly, Safety-Kleen's innovation of making grease busting a service represents conceptual rather than technical achievement.

Preparing Tomorrow's Business Leaders Today, ed. Peter F. Drucker (Englewood Cliffs, N.J.: Prentice Hall, 1969), pp. 280–81.

This is not to say that scientific invention, discovery, and application are not important. And they are not limited to "high tech" products. Henry Foster's experience in breeding defined laboratory rats at Charles River Laboratories or Frank Perdue's success in breeding the Oven-Stuffer Roaster are two triumphs of science that transformed livestock commodities into value-differentiated products. Automatic Data Processing applied the power of the computer to the world of day-to-day bookkeeping. But in each case technical technology was a means for meeting real needs—not an end in itself.

And even in our "highest tech" case study—Cray Research—the technology was conceptual. Cray's ability to use trailing-edge technology for leading-edge products convincingly demonstrates that even scientific innovation need not be based upon discovery and invention.

The second lesson is that *innovation and bureaucracy just don't mix.* Small teams and individuals, not massive projects, have brought innovation to Cray and Analog Devices—to name two of the most technically and technologically astute companies we encountered. And in each case management takes extraordinary pains to make sure that policies, procedures, systems, and structure do not get in the way of innovation.

In its most basic objective, bureaucracy as an administrative form seeks to minimize and control risk. Policies and procedures are established, often in the wake of past mistakes, to prevent errors in the future. Levels of management review and approval—pre-action reviews—are created to ensure that multiple (and perhaps more seasoned and expensive) judgments are brought to bear to avoid mistakes. But risk, the enemy of the bureaucratic administrator, is the lifeblood of the entrepreneurial innovator. And the best-performing innovators recognize that mistakes, false starts, and even embarrassments are the necessary by-products of risk-taking—an essential ingredient of the process of innovation. To take two examples, MCA and MCI, both highly innovative companies, impressed us by how they manage mistakes. MCA (Marketing Corporation of America), whose business is helping others innovate, prides itself that the people associated with its worst failures (and not coincidentally with its greatest successes) are not penalized for mistakes. At MCI, the "other" long-distance telephone company, making and learning from mistakes seems to be a central part of the management catechism. We interviewed twenty-five senior managers at MCI to discern the critical elements of its corporate culture. The first conversation was with Bill McGowan, the chief executive, who, after answering our questions, concluded the interview by saying: "Don't forget, we make a lot of mistakes around this place. Have from the beginning. But so long as somebody doesn't keep making the same mistake over and over again, we can live with it and recover." During our two dozen subsequent interviews, nineteen of the managers spoke (without prompting) of errors, mistakes, and even calamities for which each had been personally responsible. These ranged from setting up telemarketing experiments where there weren't enough people around to answer the incoming calls, to technical decisions that just flopped.

What distinguishes the way these winning companies manage mistakes is that they make them on a small scale, encourage lots of experiments, and dedicate their energy to fixing them rather than attributing fault.

The third lesson of the successful innovators is that they *regard their customers and distributors as welcome partners in the innovation process.* "Not invented here"—a term of derision within parochial bureaucratic organizations—is a form of high praise among the innovators. Although Dunkin' Donuts owns a good number of its stores, its president and chairman are quick to point out that many of its most successful new products were the ideas of franchisees—like the Munchkin doughnut holes that got started in Springfield, Massachusetts.

Fourth, *creativity is highly valued and effectively promoted.* As Professor Theodore Levitt at Harvard Business School is fond of pointing out, creativity is thinking up new ideas, while innovation is making them happen. Without new ideas there is no innovation. And without purposeful execution of new ideas, there can be no innovation. Most of the forms of business creativity we learned about—while dramatic and insightful in their examples—seem to follow commonsense patterns of experimentation that hold promise for any enterprise.

One pattern of practical creativity is thinking through analogy: What works in other industries or endeavors that might work here? Lifetime guarantees and "no questions asked—money back" return policies have been around for a long time—but it took A. T. Cross to guarantee a pen and Frank Perdue a chicken. Many of the best innovative ideas are stolen or borrowed, not from competitors, but from people in unrelated businesses.

Another pattern of creativity is contrary or opposite thinking. At its extreme, Bill McGowan, whose natural state of mind seems irreverent and contrariant, asks everyone at MCI to think about doing the opposite of its giant long-distance competitor. When earlier in his career McGowan was a venture capitalist and turnaround consultant, he developed as a rule of thumb the probability that the distressed enterprises he was seeking to fix were probably doing lots of things wrong—so why not try the opposite? In addition, he figured the organization needed shock treatment in order to allow the dramatic changes in the operation and drastic reduction in the economics of the business. If the sales force was on commission, McGowan put them on salary. If a clerical process was automated, McGowan made it manual—and vice versa. The key to the opposite experiments was to watch them closely to see if they made things better. Those "opposites" that worked were continued. At MCI, contrariant thinking is evident in many management practices. The law department is considered a profit center rather than a corporate cost center—and over the years it has been extremely profitable. MCI places its outside law firms on contingency arrangements whenever it can—a practice common among the personal-injury bar but unusual among established corporate law firms.

Still a third pattern of innovation is the "old products for new customers" point of view. We recall from an earlier chapter how Cullinet saved itself by finding a market among corporate auditors for software that the data processing specialists didn't particularly like. Cray found a market for supercomputers among geologists and among movie makers. As Peter Drucker explained a long time ago, selling refrigerators to the Eskimos to keep food cold is one thing—but selling refrigerators to the Eskimos to keep food from freezing is creative.

The fourth innovative practice centers on *creating new markets* rather than trying merely to serve old ones. Charter Medical created a nationwide market in psychiatric care. While mankind has had emotional and psychological problems ever since gaining his imagination, Charter made a for-profit—and profitable—business in treating them. Analog Devices helped create markets in computerized medical diagnosis and robotics by recognizing there was a market in making computers capable of processing real-world signals, not just binary digits.

Most of our survey respondents noted that innovation seems to get more difficult over time. It becomes complicated by the greater size, market acceptance, complexity, and company longevity that accompany success. Not surprisingly, a continuing stream of new and unique products and services becomes increasingly hard to create. But innovation continues among the winning performers—both in new products and in new markets—often by shifting to *new ways of doing business* (for instance, different production methods, imaginative marketing approaches, reconfigured distribution systems, or new ways to finance the business) —the fifth pattern of innovation.

Although size and complexity make successful innovation more challenging, they do not preclude it. Many large, high-performance corporations have noteworthy and deserved reputations for innovation. But in too many cases, the perception of innovation among larger enterprises gets lost in the shadows of sheer size.

There are two schools of thought about how innovation happens—not dissimilar to the theories of how the universe came to be. One, the "big-bang" school of innovation, sees major changes in products or in delivery systems (e.g., franchising hamburgers, radial tires, cash management accounts for individuals, quality branded chicken, or a second competitive long-distance supplier) as innovation. The second, the gradualist or "incremental" school, sees—rather than bold, dramatic innovations—smaller and modest ones (e.g., the "Big Mac" sandwich, tires with guarantees, automatic teller machines, Rock Cornish hens, or credit card machines for phone calls).

We believe that "big-bang" and "incremental" innovations differ more in perception than in kind. The impact and visibility of a smaller concern's single innovation is often perceptually enlarged, because the innovation and the firm are synonymous. Apple Computer designed and brought to market a personal computer—a conspicuous innovation. MTV pioneered in a new form of entertainment for adolescents—the rock video broadcast. But larger firms have had similarly important and successful innovations that have escaped similar high levels of public attention (e.g., Johnson & Johnson's introduction of Rhogam, a treatment that minimizes birth defects).

Thus, a larger company's incremental innovation would appear as a "big-bang" for a small company. If "Post-It Note Pads" (those neat little pieces of paper that stick to other paper but can be easily pulled off) had been developed by the new "Post-It" Company, the development would have been seen as a major risk and dramatic success and would have reverberated in the over-the-counter stock market and in the business press as a big-bang type of innovation. But for 3M, "Post-It" was just one more in a series of successful innovations—business as usual for this large professional innovator.

In truth, innovation is the product of an experimenting nature, the willingness to shoulder risk, an ingrained habit of listening, and vision about real customer needs. Whether it's big or small, whether product or service or business system-oriented, the ingredients of innovation are the same and can be accomplished in any venue.

ORCHESTRATING SPIRIT AND DISCIPLINE

Sadly, an unproductive but sometimes passionate debate about how to manage has preoccupied business theorists, practitioners, and consultants in this country. This false dichotomy centers around humanistic versus rational management. The humanist disciples on one hand, in their extreme strike a chorus of "let a hundred flowers bloom." The argument goes that by leaving employees alone and celebrating their successes, an organization will release the energies, creativity, and imagination of people—who will do the right thing if not derailed by systems, structures, and plans. Inductive thinking, intuition, and highly developed interpersonal skills are the most valued—and short-supplied—attributes. Intelligence is measured by common sense and creativity. Columbo, the television detective portrayed by Peter Falk, symbolized this kind of problem solving.

The rationalists—whose highly developed left-sided brains apply analysis as their principal problem-solving tool—tend to see the world as a microeconomic model that once mastered will bring order, method, and ultimate success. To this end, they suggest quantification when possible, and rigor and discipline always. And once the problem is solved and properly modeled for the future, systems and structure can guide decision making and action. Deductive thinking, quantitative analysis, and conceptual frameworks are the valued and developed tools. Intelligence is measured in terms of sophisticated quantitative agility, the ability to measure and manipulate "hard" facts, and the mastery of complexity. Sherlock Holmes was the fictional exemplar of rationalist detective work.*

Those who manage well have learned the lesson that each of these extremes—by itself—is dangerous and ineffective. Business—indeed, any organized enterprise—is neither the domain of pure logical positivists nor of pure phenomenologists. Management ain't science alone and it ain't art alone.

If any adjective is apt for management, the word is "practical." The practical manager in the entrepreneurial corporation draws upon both rational and humanist approaches—applying them as circumstances demand. It is, however, not the fact that they are both employed, but how, that is the key to success. This hybrid form of management does not seek to balance, trade off, or average management approach. Rather it employs both simultaneously. And the lesson we draw is that effective management is situational, selective, and synchronized.

SITUATIONAL MANAGEMENT

For each season of an enterprise's life there are special challenges and requirements for success.

*Inspector Clouseau was neither humanist nor rational. He was lucky.

In a new, one-person enterprise, the management and leadership tasks are conceptually simple but personally demanding. In the person of the entrepreneur reside the strategy, skills, shared values, systems, staff, organizational structure, and management style of enterprise.* The founder's vision of the business contains the internal shared values and strategy. He or she is the staff and the systems; the skills are his or her skills. The entrepreneur's personality is the management style that customers, suppliers, and financiers see, hear, and feel.

The next stage of growth, typically with the advent of a small group of partners, associates, and employees, is similarly straightforward as a management challenge. With such an intimate group of compatriots, the corporate heart, brain, soul, and central nervous system can most often be accommodated around a single table. As in the case of the sole proprietor, the entrepreneurial cell of a small group of kindred spirits is probably most influenced by perseverance, quick-wittedness, and hard work.

But as corporations succeed in business, the number of managers and employees grows and the complexity of the enterprise explodes. And it is during this takeoff growth stage that two disciplines of management—structure and systems—must be installed to keep the enterprise from careening out of control. For example, about half of our winning chief executives recall their enterprises being "broke or close to broke," and the strong and effective financial control systems we now find are the heritage of keeping an eye on cash and costs. As the scale and diversity of customers, functions, and activities to manage increase, some division of responsibility becomes necessary, and the burgeoning enterprise provides opportunities for specialized knowledge, experience, and attention to contribute to the work.

Success—and the renewed attention it brings from established competitors and copycat entrants—also requires that the intellectual discipline of strategy be more formally crafted, articulated, and institutionalized. "Doing what comes naturally" loses its effectiveness when multiple products are provided to multiple markets managed by multiple people. And planning, which was once easily accomplished by a series of conversations among the principals, becomes more difficult as the enterprise acquires and uses assets and makes commitments to customers and employees. But most important, more people have to make this more complex strategy work—and to do so as human beings they must con-

---

*These seven elements of organizational effectiveness were identified and assembled into the 7-S framework by our colleagues at McKinsey and are explained in greater detail in *In Search of Excellence*.

tribute to its formation, thoroughly understand its content and substance, and work cooperatively with others to achieve it.

If they are not applied with caution and care, the power and benefits of initially installing these disciplines—structure, systems, and strategy, essential to control the company during the commencement of its threshold stages—can become the beginning of the end for the larger enterprise, for a natural human reaction is that when something works—be it a cost system that keeps track of selling expenses, or a betting system at the racetrack—one should do more of the same. But when it comes to management discipline, more of the same can become too much of the same. It can be as debilitating to the corporation's vitality as more of the same miracle drug that once cured an illness but, when uncontrolled in its dosage, creates drug dependency. These servants of management—structure, systems, and formal strategy—have a way of becoming masters and inadvertent stiflers of innovation and motivation.

So for the larger enterprise—with its full complement of professional management tools—the reinforcement of the corporate spirit is what the doctor (and shareholders, employees, and customers) should order. Shared values—the philosophy, spirit, and guiding principles of the enterprise—need to be revitalized and articulated. A management style that values, exhibits, and celebrates the human touch and people-building skills becomes even more important as more and more humans must be touched as customers and employees. And most important, corporate skills—the combined skills of the people who make up the company—have to be assessed, strengthened, and updated. Thus the importance of the findings in *In Search of Excellence* and *Corporate Cultures** about the high performance of large businesses is in identifying how elements of management spirit (shared values, skills, staff, and style) unlock energy, entrepreneurial creativity, and excellence. Whether football teams, military units, or companies—both discipline and spirit are necessary for success.

SELECTIVE DISCIPLINE

The entrepreneurial executive has to discern what needs to be tightly controlled and what doesn't. The best are able to figure out which functions, activities, and tasks are essential to the business's success and are subject to direction. These are monitored, measured, controlled, inspected, supervised, and managed with great care, fre-

---

**In Search of Excellence*, op. cit.; Terrence E. Deal and Allan A. Kennedy, *Corporate Cultures: The Rites and Rituals of Corporate Life* (Reading, Mass.: Addison-Wesley Publishing Co., Inc., 1982).

quency, and attention—often by the chief executive. There are usually no more than a handful of these key factors for success, and beyond that handful, decisions are left to the common sense, judgment, and imagination of trusted managers.

For example, quality control at Perdue Farms consumes a vast amount of Frank Perdue's and his top management team's energies. Red-capped quality-control inspectors are found at every stage of chicken production—with authority to stop operations and reject product whenever something goes wrong. Because consumers inspect chickens one at a time, Perdue Farms does it that way, too—a more expensive and time-consuming method than statistical sampling, but also more effective. Sixty-seven quality standards must be met, and about 20 percent of the Perdue chicken that meets government grade "A" standards doesn't meet some Perdue standard and is therefore rejected. But quality control doesn't end at production. Perdue representatives roam grocery stores, butcher shops, and supermarkets checking on their product and buying competitors' chickens—which are analyzed at the quality laboratories side by side with Perdue birds. Awards are made to processing plants— not those that make the most money but those that achieve the highest quality. And Frank Perdue, even to this day, reads and acts on daily quality and field reports. But other decisions, such as experimenting with new equipment, figuring out the most effective feed stock, and running the company's employee suggestion system are left to those closest to those activities.

Perdue's top-management attention to the detail of a critical function is matched by other winning performers. Bob Elliot, Levitz Furniture's chief executive, keeps track daily of store inventory levels. Bill McGowan at MCI doesn't have to read in the papers which regulatory proceedings produced what decisions. And on and on. The key skill is knowing what few things to control—not trying to control everything. *The winning CEOs let general managers be general managers*—sharply limiting corporate staffs who inevitably watch, check, and second-guess the line managers.

SYNCHRONIZATION

The final lesson of balanced management is making sure things aren't set up in a such a way that one defeats another's purpose. The bigger and more disparate the organization, the more likely this is to happen. (For example, the U.S. government spends millions of dollars trying to convince its citizens not to smoke. It also spends millions of dollars subsidizing tobacco growers.)

In the realm of management, the possibilities and combinations of self-defeating practices are more subtle but just as counterproductive.

are told "get close to their customers," but then travel that permit customer visits are cut out. Innovation and risk-king are encouraged by the boss's words, but monthly profit goals and incentive plans tied to them punish small mistakes. A company decides to decentralize decision-making into small, entrepreneurial business units but fails to install accounting systems that measure performance on a business-unit basis. The possibilities are endless—and the possibilities provide for grim reality. Rhetoricians call these situations irony. We call them lousy management.

Here again, the elements of management discipline and spirit come into play. The need to ensure that they are synchronized becomes critical as companies change—as inevitably they must—to anticipate and capitalize on changing business conditions. A foolish consistency may be the hobgoblin of little minds—but consistency in reaching the objectives and outcomes of management practices is wise. Hence, when a new strategy is conceived and implemented, it must be consistent with the enterprise's shared values; it must draw upon real skills; it must have a management structure and set of systems that facilitate rather than impede its working.

The winning performers practice this consistency. Analog Devices understands that the contributions from individual technicians are important—and has a parallel career ladder that rewards and recognizes these contributions. Its personnel system is consistent with its strategy of getting the most out of individual skills. Dunkin' Donuts depends on the vitality of its franchisees—and so it involves them as partners in decision-making and beneficiaries of mass purchasing—not as third-party vendors.

As elementary as this all sounds, the playing fields of the competitive marketplace are littered with examples of those who failed. And as organizations become more complex—especially at the threshold stage and beyond—the commonsense dictum to synchronize management elements becomes more imperative.

PROVIDING ENTREPRENEURIAL LEADERSHIP

During the four years we have researched this book—and the two years we have spent writing it—our friends, colleagues, clients, and audiences have all sooner or later asked a common question along these lines: "Of all the things you have learned about these high-performing companies, which is the most important?"

It's a tough question, because becoming a winner means doing many of the right things and doing them right most of the time. As we have argued earlier, it is not one element of strategy but their combination and intensity that is powerful. Competing on value, fostering innovation, and achieving niche leadership build upon one another. And the organizational approaches that work, work in concert, not in isolation. So it's not one practice or attribute that brings success. It is how the many critical ones are orchestrated.

But *leadership at the top*—the orchestrator of strategy and organization—and the leader's *ability to instill and institutionalize that leadership throughout the enterprise* emerge in our view as the distinguishing characteristics of winning performance among midsize high-growth companies.

While it is hard to argue that leadership isn't important in any organized endeavor, it is crucial in midsize companies. Unlike some larger, well-established enterprises that can coast on their scale, power, and reputation (at least for a while), the midsize growth companies must rely on agility and quick response. They do not—and cannot—run by themselves. As with an airplane taking off, there is no place for an automatic pilot. The hands must be on the controls.

Much has been written about leadership, and business leadership in particular. Psychologists debate whether it is hereditary, learned, or forced upon one. Students of leadership cite the manifestation of human—sometimes contrary—qualities: ambition, aggressiveness, courage, compassion, integrity, hope, patience, vision, risk-taking—as the stuff of which it is made.

As U.S. Supreme Court Justice Potter Stewart observed about pornography, we are unable to define leadership, but we know it when we see it.

We observe three key practices that the leaders of midsize growth companies employ:

1. The leaders are wholeheartedly committed to the enterprise—to the point of obsession.
2. The leaders institutionalize that personal obsession into pervasive corporate values and culture.
3. The leaders bring perspective, ranging from the vision to see and act on specific opportunities to the self-knowledge of the need to replace themselves or change their roles when the time comes.

Commitment to the Point of Obsession

Despite all the talk about working smart instead of working hard, there is no substitute for both. Our observations of the most successful entrepreneurial executives is that they exhibit extraordinary devotion and commitment to their work. Understanding this phenomenon requires understanding their motivations.

More than seventy years ago, Joseph Schumpeter, the economist who first recognized the entrepreneur as the moving force of economic development, distilled the motives of entrepreneurs that lead to such levels of commitment. In his seminal work, *The Theory of Economic Development** (first published in the fall of 1911), Schumpeter dismissed material and monetary gain as a prime mover of these men, leading him to comment, "this does not seem to verify the picture of the economic man. . . ." Instead, he identified three more powerful motives, which our much more recent observations confirm:

1. "The dream and the will to found a private kingdom, usually, though not necessarily, also a dynasty."
2. "The will to conquer: the impulse to fight, . . . to succeed for the sake, not of the fruits of success, but of success itself."
3. "The joy of creating, getting things done, or of simply exercising one's energy and ingenuity."†

And our modern-day leaders appear drawn to—perhaps driven by—these same compelling and compulsive needs. In the lexicon of the social psychologist David C. McClelland, leaders of winning companies have a high need for all three of the basic motivators: achievement, power, and affiliation. They do not trade them off, as conventional wisdom has it—they optimize them all in a full-court press of personality.

The values transcending wealth creation empower the energy of the entrepreneurial business leader. Although a number of our subjects have achieved considerable personal wealth—the level of material achievement that puts some of them on the *Forbes* list of the four hundred richest Americans—wealth creation as an end in itself is low on their list of priorities. They show little evidence of conspicuous consumption. It was rare, during our wide-ranging interviews with these men and women, that the subject of making money came up. Their creeds and codes tend to subordinate profit as a goal, depict it as a necessary responsibility to shareholders, or see it as a measurement of success in

*Joseph A. Schumpeter, *The Theory of Economic Development: An Inquiry into Profits, Capital, Credit, Interest and the Business Cycle* (New York: Oxford University Press, 1934).
†Ibid., pp. 92–93.

doing the other things right. And by personal example, the material fruits of success are in many cases either downplayed or eschewed. Jim Macaleer, founder and chief executive of Shared Medical Systems, drives a six-year-old Chevy to work each day. Frank Perdue takes the New York and New Jersey Port Authority bus to Newark International Airport so he can fly on discounted People Express Airlines. Seymour Cray eats lunch at the counter in a Chippewa Falls coffee shop.

As Reynold M. Sachs, who was present during the turnaround of Digital Switch and made some $50 million in a three-year period, said in an interview with the Columbia Business School alumni magazine, "Ironically, individuals whose primary or only goal is financial gain end up failing to make the money that they dreamed about. . . . If that is your primary goal, you're more likely to fail than to succeed, perhaps because it's short-sighted and it gives you incentives to make wrong decisions."*

Some who have heard us promote this viewpoint on motivation discount it, attributing the nonchalance about money and wealth to an understandable suspicion that it's easy for a millionaire or a billionaire to say more money really isn't important. But if so, the men and women we studied fooled us. We are convinced they are more interested in making a future than in amassing a fortune and have the mentality of builders rather than of bankers. Indeed, these business leaders often see their enterprises as extensions of their own person and mortality (in many ways like a family dynasty) and accord them corresponding attention and energy.

The obsession of leaders and their contribution to success is not limited to medium-size businesses. Admiral Hyman G. Rickover was obsessed about the nuclear Navy; Casey Stengel about the fabled New York Yankees; Douglas MacArthur about victory; Martin Luther King, Jr., about equality; Thomas A. Edison about his inventions; Sam Rayburn about the House of Representatives; J. Edgar Hoover about the FBI.

But obsession per se is not enough to build an organization—and if not tempered by perspective, a trait we shall address shortly, raw obsession can be as dangerous as blind ambition. Furthermore, obsession cannot be imitated or coaxed out of someone—either you are excited and enthused about your enterprise, or you are not. And if you're not, you have no business accepting a top management role. Extraordinary commitment is the price of leadership. Conversely, commitment is one

*"The Entrepreneur Series," *Hermes, Columbia Business School Magazine* (Fall 1984), p. 28.

quality, but not the sole one, that any enterprise should use as a selection criterion for its future leaders.

Institutionalizing Values, Passion, and Leadership

Life can be lonely and frustrating for a visionary with a cause in a crowd of the dispassionate and uninterested. What distinguishes the best founders and leaders is how they transform their personal commitment and obsession into institutional obsession and energy.

Part and parcel of the temporal leadership of the winning chief executive is his or her success in instilling among others in the organization the same meaning the enterprise has for its leaders; because most important, what distinguishes the high-performance companies from the also-rans is the meanings—beyond a place to get a paycheck—these enterprises provide for those who populate them.

Esprit de corps and winning spirit are not unusual in prominent organizations—irrespective of size or endeavor. Marines, Harvard students, IBM employees, White House Office of Management and Budget professionals, *New York Times* journalists, Morgan Guaranty bankers, Goldman Sachs financiers, Sullivan & Cromwell lawyers, and Jesuit priests all tend to exhibit a special pride in the central values of excellence that imbue their organizations. But more important than sheer enthusiasm is their commitment to and understanding of the values—why these organizations can demand and get extraordinary effort and commitment.

Many, many acts—symbolic and substantive—build meanings for these companies. Who is selected to work in the company (and their fit with the culture is as important as their objective qualifications to do the job), reinforced by who is promoted to greater responsibility, are two important ways that the cause of the company is amplified rather than diminished. The distillation and propagation of corporate creeds, codes, and philosophies is another. Employee and manager stock ownership—an economic symbol of ownership and identification—is another. But the most important builder of meanings is leadership by example—how the leader makes decisions, invests his or her energies, and deals with the people.

Personal leadership by example should not be confused with charisma—defined by our friends at Webster as the "personal magic of leadership arousing special popular loyalty or enthusiasm." Although often the ultimate manifestation of transforming values and principles into actions and passionately pursued objectives, charisma is not necessary. Among the winning CEOs, some have more than their share of charisma—Bill McGowan of MCI, John Cullinane of Cullinet, and Ross Perot of Electronic Data Systems (EDS). Many more, though, are mere mortals when it comes to moving a crowd, capturing the imagination of the press, or evoking passionate followings. But their personal leadership is effective—because through more soft-stated example they instill values. They care about those values and about their people.

This should not be surprising, despite the cult of charisma that preoccupies the media. John F. Kennedy and Theodore Roosevelt were charismatic leaders—but Abraham Lincoln and Woodrow Wilson were not. Douglas MacArthur was charismatic—Omar Bradley, not. Clearly charisma helps, but the medium is not the message; substance is. And it is the substance of the values and philosophy that give meaning.

An important test we use in identifying how well understood and embraced corporate values are is to ask working people, far down in the hierarchy of an organization, what the company stands for—a test any manager can apply by talking with people on the production line, at reception desks, or on the company switchboard. Our test is to measure how congruent their explanation of the values is with those of the top management group. And the results are quite remarkable. One of us lives in Washington, D.C., the home of MCI, and he is always taken by the fact that MCI employees—on the subway, at cocktail parties, or on an airplane—sooner rather than later provide a full-blown explanation about competition in telecommunications and MCI's role in making it happen.

The important and distinguishing requirement of winning leadership, then, is convincing the other men and women who work in the enterprise of its central mission and culture through example, logic, and practice.

Perspective

Obsession without perspective is fanaticism.* And the perspective necessary for entrepreneurial leadership embraces both outward vision and internal realism.

Outward vision is the ability to see—and to get others to see and act upon—what Schumpeter termed the product of the entrepreneur: "new combinations of productive means."† Schumpeter described five new combinations that we assert even today the entrepreneurial executive must be imaginative enough to envision and practical enough to exploit: (1) new products, (2) new methods of production, (3) new markets, (4) new supply sources, and (5) new organization. And as

---

*Our favorite definition of a fanatic is "someone who having lost sight of his objective redoubles his effort."

†*The Theory of Economic Development*, p. 74.

Schumpeter observed in 1911 and as we do today, the entrepreneur's task "consists precisely in breaking up old, and creating new, tradition."*

The thin but critical line that separates such vision from hallucination is the perspective of practicality. And that practicality comes from customers—the real people and consumers of the marketplace who vote with their patronage. Whatever we buy—be it paper clips, computers, medical care, or an airline ticket—we buy to solve a problem. Practical problem-solving, then, is the substance of any business vision.

The second element of entrepreneurial perspective is internal realism—the quality of recognizing the impossible. There are few Renaissance men and women in the world—and even fewer Renaissance enterprises. Aside from the likes of Leonardo da Vinci—who excelled at science, art, and politics—and Thomas Jefferson—a master architect, scientist, educator, and public servant—few mortals have excelled in disparate fields. There are limits to achievement, no matter how burning the ambition or powerful the talent. Recognizing and accepting these natural limitations—for both the corporation and the person—make the entrepreneurial leader successful.

The perception of reality is what guides the enterprise to edge out and grow successfully but restrains it from entering and most likely failing at totally unrelated (even if exciting and superficially attractive) ventures. As we noted earlier, a fatal flaw of some growing enterprises is institutional hubris—the unabashed ambition to master products, services, and markets that are foreign to their skills and knowledge.

Succession is associated with success both etymologically and substantively. If there was a single issue that occupied the winning chief executives we interviewed, it was in preparing for the inevitable—identifying, training, and testing candidates to take command, and in preparing themselves to let go.

The perception of reality and mortality jointly demand that the effective entrepreneurial executive plan for his or her succession. In part, the vitality of the institution requires that the leader seek to attract, select, and groom potential successors even more talented than himself—acts of moral courage. And the most successful entrepreneurial executives have the organizational perspective and personal security to anticipate when the organization's future demands better, different, or new skills, talents, energy, or focus—and to stand aside when the time comes.

The brilliance of Seymour Cray and David Pall was not limited to their technical innovations or entrepreneurial successes in founding and building important businesses. In both cases they chose to turn over the

*Ibid., pp. 66, 92.

chief executive responsibilities to colleagues and devote themselves to the critical research-and-development tasks.

In our view, no enterprise has fully proved its mettle until it has successfully achieved the succession of at least one generation of top leadership.

So What?

The large majority of our readers are not associated with midsize companies; if readership follows the employment patterns of the economy, most readers will work in larger or smaller enterprises. And even fewer will be associated with enterprises whose economic performance approximates that of the companies we have examined in this volume.

Those who manage and work within the high-growth midsize companies as well as those associated with the best of the big, will undoubtedly observe a good measure of "old news" among the lessons we have discerned. Thus, the natural questions arise. How is all this relevant to me? What should I do about it?

Although this book has focused upon midsize companies, the lessons of the entrepreneurial corporation are not reserved for businesses of that size. Smaller concerns with bigger ambitions can grow and profit by understanding and selectively applying the winning practices as they prepare for—and live through—their corporate adolescence. The winning strategies—innovation as the basis of competition, niche creation and leadership, edging out into related markets and offerings, and emphasizing value—were as central to the companies we studied during their infancies as they are today. These were the well-executed strategic attributes that propelled most of our high-performing exemplars into the winners' circle of business.

For most—but not all—larger enterprises, the lessons hold value as well. Most of America's larger companies are organized these days into profit-center divisions and business units whose size and strategic characteristics approximate the entrepreneurial corporations we have chronicled. And for those businesses the lessons of strategy apply, and indeed have been applied by the decentralized businesses of some of the most entrepreneurially focused successful giant companies.* But even more important for the larger and most established businesses are our obser-

---

*There is, of course, a small minority of functionally organized scale-based businesses where integration, massive long-term investment decisions, and scale advantages predominate. For such enterprises, our strategic findings have less relevance.

vations about organization—the need to orchestrate spirit and discipline so that rigor and rejuvenation can coexist.

For all businesses—irrespective of size, age, or venue—the exercise of personal leadership by managers at all levels holds the greatest promise. Commitment and the institutionalization of that commitment into values, spirit; and guiding principles can energize employees as the reality of being associated with a special institution brings new meaning to work.

By definition, not every company can be in the top 1 percent or 10 percent of its peers—just as every golfer can't win the Masters and every nation cannot collect the most gold medals at the Olympics. Very, very few enterprises will achieve, let alone sustain, the level of winning performance we have chronicled here. But many, many enterprises can realistically aspire to and achieve better performance—if they manifest the will and develop the skill to do so.

In business, as in any human endeavor, there are "naturals" who by benefit of good fortune are endowed with exceptional natural aptitude and attitude. The natural athlete who trains, who understands and applies best practice to his or her event, and who experiments with ways to compete better and differently enhances the chances for championship performance. And the more modestly endowed who does the same may not become the champion—but usually improves his or her overall performance.

So, too, for business—the team sport of economic enterprise. Understanding, adopting, applying, refining, and indeed pushing the limits and redefining best practice, while not guaranteeing a commercial championship, will likely bring better and more satisfying results.

The lessons of the entrepreneurial corporation—innovation, orchestrating spirit and discipline, and personal leadership—can make the good better. For some enterprises, the better can become best. And the best will create a new tradition for the next generation of entrepreneurs.

Afterword

Since we completed the research for *The Winning Performance* in 1984, two years have passed and a lot has happened. In many ways past has been prologue.

At this writing, the publicly held firms that we discussed in the first edition have on average continued their winning performances*—outpacing the U.S. economy and their larger "excellent" corporate cousins. During 1984 and 1985, sales of the group we wrote about climbed nearly 20 percent a year (contrasted with 8 percent growth for the U.S. economy). The profits of our earlier subjects increased by 11 percent (vs. less than 1 percent for the economy) and employment grew at 12 percent (vs. 3 percent for the nation).

Five of the 44 companies we wrote about merged with or were acquired by larger enterprises. And two formerly public firms took themselves private.

Despite a superior overall group record, some of the companies we selected experienced the inevitable "downs" that accompany the "ups" in the volatile adolescence of the threshold enterprise. In some cases companies grew too fast and lost control; in others, the external environment shifted faster than they did; and in a couple of cases competi-

*One company was especially on the winning edge—Cray Research—which not only turned in a winning performance for its shareholders but whose product—a super computer—was used to design the boat that won back the America's Cup.

tors just innovated faster and better. We've always thought that the true test of corporate leadership is turning around a bad situation—and a handful of the management teams we chronicled will now have the chance to become candidates for the "when bad things happen to good companies" chapters of the future.

In the wake of the book's publication, the question that our friends, colleagues, clients and audiences have most often asked is "what's the most important ingredient for success?" The answer continues to be the vision, enthusiasm, and caring of the leadership team. We continue to hope that business leaders—past, present and future—can learn from what we've found and in turn create a new tradition of corporate excellence for the twenty-first century.

DKC, REC
February 1987

Appendices

Arthur Levitt well remembers the day, several years ago, that he and a group of leaders of some of the nation's largest, most prestigious companies waited outside the Roosevelt Room in the White House in advance of a meeting with President Carter to discuss the economy. The session was intended to address a broad range of issues vital to the nation's economic well-being; entrepreneurship was among the topics, but was well down the list. Furthermore, none of the nation's smaller, more entrepreneurial companies were there.

During the pre-meeting socializing, Levitt recalls that several CEOs were vociferous in their criticism of many of the Administration's business policies. But their complaints did not focus on the creation of new ideas and businesses that would generate new growth. Instead, they urged protection for older, declining businesses. Once the session started, the subject of entrepreneurship never came up. There simply was no mention made at all of programs or policies that might create incentives for innovation, either among large companies or among the smaller growing companies not represented in that room.

It was at that moment that Levitt became convinced that entrepreneurship deserved a far higher priority on the nation's agenda, and that proven entrepreneurs from midsize and smaller companies deserved a voice in public policy-making. His dream became a reality in 1980; the voice is the American Business Conference.

In important ways, the ABC as public policy advocate typifies the lessons its members (and their kindred business spirits) have learned in the course of achieving their own successes—the lessons of this book. The ABC represents a niche: the tiny proportion of the nation's businesses that are both high growth and medium size. It focuses on a very few very vital issues—tax and capital-formation policies; trade and regulatory reform—and has become generally recognized as the leader in speaking out forcefully and articulately on these matters.

By depending on its members to get its work accomplished, the ABC avoids creating its own bureaucracy. In its practice of anticipating issues and seeking to help shape public discussion of them, the ABC thinks like the policymakers who are, after all, the ultimate consumers of its ideas.

Its members are innovative in pursuing the ABC's goals—as Thermo Electron CEO George Hatsopoulos demonstrated, for example, when he spearheaded a pioneering study of the cost of capital and its impact on international competitiveness. His research demonstrated that one of the biggest contributors to America's competitive decline has been the sharp rise in the relative cost of capital, contradicting the pundits who have sought to lay the blame at the feet of American management and labor.

As is usually the case with political as well as economic entrepreneurs, the men who founded and now lead the ABC, Arthur Levitt and Jack Albertine, personify the lessons of obsession and value-institutionalization. The ABC's members likewise have instilled in the organization the values, perspective and zeal they brought to their own businesses—and in doing so have, not surprisingly, succeeded in quickly transforming a new, unknown enterprise into a powerful force of ideas and action.

Today, the ABC attracts senior public officials and other prestigious leaders from both sides of the political aisle to participate in its meetings, workshops, and conferences. And it has had a tangible impact in shaping national economic policy; for example, the ABC played an important role in passage of the Tax Equity and Fiscal Responsibility Act of 1982 and in the battles of the budgets in 1983 and 1984.

In March 1985, the American Business Conference consisted of 101 chief executives, chairman, and presidents. The list below reflects membership as of March 1985 and is alphabetized by company name.

John J. Lynch
President and CEO
Adams-Russell Company, Inc.
Waltham, Massachusetts

J. David Markley
Chairman and CEO
American First Corporation
Oklahoma City, Oklahoma

Robert J. Fierle
President
American Precision Industries, Inc.
Buffalo, New York

Ray Stata
Chairman and President
Analog Devices, Inc.
Norwood, Massachusetts

John W. Poduska, Sr.
Chairman and CEO
Apollo Computer, Inc.
Chelmsford, Massachusetts

Robert W. Philip, Jr.
Honorary Founding Member
Arthur Andersen & Company
Dallas, Texas

Sandra L. Kurtzig
Chairman and CEO
ASK Computer Systems, Inc.
Los Altos, California

Coleman Raphael
Chairman and CEO
Atlantic Research Corporation
Alexandria, Virginia

Roger D. Wellington
Chairman and CEO
Augat Inc.
Mansfield, Massachusetts

Josh S. Weston
President and CEO
Automatic Data Processing, Inc.
Roseland, New Jersey

Roland S. Boreham, Jr.
Chairman and CEO
Baldor Electric Company
Fort Smith, Arkansas

Robert H. Spilman
Chairman and CEO
Bassett Furniture Industries, Inc.
Bassett, Virginia

Earle Williams
President and CEO
BDM International, Inc.
McLean, Virginia

Emil Martini
Chairman and CEO
Bergen Brunswig Corporation
Los Angeles, California

Robert W. Van Tuyle
Chairman and CEO
Beverly Enterprises
Pasadena, California

John W. Hartman
Chairman
Bill Communications, Inc.
New York, New York

Arthur B. Birtcher
General Partner
Birtcher
Beverly Hills, California

Winton M. Blount
Chairman and CEO
Blount, Inc.
Montgomery, Alabama

Stephen R. Levy
Chairman and CEO
Bolt Beranek and Newman, Inc.
Cambridge, Massachusetts

Albert R. Snider
President and CEO
Bourns, Inc.
Riverside, California

W. L. Lyons Brown, Jr.
Chairman
Brown-Forman Corporation
Louisville, Kentucky

David Dibner
Chairman
Burndy Corporation
Norwalk, Connecticut

Thomas W. Wathen
President
California Plant Protection, Inc.
Van Nuys, California

William A. Fickling, Jr.
Chairman and CEO
Charter Medical Corporation
Macon, Georgia

J.E.R. Chilton III
Chairman
Chilton Corporation
Dallas, Texas

Henry D. Clarke, Jr.
Chairman and CEO
Clabir Corporation
Greenwich, Connecticut

James A. Collins
Chairman and CEO
Collins Food International, Inc.
Los Angeles, California

Kenneth N. Pontikes
Chairman and President
Comdisco, Inc.
Rosemont, Illinois

Stephen T. Winn
President
Computer Language Research, Inc.
Carrollton, Texas

Parker Montgomery
Chairman and CEO
Cooper Vision, Inc.
Palo Alto, California

John A. Rollwagen
Chairman and CEO
Cray Research, Inc.
Minneapolis, Minnesota

Bradford R. Boss
Chairman
A. T. Cross Company
Lincoln, Rhode Island

John J. Cullinane
Chairman and CEO
Cullinet Software
Westwood, Massachusetts

Barrie M. Damson
Chairman
Damson Oil Corporation
New York, New York

Edson de Castro
President
Data General Corporation
Westboro, Massachusetts

Marne Obernauer, Jr.
President and CEO
Devon Group, Inc.
New York, New York

John K. Castle
President
Donaldson, Lufkin & Jenrette
New York, New York

Robert E. Linton
Chairman and CEO
Drexel Burnham Lambert, Inc.
New York, New York

Robert M. Rosenberg
Chairman
Dunkin' Donuts Incorporated
Randolph, Massachusetts

J. P. Barger
President
Dynatech Corporation
Burlington, Massachusetts

Morton H. Meyerson
President
Electronic Data Systems
Dallas, Texas

Daniel Greenberg
Chairman and CEO
Electro Rent Corporation
Santa Monica, California

William F. Farley
Chairman and CEO
Farley Industries
Chicago, Illinois

Don L. Gevirtz
Chairman
The Foothill Group, Inc.
Los Angeles, California

Milton Greenberg
Chairman and CEO
GCA Corporation
Bedford, Massachusetts

Stephen C. Swid
Cochairman
General Felt Industries/
   Knoll International
New York, New York

Robert L. Tarnow
Chairman
Goulds Pumps, Inc.
Seneca Falls, New York

Gordon C. Luce
Chairman and CEO
Great American First Savings Bank
San Diego, California

Edward H. Meyer
Chairman and President
Grey Advertising, Inc.
New York, New York

Charles A. Hayes
Chairman
Guilford Mills, Inc.
Greensboro, North Carolina

Robert Marbut
President and CEO
Harte-Hanks Communications, Inc.
San Antonio, Texas

Fred R. Dusto
President and CEO
Harvey Hubbell, Inc.
Orange, Connecticut

Edgar F. Heizer, Jr.
Chairman and President
Heizer Corporation
Chicago, Illinois

James M. Hoak
President
Heritage Communications, Inc.
Des Moines, Iowa

Richard H. Hughes
Chairman
Hinderliter Industries, Inc.
Tulsa, Oklahoma

Robert H. Krieble
Chairman and CEO
Loctite Corporation
Newington, Connecticut

Gerald D. Hines
Chairman
Gerald D. Hines Interests
Houston, Texas

James R. McManus
Chairman and CEO
Marketing Corporation of America
Westport, Connecticut

Barry W. Florescue
Chairman and CEO
The Horn & Hardart Co.
New York, New York

Richard A. Manoogian
President
Masco Corporation
Taylor, Michigan

Charles R. Scott
President and CEO
Intermark, Inc.
La Jolla, California

Sheldon Weinig
Chairman
Materials Research Corporation
Orangeburg, New York

Patrick J. McGovern
Chairman
International Data Group
Framingham, Massachusetts

V. Orville Wright
President
MCI Communications Corporation
Washington, D.C.

Marvin Josephson
Chairman and CEO
Josephson International, Inc.
New York, New York

Harlan Steinbaum
President
Medicare-Glaser Corporation
St. Louis, Missouri

Michael Jaharis, Jr.
President and CEO
Key Pharmaceuticals, Inc.
Miami, Florida

Robert A. Burnett
President and CEO
Meredith Corporation
Des Moines, Iowa

Robert L. Swiggett
Chairman
Kollmorgen Corporation
Stamford, Connecticut

Max O. DePree
Chairman
Herman Miller, Inc.
Zeeland, Michigan

Lester B. Korn
Chairman
Korn/Ferry International
Los Angeles, California

Dimitri V. d'Arbeloff
Chairman
Millipore Corporation
Bedford, Massachusetts

S. Lee Kling
Chairman and CEO
Landmark Bancshares
   Corporation
St. Louis, Missouri

George P. Mitchell
Chairman, President, and CEO
Mitchell Energy & Development
   Corporation
The Woodlands, Texas

Robert M. Elliot
Chairman
Levitz Furniture Corporation
Miami, Florida

Robert A. Mosbacher
Chairman
Mosbacher Production Company
Houston, Texas

Dillard Munford
Chairman and CEO
Munford, Inc.
Atlanta, Georgia

Burke Mathes
Chairman and CEO
Pacific Stereo Company
Emeryville, California

Abraham Krasnoff
President and CEO
Pall Corporation
Glen Cove, New York

Edward Green
Chairman
Pandick, Inc.
New York, New York

Larry D. Horner
Chairman and CEO
Peat, Marwick, Mitchell & Company
New York, New York

Jerome A. Lewis
Chairman and CEO
Petro-Lewis Corporation
Denver, Colorado

Robert G. Tointon
President
Phelps, Inc.
Greeley, Colorado

Burton P. Resnick
President
Jack Resnick & Sons, Inc.
New York, New York

Ernest J. Nagy
Chairman & President
Riblet Products Corporation
Elkhart, Indiana

Melvyn N. Klein
President
Rockwood Holding Company
Corpus Christi, Texas

Donald W. Brinckman
President and CEO
Safety-Kleen Corporation
Elgin, Illinois

Jack L. Bowers
Chairman and CEO
Sanders Associates, Inc.
Nashua, New Hampshire

T. J. Dermot Dunphy
President and CEO
Sealed Air Corporation
Saddle Brook, New Jersey

R. James Macaleer
Chairman
Shared Medical Systems
Malvern, Pennsylvania

Stuart D. Buchalter
Chairman
Standard Brands Paint Company
Torrance, California

Wendell W. Gamel
Chairman and President
Tech-Sym Corporation
Houston, Texas

Alexander V. d'Arbeloff
President
Teradyne, Inc.
Boston, Massachusetts

George N. Hatsopoulos
Chairman and President
Thermo Electron Corporation
Waltham, Massachusetts

J. David Parkinson
Chairman
Thomas & Betts Corporation
Raritan, New Jersey

G. Allen Mebane
Chairman and CEO
Unifi, Inc.
Greensboro, North Carolina

Arthur H. Stromberg
Chairman, President, and CEO
URS Corporation
San Mateo, California

C. Angus Wurtele
Chairman and CEO
The Valspar Corporation
Minneapolis, Minnesota

Roger W. Johnson
Chairman, President, and CEO
Western Digital Corporation
Irvine, California

Stanley A. Wainer
Chairman, President, and CEO
Wyle Laboratories
El Segundo, California

Lester L. Colbert, Jr.
President and CEO
Xidex Corporation
Sunnyvale, California

Appendix B
119 Fastest-Growing Publicly Listed Midsize Companies in the United States (1983)*

Adobe Oil & Gas Corp.
Advanced Micro Devices, Inc.
Alaska Airlines, Inc.
Allegheny Beverage
Alpha Industries, Inc.
Ames Department Stores, Inc.
Analog Devices, Inc.
Applied Data Research, Inc.
Atwood Oceanics, Inc.
Augat Inc.
Automatic Data Processing, Inc.
Basix Corp.
California Microwave, Inc.
Charming Shoppes, Inc.
Charter Medical Corp.
Coachmen Industries, Inc.
Cobe Laboratories, Inc.
Comdisco, Inc.
Commodore International Ltd.
Community Psychiatric Centers
Comprehensive Care Corp.
Computer Consoles, Inc.
Computer Horizons Corp.
Computer Products, Inc.
Computervision Corp.

Conair Corporation
Cox Communications, Inc.
CPT Corporation
Damson Oil Corp.
Data Card Corporation
Data-Design Laboratories
Datapoint Corp.
Dillard Department Stores, Inc.
Diversifoods Inc.
D.O.C. Optics Corp.
Donaldson, Lufkin & Jenrette, Inc.
Dreyfus Corp.
Dynascan Corp.
Dynatech Corporation
A. G. Edwards & Sons, Inc.
EG&G, Inc.
Electrospace Systems, Inc.
Emerson Radio Corp.
Fay's Drug Company
Flightsafety International, Inc.
Fort Howard Paper Co.
General Datacomm Industries, Inc.
Gerber Scientific Inc.
Global Marine Inc.
Golden Nugget, Inc.

*Companies listed by Compustat with 1983 sales between $25 million and $1 billion, and with 1973–83 sales *and* profit compound annual growth over 20 percent.

Great Lakes Chemical Corp.
John H. Harland Co.
Hechinger Co.
The Horn & Hardart Co.
Impell Corporation
Jerrico, Inc.
Kaneb Services, Inc.
Mary Kay Cosmetics, Inc.
Key Pharmaceuticals Inc.
Kinder-Care Learning Centers, Inc.
Knogo Corp.
La Quinta Motor Inns, Inc.
Loral Corp.
Luby's Cafeterias Inc.
Lynden Incorporated
M/A-Com Inc.
Manor Care, Inc.
MEI Corp.
Herman Miller, Inc.
Mitchell Energy & Development Corp.
Molex Incorporated
National Education Corp.
National Medical Care, Inc.
Newcor, Inc.
Nicolet Instrument Corp.
Nordstrom, Inc.
Ocean Drilling & Exploration Co.
Optical Radiation Corp.
Pacific Telecom Inc.
Pall Corp.
Pauley Petroleum Inc.
Payless Cashways, Inc.
Petro-Lewis Corp.
PHH Group, Inc.
Pic 'N' Save Corp.

Piedmont Aviation, Inc.
Public Service Co. of New Mexico
Pulte Home Corp.
Pyro Energy Corp.
Republic New York Corp.
Resorts International Inc.
Adams Russell Co., Inc.
Ryland Group Inc.
Sabine Corp.
Science Applications International Corp.
Scurry-Rainbow Oil Ltd.
Sealed Air Corp.
Sensormatic Electronics Corp.
Servicemaster Industries Inc.
Shaklee Corp.
Shared Medical Systems Corp.
Shoney's Inc.
Shop & Go, Inc.
Southland Royalty Co.
Southwest Airlines Co.
Staff Builders Inc.
Survival Technology, Inc.
Telecredit, Inc.
Timeplex, Inc.
Torotel, Inc.
Transtechnology Corp.
Tyco Laboratories Inc.
Valtek Incorporated
Viacom International Inc.
Wavetek Corporation
WD-40 Company
Western Steer Mom 'N' Pop's, Inc.
Winners Corp.
Worthington Industries, Inc.

APPENDIX C
TECHNICAL NOTES ON APPROACH AND ANALYSIS

Some readers may be interested in more detail about our approach to preparing this book and the findings that support it. To this end, in this appendix we describe:

1. the methodology we employed
2. the sources of data that support our findings
3. details of our analysis and findings (including thirty-six statistical exhibits)

I. METHODOLOGY

We believe that our examination of the winning performance of the high-growth midsize companies has been rigorous, disciplined, and comprehensive—but not "scientific research" in its classic sense.

Our approach was twofold. First, we sought to discern firsthand which strategic, organizational, and leadership practices are typically found among superior-performing midsize companies. With those identified, we subsequently tested our findings wherever possible with broader samples of enterprises with varying records of performance. Those practices that met the test of being employed at high-performance enterprises *and* that were absent or less pronounced in average and below-average performers are the ones we wrote about.

Practices Among the Winners

Our prime "focus group" of superior-performance midsize enterprises was the members of the American Business Conference. Guidelines for membership in this group of one hundred business leaders required that companies have sales in the $25 million to $1 billion range *and* annual compound growth records of 15 percent in either sales or earnings for five years prior to admission. In the case of publicly held companies, individual performance is easily verifiable through annual reports, SEC filings, and widely used data bases such as Compustat or Dun & Bradstreet. For privately held companies, the ABC relies on the appraisal of the company's auditors.

On average, the eighty-one publicly held ABC companies have greatly exceeded the 15 percent minimum growth rates over the preceding five years. Their collective average performance, which is measured in Exhibits 19 through 25 to this appendix, show that they have outpaced the economy, the *Fortune* 500, and even the "excellent companies" chronicled in *In Search of Excellence* by Peters and Waterman, by substantial margins in growth rates in sales, income, market value, assets, employment, and capital spending during the 1978–83 period (the most recent five-year period for which publicly available data have been collected). With respect to return on equity, one standard measurement of profitability, the ABC sample exceeded the economy and *Fortune* 500, but lagged behind the "excellent companies" by 1.3 percent.

Although the ABC sample on average achieved growth records that placed it solidly among the top quarter of all midsize companies (those 6,117 midsize companies with five-year data available from Dun & Bradstreet) and a majority of them ranked among the top quartile of their industry competitors in sales growth and return on equity, within the ABC there were wide ranges of performance. The companies that serve as primary examples in the text were those whose long-term performance records ranked high among the ABC sample and whose leadership volunteered to cooperate in the interviews, the survey, and the fact-finding process.

As is the case with most any voluntary organization, there are changes in membership over time. For example, three companies in the sample—EDS, Charles River Laboratories, and Lenox—have recently merged with other firms. For the purposes of statistical comparisons we used the ABC membership list as of February 1984. Additionally, a few non-ABC members are drawn upon to illustrate certain practices; in each case their performance record equals or exceeds the ABC sample average.

Our initial fact-finding approach was to interview the leaders of the companies during the period 1981–83, when we undertook the study (whose results were published in our report *The Winning Performance of the Midsized Growth Companies*). These interviews, designed to identify "best practices," were conducted individually and in small groups. They were supplemented by an eighty-two-question survey as well as numerous discussions with managers, employees, and board members; people who did business with our sample (such as distributors and customers); and those formerly associated with the enterprises. In every case we also compiled a dossier of material published about the company, and further broadened our perspective and understanding in many cases by discussions with informed observers (financial analysts, competitors, academics, and journalists). During the 1983–85 period, when we prepared this book, we essentially carried out the same process again. We conducted hundreds of interviews—one hundred of them with presidents and/or chairmen—during the course of our investigation and assembled four file cabinets full of documentation.

Interview subjects and survey participants were assured the confidentiality of proprietary data—and we checked our facts with those who participated and gained permission to quote individuals.

From these interviews, survey results, and published material we synthe-sized our observations of winning practices.

Testing the Findings

It was necessary to test the validity of our initial findings about success-ful management practices for two reasons. First, the practices and attributes we uncovered might be universal to all businesses—regardless of performance. Second, many of our findings either contradicted or transcended some of the popular theories of management. Our approach to testing and validating our findings was both quantitative and qualitative.*

With respect to testing our strategic findings, we conducted a series of disciplined statistical analyses. For example, to confirm or deny our finding that business success is largely independent of industry sector, we analyzed the business performance of 6,117 midsize companies in 58 primary Standard Industrial Classifications. And we examined published lists of high-performance companies in leading journals (such as the annual *Inc.* and *Forbes* profiles of high performers).

The PIMS data base proved to be an excellent—though not perfect—vehicle for testing other strategic findings. Its 525 midsize business units encompass a wide range of industries and records of business performance. In this case we were limited to information already collected by the Strategic Planning Institute, but fortunately much of that data base lent itself to testing hypotheses we sought to vali-date. For example, our findings about new-product innovation were corroborated by PIMS data on market-entry timing, and our value findings by product quality. In all, we conducted seven principal analyses to correlate strategic traits found in the winning performers with corresponding PIMS attributes. And in all seven cases we found that profit performance (measured by four-year average return on investment) among the 525 PIMS business units confirmed our findings. PIMS participants which reported attributes like those of our winning practices had higher profitability—those that did not recorded lower returns.

Not all of our findings lend themselves to quantification (e.g., the passion of chief executives or the strongly held shared values among employees). In these cases, we drew upon our own forty combined years of consulting experi-ence to test those "softer" attributes. In the text we have included numerous nameless examples of organizations that followed contrary practices. We also enlisted the help of some twenty senior members of McKinsey & Company—collectively having hundreds of years of professional consulting experience—to react to our findings. While we did not receive universal agreement on every finding, we did elicit high levels of general agreement.

Finally, we tested our findings with the business community. During the past four years we have presented our findings scores of times to audiences

*We tested our findings in a variety of ways—drawing upon statistical data-base analyses, comparative case studies, published accounts, and professional experi-ence. A more precise method to assess our findings would have been to identify and examine through interviews, surveys, and collaborating evidence a sample of one hundred "losers"—to compare and contrast their practices with our "winning" sam-ple. Although theoretically appealing, such an exercise is impractical because gain-ing the candid and enthusiastic cooperation of "losers" would have defied human nature. Few people or institutions are eager to discuss why they fail, especially for publication.

ranging from management groups of companies not in our sample through faculty and student audiences at leading business schools, and to trade and professional association meetings across the United States. These presentations almost always included give-and-take discussions in which we encouraged practitioners to challenge or confirm our findings. In the same vein we distributed some three thousand copies of the original report to anyone who asked for one—managers, academicians, researchers, government officials, and the like. Finally, the report received considerable coverage in the business and general press. In almost all of these instances, the findings were confirmed by those who read or heard of them.

All this is to say that while our findings may not be based on absolutely perfect scientific research, we believe that they are supported by a reasonable measure of rigorous analysis and that they have benefited by the test of expert and public examination.

II. Description of Data Sources

The statistical analyses of this book drew upon five major sources of data.

1. ABC Member Survey

We developed and administered an eighty-two-question survey that was completed by forty-six members of the American Business Conference. The questionnaire addressed topics such as market attributes, corporate values, organization, and compensation. The results were tabulated and used as one source for determining the common characteristics of high-growth midsize companies.

2. Compustat

Compustat, a data base managed by Standard & Poor's, contains 175 categories of financial information for periods of up to twenty years on more than six thousand publicly owned companies.

Because Compustat includes all 81 of the publicly held ABC companies, more than 2,500 other midsize companies, and virtually all of the *Fortune* 500, we used it frequently to calculate comparative averages and historical trends.

3. Dun & Bradstreet

Dun & Bradstreet maintains a data base describing more than 5 million business enterprises. Of these companies, roughly 15,000 are midsize. We analyzed the size, distribution, and economic impact of these companies in preparation for the 1983 report *The Winning Performance of the Midsized Growth Companies;* 6,117 of the midsize enterprises in the D&B data base were sufficiently well documented to allow growth patterns to be computed as well.

4. IRS Statistics

In order to determine the number of businesses in America, we used data from the Internal Revenue Service's "Statistics of Income." This compilation includes estimates of the number of corporations, partnerships, and sole proprietorships filing income-tax returns in the United States.

5. PIMS

PIMS (Profit Impact of Market Strategy) is a research-and-application program operated by the Strategic Planning Institute (SPI) of Cambridge, Massachusetts. SPI granted us permission to carry out a wide range of analyses of the midsize business units in the PIMS data base. This data base includes operating and performance data on some 2,500 business units supplied by a group of 200 participating companies.

The 525 midsize business units (those with between $25 million and $1 billion in sales) were separated out. They were then analyzed to assess the impact of various marketing strategies and business conditions on return on investment.

To SPI's and our knowledge, this was the first time this segment of its data base had ever been isolated and analyzed.

III. DESCRIPTION OF DATA ANALYSES AND FINDINGS

The quantitative analyses used over the two years of the original ABC study and the additional analyses underlying this book fall into three major categories:

- analysis of all midsize companies
- analysis of high-growth midsize companies
- analysis of ABC member companies.

ANALYSIS OF ALL MIDSIZE COMPANIES

We sought to determine the importance of midsize companies and their distribution throughout the United States economy. Statistics on 15,000 midsize companies were extracted from Dun & Bradstreet's 5-million-company data base. The findings from analyses of these statistics are illustrated in the exhibits that follow.

Exhibit 1: For a segment that represents a small fraction of a percent of all companies in the American economy, the midsize companies make a disproportionately large contribution in sales, assets, and employment.

Exhibit 1
MIDSIZE COMPANIES IN THE U.S. ECONOMY

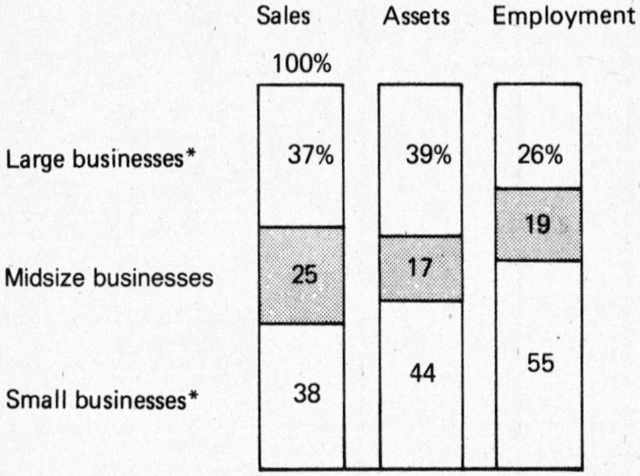

Sales
Assets
Employment
100%
Large businesses*
Midsize businesses
Small businesses*
37%
39%
26%
25
17
19
38
44
55

* Estimated

Note: Midsize defined as having total sales between $25 million and $1 billion; excludes the financial sector

Sources: Dun & Bradstreet; *Statistical Abstract of the United States;* IRS statistics of income; *Forbes; Fortune:* McKinsey analysis

Exhibit 2: Similarly, the nation's midsize *financial institutions* hold a disproportionately large proportion of assets.

Exhibit 2
ESTIMATED PORTION OF FINANCIAL SECTOR ASSETS HELD BY MIDSIZE FINANCIAL COMPANIES
1982 data

Small
27%
38%
Midsize
35%
Large

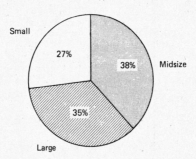

Sources: 1983 Savings & Loan Sourcebook; 1982 Statistics on Banking; Moody's Bank and Finance Manual; McKinsey analysis

Note: Midsize defined as assets between $250 million and $8 billion

Exhibit 3: Overall, the broad sectors in which the midsize companies operate broadly reflect the distribution of all businesses.

Exhibit 3
DISTRIBUTION OF MIDSIZE COMPANIES COMPARED TO THE U.S. ECONOMY

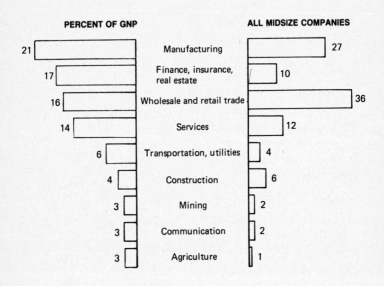

PERCENT OF GNP		ALL MIDSIZE COMPANIES
21	Manufacturing	27
17	Finance, insurance, real estate	10
16	Wholesale and retail trade	36
14	Services	12
6	Transportation, utilities	4
4	Construction	6
3	Mining	2
3	Communication	2
3	Agriculture	1

Sources: Dun & Bradstreet; U.S. Survey of Current Business, August, 1984; McKinsey analysis

Exhibit 4: The midsize companies' locations are dispersed throughout the nation.

Exhibit 4
NUMBER OF MIDSIZE COMPANIES IN THE UNITED STATES

STATE	NUMBER OF FIRMS	STATE	NUMBER OF FIRMS
Alabama	151	Nebraska	87
Alaska	28	Nevada	40
Arizona	102	New Hampshire	37
Arkansas	77	New Jersey	554
California	1,437	New Mexico	34
Colorado	172	New York	1,195
Connecticut	274	North Carolina	226
Delaware	37	North Dakota	23
District of Columbia	50	Ohio	635
Florida	363	Oklahoma	218
Georgia	253	Oregon	141
Hawaii	34	Pennsylvania	712
Idaho	21	Puerto Rico	55
Illinois	885	Rhode Island	48
Indiana	270	South Carolina	98
Iowa	137	South Dakota	19
Kansas	158	Tennessee	258
Kentucky	133	Texas	1,234
Louisiana	202	Utah	73
Maine	45	Vermont	9
Maryland	160	Virginia	218
Massachusetts	394	Virgin Islands	2
Michigan	484	Washington	226
Minnesota	321	West Virginia	55
Mississippi	68	Wisconsin	337
Missouri	315	Wyoming	8
Montana	25	Total	13,188

Note: 1982 data; excludes financial sector; these are minimum values - i.e., they represent those firms that could be specifically identified

Sources: Dun & Bradstreet; McKinsey analysis

Exhibit 5: Comparing the performance of 6,117 midsize companies with that of the top half of the *Fortune* 500 shows that the midsize companies outperform the nation's industrial giants in sales growth and in return on equity. (Of the 15,000 midsize companies in the Dun & Bradstreet data base, 6,117 were sufficiently well documented to enable these calculations to be made.)

Exhibit 5
GROWTH AND RETURNS IN MIDSIZE COMPANIES COMPARED WITH THE "FORTUNE 250"
1981-82

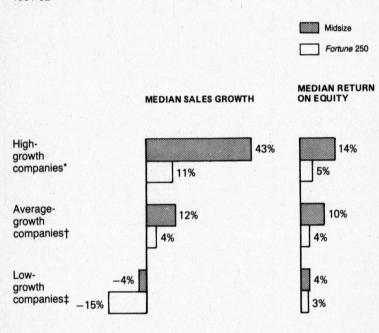

* Defined as those companies in the top quartile of the samples in terms of sales growth rate
† Defined as those companies in the middle two quartiles of the samples in terms of sales growth rate
‡ Defined as those companies in the bottom quartile of the samples in terms of sales growth rate

Note: Excludes finance, insurance, and real estate; 6,117 midsize companies and 250 *Fortune* companies analyzed

To determine the critical variables that contribute to superior business performance among the midsize companies, we evaluated 525 midsize business units in the PIMS data base. Correlating return on investment with other variables yields several findings illustrated in Exhibits 6 through 12.

Exhibit 6: There is little relationship, if any, between ROI and rate of overall market growth.

Exhibit 6
REAL MARKET GROWTH RATE AND BUSINESS PERFORMANCE
Four year average return on investment*

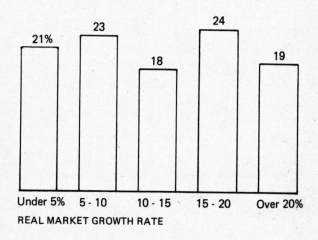

REAL MARKET GROWTH RATE

* Before interest expense and corporate overhead; 525 midsize businesses
Source: PIMS Program

Exhibit 7: . . . A strong directional relationship between a company's ROI and the extent to which it demonstrates "winning" characteristics exists.

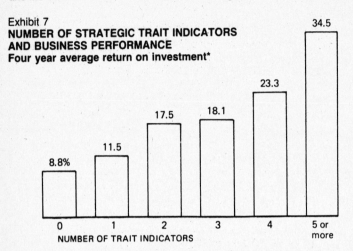

Exhibit 7
NUMBER OF STRATEGIC TRAIT INDICATORS
AND BUSINESS PERFORMANCE
Four year average return on investment*

* Before interest expense and corporate overhead; 525 midsize businesses

Note: Six variables were used as indicators of a company exhibiting a strategic trait; e.g., having a market share rank of one or two was considered an indicator of a market leader

Source: PIMS Program

Exhibit 8: . . . in the propensity to be a pioneer in its markets.

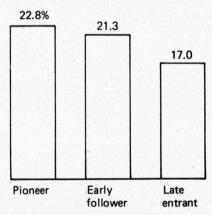

Exhibit 8
TIMING OF MARKET ENTRY AND BUSINESS PERFORMANCE
Four year average return on investment*

* Before interest expense and corporate overhead; 525 midsize businesses

Source: PIMS Program

Exhibit 9: High ROI also correlates with smaller—"niche"—markets . . .

Exhibit 9
SIZE OF MARKET AND BUSINESS PERFORMANCE
Four year average return on investment*

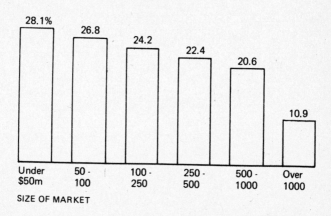

* Before interest expense and corporate overhead; 525 midsize businesses

Source: PIMS Program

Exhibit 10: . . . and with product quality . . .

Exhibit 10
RELATIVE PRODUCT QUALITY AND BUSINESS PERFORMANCE
Four year average return on investment*

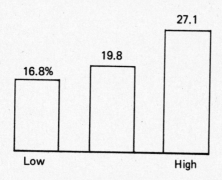

* Before interest expense and corporate overhead; 525 midsize businesses

Source: PIMS Program

Exhibit 11: . . . with market share . . .

Exhibit 11
MARKET SHARE RANK AND BUSINESS PERFORMANCE
Four year average return on investment*

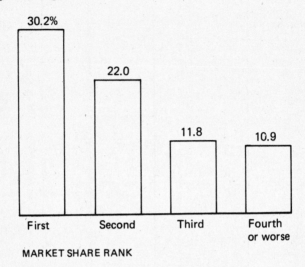

MARKET SHARE RANK

* Before interest expense and corporate overhead; 525 midsize businesses

Source: PIMS Program

Exhibit 12: . . . and with high product price.

Exhibit 12
RELATIVE PRICE OF PRODUCTS AND BUSINESS PERFORMANCE
Four year average return on investment*

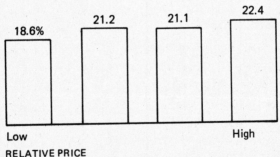

RELATIVE PRICE

* Before interest expense and corporate overhead; 525 midsize businesses

Source: PIMS Program

ANALYSIS OF HIGH-GROWTH MIDSIZE COMPANIES

Having established the importance of the midsize sector of the economy, we then turned our attention to the "winning performance" of high-growth midsize companies, using Compustat and Dun & Bradstreet data bases, with results as shown in Exhibits 13 through 15.

Exhibit 13: For the most part, the overall midsize economy and the high-growth midsize players follow similar industry distributions.

Exhibit 13
**DISTRIBUTION OF NUMBERS OF MIDSIZE COMPANIES
AND "HIGH-GROWTH" MIDSIZE COMPANIES**

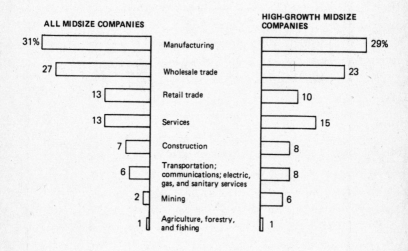

ALL MIDSIZE COMPANIES / HIGH-GROWTH MIDSIZE COMPANIES

	All Midsize Companies	High-Growth Midsize Companies
Manufacturing	31%	29%
Wholesale trade	27	23
Retail trade	13	10
Services	13	15
Construction	7	8
Transportation; communications; electric, gas, and sanitary services	6	8
Mining	2	6
Agriculture, forestry, and fishing	1	1

Note: Finance, insurance, and real estate excluded; 1981-82 growth figures utilized

Sources: Dun & Bradstreet; McKinsey analysis

Exhibit 14: Among companies contained in the Compustat data base, a disproportionate percentage of high-growth companies is found in the midsize sector.

Exhibit 14
HIGH-GROWTH COMPANIES AS PERCENT OF SAMPLE
1973-83 AND 1980-83 DATA COMBINED
The midsize company group contains the largest concentration
of high-growth companies

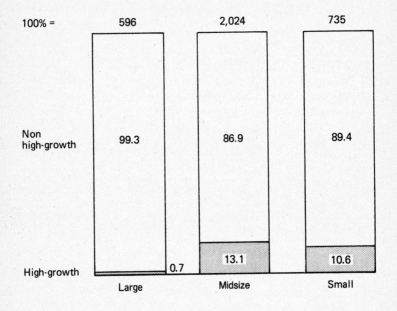

Growth figures are for sales growth 1973-83 or 1980-83 where 1973 data were not available.
High-growth is annual compound growth exceeding 20%

Sources: Compustat 3355 company sample; McKinsey analysis

Exhibit 15: In order to gain insight into the problem of sustaining high growth, we traced one hundred of 1973's star performers over the following half decade and decade. After ten years, only twenty-seven of the 1973 star performers could still claim that distinction.

Exhibit 15
THE STAR PERFORMERS* OF 1973
100% = 100 companies

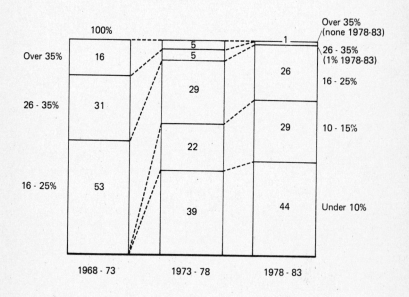

* Star performers defined as the fastest growing midsize companies in terms of sales growth 1968-73 and still in existence in 1982

Sources: Compustat; McKinsey analysis

ANALYSIS OF ABC MEMBER COMPANIES

Since the ABC companies are a major focus of this book, we subjected their attributes and performance to extensive analysis. Much of this analysis draws upon data contained in the Compustat data base on the eighty-one publicly owned ABC companies.

Like the midsize sector of which they are a subset, the members of the American Business Conference are widely distributed throughout the United States economy, as Exhibits 16 through 18 illustrate.

Exhibit 16: . . . geographically . . .

Exhibit 16
NUMBER OF ABC MEMBERS IN THE FIFTEEN MOST POPULATED STATES
1984

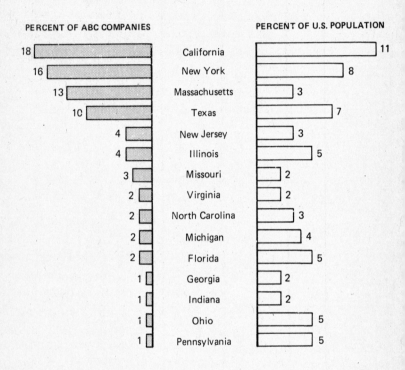

Note: These 15 states comprise 85% of the U.S. population; ABC companies are headquartered in
      25 states and the District of Columbia

Sources: 1984 Statistical Abstract of the U.S; McKinsey analysis

Exhibit 17: . . . and by industry sector.

Exhibit 17
ABC REPRESENTATION BY ECONOMIC SECTOR

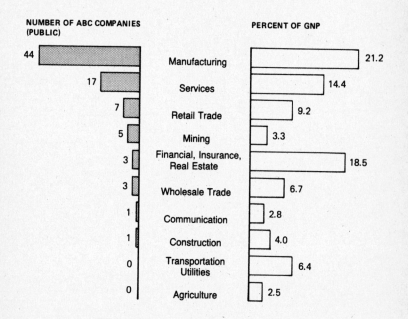

Note: ABC membership as of February 1984

Sources: U.S. Survey of Current Business, August 1984; Compustat; McKinsey analysis

Exhibit 18: Relative to their respective industries, most ABC companies are superior performers.

Exhibit 18
**PERFORMANCE OF ABC COMPANIES RELATIVE TO
THEIR INDUSTRIES**
1978-83

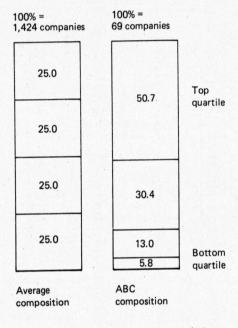

Note: Performance measurement is the sum of sales growth rate and return on equity.
ABC membership as of February 1984.

Sources: Compustat; McKinsey analysis

As a general performance evaluation, we compared the growth rates of the ABC companies with those of the "excellent companies" described in *In Search of Excellence*, the *Fortune* 500, and where available, the United States economy. These calculations were made using data from the Compustat data base and programs written in both the FOCUS data manipulation language and the Statistical Analysis System (SAS). The ABC members outperformed those other groups in all measures of growth except return on equity, as shown in Exhibits 19 through 25.

Exhibit 19: . . . first in sales growth . . .

Exhibit 19
SALES GROWTH
Annualized 1978-83

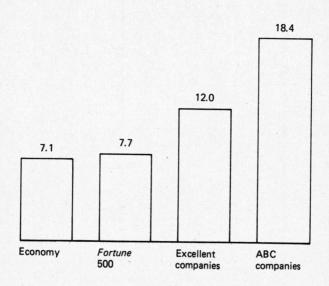

Note: ABC membership as of February 1984 represented, median values depicted. *Fortune* 500 figures derived from 470 company database.

Sources: Compustat; *Fortune; In Search of Excellence;* Economic Indicators

Exhibit 20: . . . first in growth in net profits . . .

Exhibit 20
NET INCOME GROWTH
Annualized 1978-83

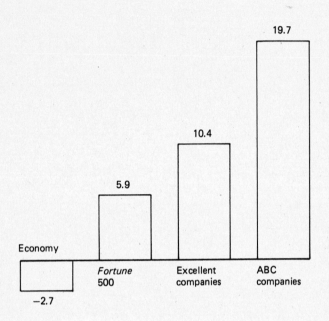

Note: ABC membership as of February 1984 represented, median values depicted. *Fortune* 500 figures derived from 470 company database.

Sources: Compustat; *Fortune; In Search of Excellence;* Economic Indicators

Exhibit 21: . . . first in increased market value . . .

Exhibit 21
MARKET VALUE GROWTH
Annualized 1978-83

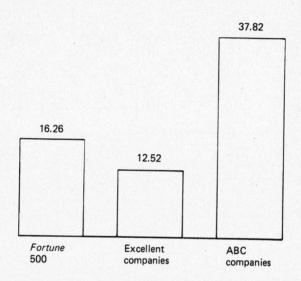

Note: ABC membership as of February 1984 represented, median values depicted. *Fortune* 500 figures derived from 470 company database.

Sources: Compustat; *Fortune; In Search of Excellence;* Economic Indicators

Exhibit 22: . . . second (to the "excellent companies") in return on equity . . .

Exhibit 22
RETURN ON EQUITY
Average annual 1978-83

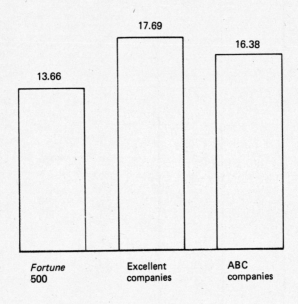

Note: ABC membership as of February 1984 represented, median values depicted. *Fortune* 500
    figures derived from 470 company database.

Sources: Compustat; *Fortune; In Search of Excellence*

Exhibit 23: . . . first in asset growth . . .

Exhibit 23
ASSET GROWTH
Annualized 1978-83

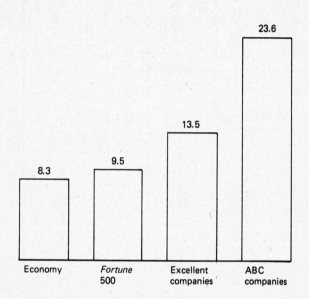

Note: ABC membership as of February 1984 represented, median values depicted. *Fortune* 500
figures derived from 470 company database.

Sources: Compustat, *Fortune, In Search of Excellence,* Economic Indicators

Exhibit 24: . . . first in job creation . . .

Exhibit 24
GROWTH RATES IN EMPLOYMENT
Annualized 1978-83

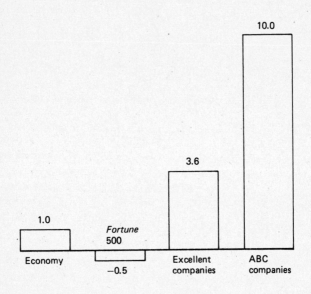

Note: ABC membership as of February 1984 represented, median values depicted. *Fortune* 500
   figures derived from 470 company database.

Sources: Compustat, *Fortune, In Search of Excellence,* Economic Indicators

Exhibit 25: . . . and first in growth in capital spending.

Exhibit 25
CAPITAL SPENDING GROWTH
Annualized 1978-83

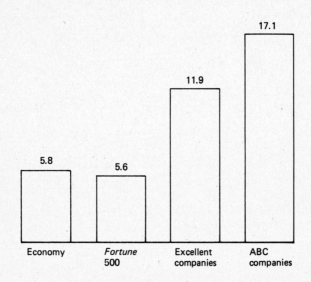

Note: ABC membership as of February 1984 represented, median values depicted. *Fortune* 500
figures derived from 470 company database.

Sources: Compustat, *Fortune, In Search of Excellence,* Economic Indicators

We completed our analysis of the ABC by evaluating an eighty-two-question survey of its members. Our forty-six responses allowed us to construct a data base of the reported attributes of success related to such factors as strategy, marketing philosophy, and organization. Among the significant findings were those illustrated in Exhibits 26 through 36.

Exhibit 26: Three quarters attribute their initial success to innovation.

Exhibit 26
PORTION OF RESPONDENTS ATTRIBUTING INITIAL SUCCESS TO A UNIQUE FACTOR

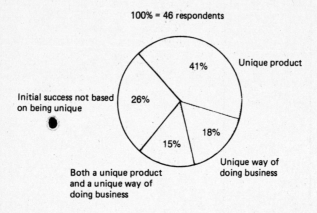

100% = 46 respondents

Unique product — 41%

Initial success not based on being unique — 26%

Both a unique product and a unique way of doing business — 15%

Unique way of doing business — 18%

Source: Survey of ABC membership

Exhibit 27: The sample overwhelmingly endorsed the strategic notions of innovation, niche competition, and competing on the basis of value instead of price.

Exhibit 27
STRATEGIC TRAITS IN ABC COMPANIES

	"TRUE OF MY COMPANY"	IMPORTANCE OF		
		Very	Moderate	Low
Frequent innovation	84%	63%	34%	3%
Niche competition	81	59	32	9
"Overspending" on critical functions	59	31	34	35
Value, not price	97	80	20	0

Sources: Survey of ABC membership; McKinsey analysis

Exhibit 28: Over time, innovation focuses on new ways of doing business rather than on new products.

Exhibit 28
CONTINUING INNOVATORS*:
THE SHIFTING NATURE OF INNOVATION

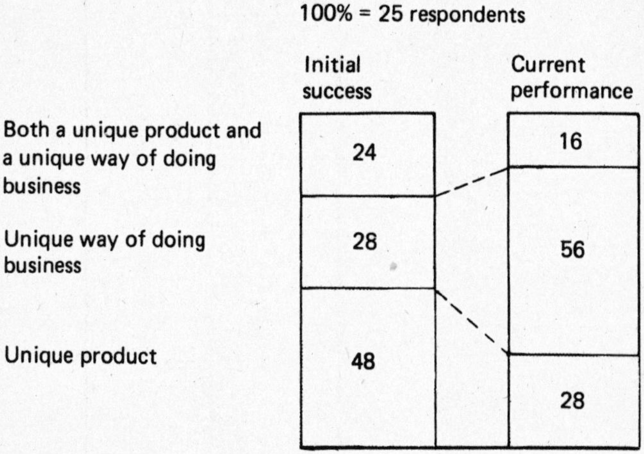

100% = 25 respondents

	Initial success	Current performance
Both a unique product and a unique way of doing business	24	16
Unique way of doing business	28	56
Unique product	48	28

* Continuing innovators are defined as those companies that attribute both their initial success and current performance to innovation

Source: Survey of ABC membership

Exhibit 29: Continuing innovation is difficult to sustain.

Exhibit 29
IMPORTANCE OF UNIQUE FACTORS TO INITIAL SUCCESS AND
CURRENT PERFORMANCE FROM SURVEY

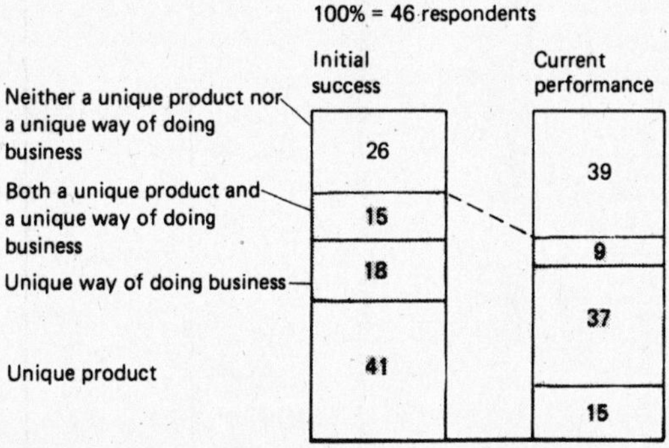

100% = 46 respondents

	Initial success	Current performance
Neither a unique product nor a unique way of doing business	26	39
Both a unique product and a unique way of doing business	15	9
Unique way of doing business	18	37
Unique product	41	15

Source: Survey of ABC membership

Exhibit 30: Virtually none continue to rely on a single product sold in a single market—most have participated in related diversification of products and/or markets.

Exhibit 30
SIMILARITY OF MARKETS AND PRODUCTS

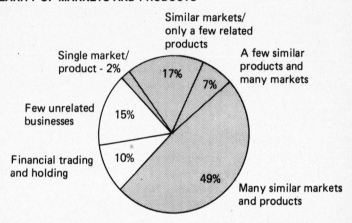

Source: Survey of ABC membership

Exhibit 31: Three quarters have grown by acquisition, and half by acquiring more than one or two companies.

Exhibit 31
DISTRIBUTION OF NUMBER OF ACQUISITIONS MADE BY SURVEY RESPONDENTS IN THE LAST TEN YEARS

100% = 45 Respondents

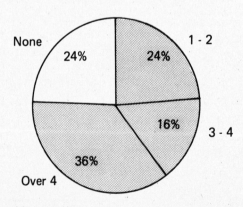

Source: Survey of ABC membership

Exhibit 32: There is extremely strong consensus on the importance of a handful of organizational traits.

Exhibit 32
ORGANIZATIONAL CHARACTERISTICS OF ABC MEMBERS

	"TRUE OF MY COMPANY"	"CONTRIBUTION TO MY SUCCESS"		
		Very important	Moderately important	Relatively unimportant
Sense of mission and shared values	91%	69%	25%	6%
People management at the top	91	83	14	3
Action orientation	91	89	8	3
Market driven/close to the customer	97	89	11	0
Strong incentives	95	61	39	0

Sources: Survey of ABC membership; McKinsey analysis

Exhibit 33: They emphasize shared values.

Exhibit 33
SHARED VALUES IN ABC COMPANIES

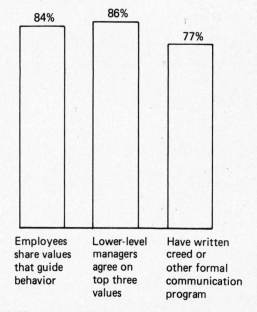

Sources: Survey of ABC membership; McKinsey analysis

Exhibit 34: They limit the existence and size of corporate staff units.

Exhibit 34
SIZE OF STAFF FUNCTIONS IN ABC COMPANIES

	SIZE OF DEPARTMENT			
	Do not have one	Small	Moderate	Large
Government relations	80%	18%	2%	0%
Internal communications	64	24	9	3
Public affairs	58	38	4	0
Investor relations	55	45	0	0
Corporate planning	40	51	9	0
Legal affairs	33	42	22	3
Personnel	7	31	53	9

Sources: Survey of ABC membership; McKinsey analysis

Exhibit 35: Employee ownership is broadly based in ABC companies, whether closely or widely held.

Exhibit 35
EMPLOYEE STOCK OWNERSHIP IN ABC COMPANIES
Percentage of total outstanding stock

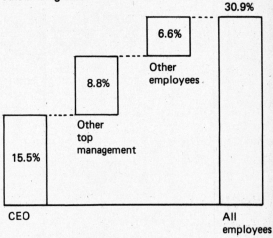

Sources: Survey of ABC membership; McKinsey analysis

Closely held*

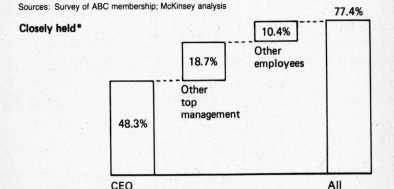

Not closely held†

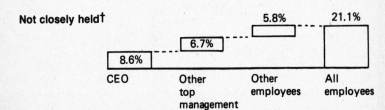

* Employee ownership exceeds 50%; seven companies represented
† Employee ownership is under 50%; 33 companies represented

Sources: Survey of ABC membership; McKinsey analysis

Exhibit 36: Incentive pay accounts for a substantial portion of management compensation.

Exhibit 36
PERCENT OF TOTAL COMPENSATION PAID AS AN INCENTIVE BY ABC COMPANIES

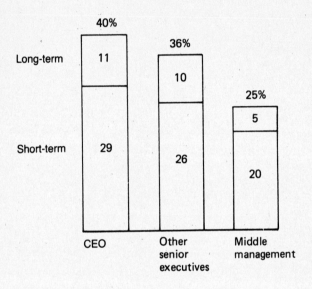

Sources: Survey of ABC membership; McKinsey analysis

INDEX

ABOUT THE AUTHORS

DONALD K. CLIFFORD, JR., for twenty-five years a management consultant with McKinsey & Company, began his work with, research on, and writings about midsize growth companies in the early 1970s. He coined the term "threshold companies" in his 1979 *Harvard Business Review* article and for years led McKinsey's practice in helping entrepreneurs master professional management. Educated at Yale College and Harvard Business School, Clifford is active in civic affairs as a hospital trustee, trustee and secretary of Quebec Labrador Foundation, trustee of Sarah Lawrence College, and member of the Council on Foreign Relations. Today Clifford has established Threshold Management, Inc., and is a director of several companies and active in venture capital. He is married to Mary Lawrence, has five children, and with his family makes his home in Westchester County. When he's not working or writing, Clifford is a committed outdoorsman.

RICHARD E. CAVANAGH is Executive Dean of the John F. Kennedy School of Government at Harvard, and has served both public enterprises and corporations around the world. Formerly a principal in McKinsey & Company's Washington office, Cavanagh is a graduate of Wesleyan University and Harvard Business School. Cavanagh is a member of the Board of Visitors to the Georgetown University Business School, and has been a member of the Business Advisory Committee to the Brookings Institution and the Executive Committee of the Grace Commission. During a leave of absence from McKinsey, Cavanagh held executive positions in the U.S. Office of Management and Budget—as executive director of Federal Cash Management (where he was credited with saving $12 billion) and as domestic coordinator of the President's Reorganization Project. A native of New Jersey, where his mother and brother live, Cavanagh drives a 1959 Edsel.

Together and separately, Clifford and Cavanagh have published articles on management in the *Harvard Business Review, Management Review, Organization Dynamics, Planning Review,* and *The Wall Street Journal,* and each is a frequent speaker before business management audiences.